Lone P

Perennials
for
Saskatchewan
and
Manitoba

Patricia Hanbidge
Laura Peters

The Publisher: Lone Pine Publishing
10145 – 81 Avenue
Edmonton, AB, Canada   T6E 1W9

Website: www.lonepinepublishing.com

Library and Archives Canada Cataloguing in Publication
Peters, Laura, 1968–
      Perennials for Saskatchewan and Manitoba / Laura Peters, Patricia Hanbidge.

Includes index.
ISBN–13: 978–1–55105–325–7.—ISBN–10 1–55105–325–X

      1. Perennials—Saskatchewan. 2. Perennials—Manitoba.
I. Hanbidge, Patricia II. Title.

SB434.P485 2005   635.9'32'097124   C2004–905634–4

Editorial Director: Nancy Foulds
Project Editor: Sandra Bit
Illustrations Coordinator: Carol Woo
Photo Coordinator: Don Williamson
Production Manager: Gene Longson
Book Design: Heather Markham
Layout & Production: Curtis Pillipow, Heather Markham
Cover Design: Gerry Dotto
Production Support: Elliot Engley, Trina Koscielnuk
Scanning & Electronic Film: Elite Lithographers Co.

All photos by Laura Peters, Tamara Eder, Tim Matheson and Allison Penko except: Sandra Bit 10, 11, 15, 213a; Therese D'Monte 299b&c; Joan de Grey 104, 105b; Elliot Engley 45a,b,&c, 46; Derek Fell 108, 298b, 331b, 332; Erika Flatt 47a, 48a&c, 69, 167a, 210a, 211a, 212a, 213b, 222b, 250; Kevin Frey 209b, 211b; Anne Gordon 107a, 246a, 298a; Patricia Hanbidge 131a; Liz Klose 78b, 123b, 129b, 258b; Debra Knapke 339b; Horticolor (N0901048) 295; Horticultural Photography 246b; Colin Laroque 112b; Dawn Loewen 17b; Janet Loughrey 105a, 106a&b, 119b, 232, 309a, 335a; Kim O'Leary 263b, 321a; PPA 253a, 265b, 286b; Robert Ritchie 61, 63b, 65, 80, 81a&b, 119a, 196, 197b, 238a, 239b, 268b, 290a; Leila Sidi 280; Peter Thompstone 70, 71b, 150, 173a, 188a, 187b, 214, 236, 237, 269a&b, 272a, 325b; Mark Turner 299a; Valleybrook Gardens 294; Don Williamson 148b, 178, 238b, 245b.

Cover photos by Tim Matheson except where noted. *Clockwise from top left:* bleeding heart, bellflower, pincusion flower (Tamara Eder), columbine (Tamara Eder), daylily, clematis (Tamara Eder), prairie mallow (Tamara Eder), cranesbill.

Hardiness map information taken from The Atlas of Canada (http://atlas.gc.ca) © 2004. Her Majesty the Queen in Right of Canada with permission from Natural Resources Canada.

This book is not intended to be a 'how-to' guide on eating garden plants. No plant or plant extract should be consumed unless you are certain of its identity and toxicity and of your potential for allergic reactions.

We acknowledge the financial support of the Government of Canada through the Book Publishing Industry Development Program (BPIDP) for our publishing activities.

PC: P1

Contents

ACKNOWLEDGEMENTS 4
THE FLOWERS AT A GLANCE.... 5
INTRODUCTION 11
  Climate, Geography and Soil 11
  Microclimates 13
  Perennial Gardens 15
  Getting Started.......................... 19
    Light... 20
    Soil 21
    Exposure 23
  Preparing the Garden 25
    Composting.............................. 25
  Selecting Perennials 29
  Planting Perennials 32
    Potted Perennials..................... 32
    Bare-Root Perennials.............. 33
    Root Types 34
    Containers 34
  Caring for Perennials 37
    Weeding................................... 37
    Mulching 38
    Deadheading 39
    Pruning 40
    Staking..................................... 41

  Watering 43
  Fertilizing................................. 43
  Propagating Perennials 44
    Seeds 44
    Cuttings 49
    Stem Cuttings 50
    Basal Cuttings 53
    Root Cuttings 54
    Rhizomes 55
    Divisions 56
  Problems & Pests 58
  Glossary of Pests and Diseases 60
    Pests 60
    Diseases 63
  Pest Control Alternatives.......... 66
  About This Guide 68
THE PERENNIALS
  FOR SASKATCHEWAN
  AND MANITOBA................. 69
OTHER PLANTS
  TO CONSIDER 338
QUICK REFERENCE CHART.. 340
GLOSSARY 346
INDEX....................................... 348

Acknowledgments

My evolution as a gardener has been greatly influenced by countless experiences over the years. A great Master Gardener and mentor of many—Ruthanne Hanbidge, whom I am fortunate enough to also call my mother—is awarded the great honour of first nurturing my love of all gardens. This love evolved with the help of numerous educational and industry colleagues, fellow gardeners and, of course, my Master Gardeners. Special thanks to Lone Pine and to my co-author Laura Peters for her always sunny approach to both gardening and the endless deadlines associated with publishing. —*Patricia Hanbidge*

I would like to thank my parents, Gary and Lucy Peters, for their continued support and encouragement. I would also like to thank Barry Greig and Linda Hewlett from the University of Alberta Devonian Botanic Garden for their assistance, the Voogds from Sunstar Nurseries and Kevin Frey from Estate Perennials for his vast knowledge of lilies and all things green. A special thanks to Patricia Hanbidge for her enthusiasm, hard work, sense of humor and wonderful gardening stories. Thanks to all who contributed photos and allowed us to photograph their gardens. I would also like to acknowledge those fellow prairie gardeners who have shared their love of gardening with me over the years. I would like to dedicate this book to my grandma, Annie Urban, a dedicated gardener and an inspiration not only to me, but to anyone who had the pleasure of knowing her. My family's heritage began on the prairies, on my grandparents' farm just outside of Prince Albert, Saskatchewan. I know she'd be so proud of this accomplishment. I hope you enjoy what this book has to offer and use it frequently over the years. Experiment, have fun and happy gardening to all. —*Laura Peters*

The Flowers at a Glance

Pictorial Guide in Alphabetical Order

Arabis
p. 70

Artemisia
p. 72

Astilbe
p. 76

Baptisia
p. 80

Bellflower
p. 82

Bergamot
p. 86

Bergenia
p. 90

Bishop's Hat
p. 94

Bitterroot
p. 96

Bleeding Heart
p. 98

Buttercup
p. 102

Chrysanthemum
p. 104

Columbine
p. 116

Coral Bells
p. 120

Cimicifuga
p. 108

Clematis
p. 110

Corydalis
p. 124

Cranesbill
p. 126

Crocus
p. 130

Cupid's Dart
p. 132

Daylily
p. 134

Delphinium
p. 138

Elephant Ears
p. 142

Euphorbia
p. 146

Evening Primrose
p. 150

False Solomon's Seal
p. 152

Flax
p. 154

Fleece-Flower
p. 156

Forget-Me-Not
p. 158

Foxglove
p. 160

Gaillardia
p. 164

Gentian
p. 166

Globe Thistle
p. 168

Goat's Beard
p. 170

Goutweed
p. 174

Hens and Chicks
p. 176

Hops
p. 178

Hosta
p. 180

Iris
p. 186

Jacob's Ladder
p. 190

Japanese Painted Fern
p. 192

Japanese Spurge
p. 194

Joe Pye Weed
p. 196

Lady's Mantle
p. 198

Lamb's Ears
p. 200

Lamium
p. 202

Liatris
p. 206

Lily-of-the-Valley
p. 214

Lupine
p. 216

Lysimachia
p. 220

Lily
p. 208

Mallow
p. 224

Maltese Cross
p. 228

Marsh Marigold
p. 230

Masterwort
p. 232

Meadow Rue
p. 234

Meadowsweet
p. 236

Monkshood
p. 240

Mullein
p. 244

Obedient Plant
p. 248

Peony
p. 256

Phlox
p. 260

Ostrich Fern
p. 250

Penstemon
p. 252

Pincushion Flower
p. 264

Pinks
p. 266

Potentilla
p. 274

Prairie Mallow
p. 276

Poppy
p. 270

Prickly Pear Cactus
p. 278

Primrose
p. 280

Purple Coneflower
p. 284

Sandwort
p. 294

Rudbeckia
p. 288

Russian Sage
p. 292

Saxifrage
p. 296

Sea Holly
p. 300

Sea Lavender
p. 302

Sedum
p. 304

Siberian Bugloss
p. 308

Snow-in-Summer
p. 310

Soapwort
p. 312

Sweet Woodruff
p. 322

Solomon's Seal
p. 314

Speedwell
p. 316

Spiderwort
p. 320

Thrift
p. 324

Thyme
p. 326

Tiarella
p. 330

Trollius
p. 332

Viola
p. 334

Windflower
p. 336

Introduction

PERENNIALS ARE PLANTS THAT TAKE THREE OR MORE YEARS TO complete their life cycles. This broad definition includes trees and shrubs. More narrowly, we refer to herbaceous perennials as perennials. Herbaceous perennials live for three or more years, but they generally die back to the ground at the end of the growing season and start fresh with new shoots each spring. Some perennials do not die back completely and still others remain green all winter. Subshrubs such as thyme, and evergreen perennials such as pinks, are examples of other plants categorized as perennials. Although winter conditions vary widely across Saskatchewan and Manitoba, many perennials will flourish in any conditions, providing the gardener with an almost limitless selection of colours, sizes and forms. This versatility, along with the beauty and permanence of perennials, lies at the root of their continued and growing popularity.

Climate, Geography & Soil

Many prairie gardeners are aware of the vast range of perennials that they can grow. In fact, Manitoba and Saskatchewan possess some of the most enthusiastic gardeners in the country. An array of horticultural societies and gardening clubs exists throughout the two provinces, catering to every level of gardening interest. A large chunk of the population, however, is still unaware of the potential growing material available to prairie gardeners. Our continental climate in Saskatchewan and Manitoba may sometimes be harsh, but it's also diverse and varied, allowing for growing opportunities that should be explored. Both provinces have a reasonably lengthy season, including areas with 90–140 frost-free days, suitable for growing a wide variety of perennials. Gardeners across the prairies experience many of the same climatic features, but temperature and soil conditions can vary.

The geography of Saskatchewan and Manitoba varies, from the general flatness of the Interior Plains to the rocky, forested expanses of the Canadian Shield. The soils change from one region to another, and the weather becomes more extreme the farther north one goes, as the soil, vegetation and human population begin to thin. The central portion of each province receives slightly colder temperatures in winter and maintains its snow coverage for longer periods, which allows for better winter protection for tender or semi-hardy perennials in sheltered microclimates. The southern parts of each province are generally drier and milder and have less reliable snow coverage. We may resent snow sometimes, but without it, fewer perennials would grow successfully in our climate. Good snow cover can be a gardener's best friend, along with the fabulous light of our sweeping prairie skies.

One of the many factors that affect one's ability to successfully grow a plant is soil type. Luckily, our native soils are, in general, very good for growing all kinds of plants. Soil characteristics vary across Saskatchewan and Manitoba, ranging from heavy clay to sandy silt, depending on the region. You probably already know if your soil is sandy, heavy clay or loamy.

Hardiness Zones Map

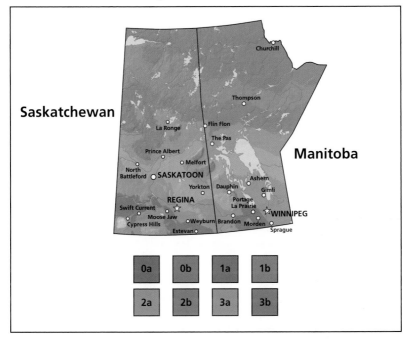

Taking what you have and amending it with organic matter is a step in the right direction, but before doing that, consider having your soil tested by a soil-testing lab, usually connected to a university. Contact the lab nearest you to ask for a soil-testing kit and directions on how to submit your sample. The results of such a test will give you the exact specifications of your soil's pH, macronutrient content and percentage of organic material, in addition to directions on how to alter the soil's characteristics to better grow your perennials and other plants. A soil test done by a qualified lab gives more accurate, comprehensive results and better recommendations than a do-it-yourself soil-testing kit.

Microclimates

Contrary to popular belief, more Saskatchewan and Manitoba gardeners are successfully growing tender perennials that survive our colder winters and are not limiting themselves to plants hardy only to zones 2–4. That's partly because all gardeners have the ability to create microclimates in their gardens, or to exploit existing ones. It's truly exciting to experiment with microclimates once you discover them.

Microclimates are small areas created by the topography in the garden that may be more or less favourable for growing different plants. Microclimates can be created, for example, in the shelter of a building or stand of evergreen trees; in a low, still hollow; at the

top of a barren, windswept hill, or close to a large body of water. Microclimates that raise the zone level a notch give gardeners almost anywhere in Saskatchewan and Manitoba the possibility of growing perennials that people who live in milder climates claim won't grow here.

Challenging the assumption of what's hardy and what's not is part of the fun of growing perennials. Those who experiment with various perennials discover that the possibilities often far exceed original expectations. Perennials are not limited to growing in the ground, either. They can be grown in a variety of containers as well. It is all a matter of exploring and learning not to become discouraged when you experience failures from time to time. That is only part of the gardening adventure. Unlike trees and shrubs, perennials are relatively inexpensive and easy to share with friends and neighbours, so the more varieties you try, the more likely you'll discover what loves to grow in your garden. When it comes to perennials, the best advice is to dig in and 'just grow for it.'

Perennial Gardens

A GOOD PERENNIAL GARDEN IS ABOUT MORE THAN JUST FLOWERS, and it can be interesting throughout the entire year.

Perennials can be used alone in a garden or combined with other plants such as trees, shrubs and annuals. They can form a bridge in the garden between the permanent structure provided by trees and shrubs and the temporary colour provided by annuals. They often flower for longer and grow to mature size more quickly than shrubs do. In many cases, they require less care and are less prone to pests and diseases than annuals.

Perennials can be included in any type, size or style of garden. From the riot of colour in a cottage garden, to the cool, soothing greens of a woodland garden, to a welcoming cluster of pots on a front doorstep, perennials open up a world of design possibilities for even the most inexperienced gardener.

A variety of textures adds interest to your garden.

When planning your garden, it is very important to decide what you like. If you enjoy the plants that are in your garden, then you are more likely to take proper care of them. Decide what style of garden you like as well as what plants you like. Think about the gardens you have most admired in your neighbourhood, in books or while visiting friends. Use these ideas as starting points for planning your own garden.

Select perennials that flower at different times so that some part of your garden flowers all season. Next, consider the size and shape of the perennials you choose. A variety of forms will make your garden more interesting. The size of your garden influences these decisions,

but do not limit a small garden to small perennials or a large garden to large perennials. Use a balanced combination of plant sizes in scale with their specific location.

Perennials come in many colours, and it's interesting to consider the varying effects that different colours have on our senses. Cool colours like blue, purple and green are soothing and make small spaces seem bigger. Warm colours like red, orange and yellow are more stimulating and appear to fill large spaces. Crisp and clean colours like white, grey and silver can tie it all together while accentuating brighter colours.

For more information about plant flowering times, heights and colours, see the Quick Reference Chart on p. 340.

Always consider the foliage of the perennials you want to use. Foliage can be bold or flimsy, shiny, fuzzy, silky, rough or smooth; it can be big or small, light or dark; its colour can vary from yellow or purple to a multitude of greens, and it can be striped, splashed, edged, dotted or mottled. The famous white gardens at Sissinghurst, England, were designed not to showcase a haphazard collection of white flowers, but to remove the distraction of colour and allow the eye to linger on the foliage, to appreciate its subtle appeal. Flowers come and go, but a garden planned with careful attention to foliage will always be interesting.

Textures can also create a sense of space. Larger leaves are considered coarse, and their visibility from a greater distance makes spaces seem smaller and more shaded. Small leaves, or those that are finely divided, are considered fine and create a greater sense of space and light. Some gardens are designed solely by texture.

Coarse-textured Perennials

Bishop's Hat
Coral Bells
Daylily
Elephant Ears
Hops
Hosta
Lamb's Ears
Purple Coneflower
Sedum 'Autumn Joy'
Siberian Bugloss

Hops

Sedum 'Autumn Joy'

Fine-textured Perennials

- Artemisia
- Astilbe
- Bleeding Heart
- Columbine
- Cranesbill
- Goat's Beard
- Lady's Mantle
- Meadow Rue
- Snow-in-Summer
- Thyme

Astilbe

Coral Bells

Decide how much time you will have to devote to your garden. With good planning and preparation, you can enjoy a low-maintenance perennial garden. Consider using plants that perform well with little care and ones that are generally pest and disease free.

Low-maintenance Perennials

- Bergamot*
- Bernia
- Bleeding Heart
- Coral Bells
- Daylily*
- Foxglove*
- Globe Thistle
- Hosta
- Japanese Spurge
- Lamium*
- Pinks
- *may become invasive

Foxglove

Getting Started

ONCE YOU HAVE SOME IDEAS ABOUT WHAT YOU WANT IN YOUR
garden, consider the growing conditions. Plants grown in ideal conditions,
or conditions as close to ideal as you can get them, are healthier and less
prone to pest and disease problems than plants growing in stressful conditions. Some plants considered high maintenance become low maintenance
when grown in the right conditions.

Do not attempt to make your garden match the growing conditions
of the plants you like. Choose plants
to match your garden conditions.
The levels of light, the type of soil
and the amount of exposure in your
garden provide guidelines that make
plant selection easier. A sketch of
your garden, drawn on graph paper,
may help you organize the various
considerations you want to keep in
mind as you plan. Start with the

garden as it exists. Knowing your growing conditions can prevent costly mistakes—plan ahead rather than correct later. You will still make mistakes, but there will be fewer of them. That is all part of the learning process.

Light

Buildings, trees, fences and even the time of day all influence the amount of light that gets into your garden. The four basic categories of light in the garden are full sun, partial shade, light shade and full shade. Knowing what light is available in your garden will help you decide where to put each plant.

Full sun locations, such as a south- facing wall, receive direct sunlight all or most of the day. Partial shade or partial sun locations receive direct sun for part of the day and shade for the rest. An east- or west-facing wall gets only partial sun. Light shade locations receive shade most or all of the day, but some sun gets through to ground level. The ground under a small-leaved tree is often lightly shaded, and small dapples of sun are visible on the ground beneath the tree. Full shade locations receive no direct sunlight. The north side of a house is considered to be in full shade.

Remember that the intensity of the full sun can vary. For example, between buildings in a city, heat can become trapped and magnified, baking all but the most heat-tolerant of

Sedum

plants in a concrete oven. The sun is generally in a higher position for longer periods of time. A fully exposed area can receive up to 16 hours of sunlight a day. Even a shaded northern exposure can receive a touch of sunlight early in the morning and later in the evening. Plants that normally wouldn't be prone to burning or scalding, such as certain sun-loving perennials, cannot fully tolerate intense prairie sunlight, so provide a shadier location for touchy plant material.

Phlox

Perennials for Full Sun
- Artemisia
- Daylily
- Hens and Chicks
- Phlox
- Russian Sage
- Sedum
- Thyme

Perennials for Full Shade
- Astilbe
- Bleeding Heart
- Elephant Ears
- Foamflower
- Hosta
- Lamium
- Monkshood
- Siberian Bugloss
- Solomon's Seal

Lamium

Soil
Plants and the soil they grow in have a unique relationship. Many plant functions go on underground. Soil holds air, water, nutrients and organic matter. Plant roots depend upon these resources while using the soil to hold themselves upright. Soil is the backbone of your garden, so invest in the best soil available and your plants will be amply rewarded.

Soil is made up of particles of different sizes. Sand particles are the largest. Water drains quickly out of sandy soil and nutrients are quickly washed away. Sand has lots of air space and doesn't compact easily. Clay particles are the smallest and can only be seen through a microscope. Water penetrates clay very slowly and drains very slowly. Clay holds the most nutrients, but there is very little room for air, so clay compacts quite easily. Most soil is made up of a combination of different particle sizes. This soil is called loam.

Perennials for Sandy Soil

Artemisia
Euphorbia
Flax
Globe Thistle
Penstemon
Pinks
Poppy
Russian Sage
Thyme

Perennials for Clay Soil

Bergenia
Bishop's Hat
Cranesbill
Daylily
Foamflower
Goat's Beard
Hosta
Lamium
Windflower

The other aspect of soil to consider is the pH, the scale on which the level of acidity or alkalinity is analyzed. Soils in Saskatchewan and Manitoba vary from very acidic to slightly alkaline. You can test your soil if you plan to amend it, but be aware that the testing kits available at most garden centres are not especially reliable or detailed. A more comprehensive lab test (see p.13) may cost a bit more, but it also provides much more information and, more importantly, explains how to correct your soil's problems. Soil acidity influences which nutrients are available for plants. Soil can be made more alkaline with the addition of horticultural lime. Soil acidity can be increased with the addition of acidic materials such as peat moss or pine needles. Altering the pH of your soil takes a long time, often many years, and is not easy. If only one or two plants you are trying to grow require a more or less acidic soil, consider growing them in a container or raised bed where it will be easier to control and amend

Goat's beard

Penstemon

the pH as needed. Most plants prefer soil pH between 5.5 and 7.5.

Another thing to consider is how quickly the water drains out of your soil. Rocky soil on a hillside will probably drain very quickly and should be reserved for those plants that prefer a very well-drained soil. Low-lying areas tend to retain water longer, and some areas may rarely drain at all. Moist areas can be used for plants that require a consistent water supply, and the areas that stay wet can be used for plants that prefer boggy conditions. Drainage can be improved in very wet areas by adding organic matter, compost or by building raised beds. Water retention in sandy soil can be improved through the addition of organic matter.

Perennials for Moist Soil

- Astilbe
- Bleeding Heart
- Elephant Ears
- Goat's Beard
- Hosta
- Iris
- Lady's Mantle
- Marsh Marigold
- Meadowsweet
- Monkshood

Bleeding heart

Lamb's ears

Perennials for Dry Soil

- Artemisia
- Globe Thistle
- Hens and Chicks
- Lamb's Ears
- Lupine
- Pinks
- Russian Sage
- Sedum
- Thrift

Exposure

Finally, consider the exposure in your garden. Wind, heat, cold and rain are some of the elements your garden is exposed to, and different plants are better adapted than others to the potential damage these forces can cause. Buildings, walls, fences, hills, hedges and trees can all influence your garden's exposure.

Wind in particular can cause extensive damage to your plants. Plants can become dehydrated in windy locations because they may not be able to draw water out of the soil fast enough to replace the water that is lost through the leaves. Tall, stiff-stemmed perennials can be knocked over or broken by strong winds. Some plants that do not require staking in a sheltered location may need to be staked in a more exposed one. Use plants that are recommended for exposed locations or temper the effect of the wind with a hedge or some trees. A solid wall will create turbulence on the leeward side, but a looser structure, like a hedge, breaks up the force of the wind and protects a larger area.

Map out your garden's various growing conditions, identifying shaded, wet and windy areas. This guideline will help you recognize where your plants will do best.

Perennials for Exposed Locations

Candytuft
Columbine
Creeping Phlox
Daylily
Euphorbia
Flax
Penstemon
Purple Coneflower
Sedum (groundcover species)
Thyme

Thyme

Columbine

Preparing the Garder

TAKING THE TIME BEFORE YOU START PLANTIN
prepare the flowerbeds will save you time later on. Removing
amending the soil with organic matter prior to planting is the first ste
caring for your perennials. Thoroughly digging over a bed and picking out
all the weeds by hand is the best technique.

Turning compost into beds

Removing weeds & debris

Composting

Compost is known as black gold for a reason. All soils, from the heaviest clay to the lightest sand, benefit from the addition of organic matter. Some of the best organic additives are compost, well-rotted manure and composted bark or mulch because they add nutrients as well as improve the soil. These additives improve heavy clay soils by loosening them and allowing air and water to penetrate. Organic matter improves sandy or light soils by increasing the ability of the soils to retain water, which allows plants to absorb nutrients before they are leeched away. Mix organic matter into the soil with a garden fork. Within a few months, earthworms and other decomposer organisms

will break down the organic matter; at the same time, their activities will keep the soil from compacting.

In forests, meadows or other natural environments, organic debris such as leaves and various plant bits break down on the soil surface, and the nutrients are gradually made available to the plants that are growing there. In the home garden, where pests and diseases may be a problem and where untidy debris isn't practical, a compost pile or bin is useful. Compost is a great regular additive for your perennial garden and good composting methods will help reduce pest and disease problems.

Compost can be made in a pile, in a wooden box or in a purchased composter, and the process is not complicated. A pile of kitchen

Wooden compost bins

Brown matter includes chopped straw, shredded leaves or sawdust, and green matter may be vegetable scraps, grass clippings or pulled weeds. Green matter breaks down quickly and produces nitrogen, which composting organisms use to break down brown matter. Spread the green materials evenly throughout the pile by layering them between brown materials.

Layers of soil or finished compost will introduce the organisms that are necessary to break down the compost pile properly. Fertilizers available at garden centres can help speed up the composting process. If the pile seems very dry, add a bit of water as you layer. The pile needs to be moist but not soggy.

scraps, grass clippings and fall leaves will eventually break down if simply left alone. The process can be sped up if a few simple guidelines are followed.

Use brown (dry) as well as green (fresh) materials with a higher proportion of brown to green matter.

To speed up decomposition, introduce air into the pile by turning

Plastic compost bins

Material for compost

it over or poking holes into it with a pitch fork every week or two. A well-aerated compost pile will generate a high degree of heat. Use a thermometer attached to a long probe, like a meat thermometer, to take the temperature near the middle of the pile. Compost can easily reach temperatures of 71° C (160° F) while decomposing. At this temperature, weed seeds are destroyed and many damaging soil organisms killed. Most beneficial organisms are not killed unless the temperature rises above this temperature. Once your pile reaches 71° C (160° F), let it sit. When the temperature drops significantly, turn the pile to aerate it and stimulate the process again.

Your compost has reached the end of its cycle when you can no longer recognize the matter that went into it, and when the temperature no longer rises when you turn the pile. It may take as little as one month to reach this stage and be ready to spread onto your perennial garden. It will have a good mixture

An active (hot) compost bin

Finished compost

of nutrients and be rich in beneficial organisms.

Avoid putting any diseased, pest-ridden materials into your compost pile. By adding this material, you risk spreading problems throughout your entire garden. If you do put questionable material in the pile, put it as near to the centre as possible, where the temperatures are highest. Egg shells, coffee grounds and filters, tea bags, fish bones,

Compost worms

shrimp shells and lint from your vacuum cleaner and dryer are all beneficial additions, but do not add dog or cat feces, kitty litter, fats, dairy or meat to the mix. These items will attract pests and will begin to smell, resulting in a mess. Remember the basics and you'll end up with black gold: layers of wet, dry, green and brown and smaller pieces that break down quickly.

If you have limited space, you can still make compost using red worms, which are available at any bait shop. Follow this simple process: get a large plastic container and drill drainage and air holes into it. Place shredded, lightly moistened newspaper (no glossy newsprint) into the container and bury the worms with cut-up kitchen scraps. Start with $1/2$ kg (1 lb.) of worms, and they will multiply to fill their space. The composter won't smell if the worms are not overloaded with too many scraps. The worms will create usable, nutrient-rich compost in as little as six weeks.

Selecting Perennials

PLANTS CAN BE PURCHASED OR STARTED FROM SEED. PURCHASED plants may begin flowering the same year they are planted, while plants started from seed may take several years to mature. Starting plants from seed is more economical if you want large numbers of plants. (See how to start seeds in the Propagation section, p. 44.)

Plants and seeds are available from many sources. Garden centres, the Internet, mail order catalogues and even friends and neighbours are excellent sources of perennials. Garden clubs or societies promote the exchange of traditional and unusual seeds and plants, and many public gardens sell seeds from rare plants.

Get your perennials from a reputable source and be sure that the plants are not diseased or pest-ridden.

Purchased perennials come in two main forms. They are sold in pots or they are sold bare-root, usually packed in moist peat moss or sawdust. Potted perennials are actively growing and have likely been raised

Plant on left is root-bound; plant on right is healthy.

in the pot. Bare-root perennials are typically dormant (without top growth), although some of the previous year's growth may be evident, or there may be new growth starting. Sometimes the piece of root has no signs of obvious growth. Both potted and bare-root perennials are good purchases. In each case, look for certain things to make sure that you are getting a plant of the best quality.

Potted plants come in many sizes. Perennials in larger containers may take a little longer to establish and may experience more extensive transplant shock. The up side is that you're likely to have a fully mature plant in less time. Many factors are involved in what size of perennial to choose. Is budget a factor? Are you in a hurry to have a mature-looking plant? In the long run, perennials are

going to reach their mature size regardless of what size plant you begin with, so choose what's best for you.

Most perennials grow quickly once they are planted in the garden. Select plants that seem to be a good size for the pot they are in. When tapped lightly out of the pot, the roots should be visible but not winding and twisting around the inside of the pot. The leaves should be a healthy colour.

If the leaves appear to be chewed or damaged, check carefully for insects or diseases before you purchase any plant. If you find insects on the plant, you may not want to purchase it unless you are willing to cope with the hitchhikers you are taking home. If the plant is diseased, do not purchase it. Deal with any pest problems before you move the plant into the garden to prevent spreading the pest.

Once you get your plant home, water it if it is dry, and keep it in a lightly shaded location until you plant it. Remove any damaged growth and discard it. Try to plant your new perennial into the garden as soon as possible.

Bare-root plants are most commonly sold through mail order, but some are available in garden centres, usually in the spring. Choose roots that are dormant because a plant may take longer to establish itself if it is growing before being placed in the garden. It may have too little energy to recover after trying to grow in the stressful conditions of a plastic bag.

Cut off any damaged parts of the roots with a very sharp knife. Bare-root perennials need to be planted more quickly than potted plants because they will dehydrate quickly out of soil. Soak the roots in lukewarm water and either plant them directly in the garden or into pots with good-quality potting soil until they can be moved to the garden.

It can be difficult to distinguish the top from the bottom of some bare-root plants. Usually there is a tell-tale dip or stub from which the plant previously grew. If you can't find any distinguishing characteristics, lay the root in the ground on its side and the plant will send the roots down and the shoots up.

Root mass of root-bound plant

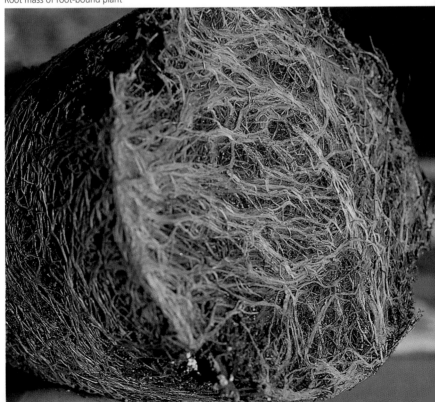

Planting Perennials

ONCE YOU HAVE YOUR GARDEN PLANNED, THE SOIL WELL PREPARED
and the perennials ready, it is time to plant.

Potted Perennials

Perennials in pots are convenient because you can space them out across the bed or rearrange them before you start to dig. Once you have the collection organized, you can begin planting. Ensure that the rootball is moist prior to planting, and do not remove the plant from the pot before you transplant to prevent the roots from drying out.

To plant potted perennials, start by digging a hole about the width and depth of the pot. Remove the perennial from the pot. If the pot is small enough, you can hold your hand across the top of the pot, letting your fingers straddle the stem of the plant, and then turn it upside-down. Never pull on the stem or leaves to get a plant out of a pot. Cut a difficult pot off rather than risk damaging the plant. Tease a few roots out of the soil ball to get the plant growing in the right direction. If the roots have become densely wound around the inside of the pot, you should cut into the root mass with a sharp knife to encourage new growth into the surrounding soil. The process of cutting into the bottom half of the rootball and spreading the two halves of the mass outward like butterfly wings is called butterflying the roots and is a very effective way to promote fast growth of pot-bound perennials that are being transplanted. Place the plant into the prepared hole. It should be buried to the same level as it was in the pot, or a little higher, to allow for the soil to settle. If the plant is too low in the ground, it may rot when rain collects around the crown. Fill the soil in around the roots and firm it down. Water the plant well and regularly as soon as you have planted it until it establishes itself.

If your perennials have identification tags, poke them into the soil next to the newly planted perennials. Next spring, when most of your perennial bed is nothing but a few stubs of green, the tags will help you with identification and remind you that there is indeed a plant in that bare patch of soil.

Bare-root Perennials

Support plant as you remove pot (above)

During planting, bare-root perennials should not be spaced out across the bed unless you have planted them in temporary pots. Roots dry out very quickly if you leave them lying about waiting to be planted. If you want to visualize your spacing, you can poke sticks into the ground or put rocks down to represent the locations of your perennials.

If you have been keeping your bare-root perennials in potting soil, you may find that the roots have not grown enough to knit the soil together and that all the soil falls away from the root when you remove it from the pot. Don't be concerned. Simply follow the regular root-planting instructions. If the soil does hold together, plant the root the way you would a potted perennial.

Loosen rootball before planting (above)

Root Types

The type of hole you need to dig will depend on the type of roots the perennial has. Plants with fibrous roots will need a mound of soil in the centre of the planting hole over which the roots can be spread out evenly. The hole should be dug as deep as the longest roots. Mound the soil into the centre of the hole up to ground level. Spread the roots out around the mound and cover them with loosened soil. If you are adding just one or two plants and do not want to prepare an entire bed, dig a hole twice as wide and deep as the rootball. Add a little peat moss for improved air circulation, water retention and to lighten up heavy, clay-based soils. Add slow-release organic amendments, including compost or a mycorrhizae-based product, to the backfill of soil that you spread around the plant.

Plants with a taproot need a hole that is narrow and about as deep as the root is long. The job is easily done with the help of a trowel: open up a suitable hole, tuck the root into it and fill it in again with the soil around it. If you can't tell which end is up, plant the root on its side.

Some plants, such as irises, have roots that appear to be taproots, but the plant seems to be growing off the side of the root rather than upwards from one end. These roots are called rhizomes. Rhizomes should be planted horizontally in a shallow hole and covered with soil.

In most cases, you should try to get the crown at or just above soil level and loosen the surrounding soil in the planting hole. Keep the roots thoroughly watered until the plants are well established.

Whether the plants are potted or bare-root, leave them alone and let them recover from the stress of planting. In the first month, you will need only to water the plant regularly, weed it and watch for pests. A mulch spread on the bed around your plants will improve moisture retention in the soil and control weeds.

If you have prepared your beds properly, you probably won't have to fertilize in the first year. If you do want to fertilize, wait until your new plants have started healthy new growth, and apply a weak fertilizer to avoid damaging the new root growth.

Containers

Perennials can also be grown in planters for portable displays that can be moved around the garden. They can be used on patios or decks, in gardens with very poor soil or in yards where kids and dogs might destroy a traditional perennial bed. Many perennials, such as hostas and

Artemisia ORIENTAL LIMELIGHT

daylilies, can grow in the same container without any fresh potting soil for five or six years. Be sure to fertilize and water perennials in planters more often than those growing in the ground. Dig your finger deep into the soil around the perennial to make sure it needs water. Too much water in the planter causes root rot.

Always use a good-quality potting mix or a soil mix intended for containers in your planters. Garden soil quickly loses its structure and becomes a solid lump in a container, preventing air, water and roots from penetrating into the soil. Plants will never thrive in a container if planted in soil from the garden. At the very least, combine half garden soil with half peat moss, and mix the two together well.

When designing a planter garden, you can either keep one type of perennial in each planter and display many planters together, or mix different perennials in large planters along with annuals and bulbs. The latter choice results in a dynamic bouquet of flowers and foliage. Keep tall, upright perennials such as garden phlox (*Phlox paniculata*) in the centre of the planter, the rounded or bushy types like coreopsis (*Coreopsis verticillata*) around the sides and low-growing or draping perennials such as species candytuft (*Iberis sempervirens*) along the edge of the planter. Perennials that have long bloom times or attractive foliage are good for planters.

Choose hardy perennials that can tolerate difficult conditions. Planters are exposed to extremes of our variable weather. They bake and dry out quickly in hot summer weather, become waterlogged after a couple of rainy days and freeze in cold winter winds. Not all perennials are tough enough to survive in these extreme conditions. Some of the more invasive perennials are a good choice, because their spread is controlled by the container, but at the same time they are tough to kill.

Perennials in planters are more susceptible to winter damage because the exposed sides of the container allow for greater fluctuations in temperature and provide very little insulation for roots. The container itself may even crack when exposed to a deep freeze. Don't despair; there are plenty of things you can do to get planters through a tough Saskatchewan and Manitoba winter in great shape. You can simply move the planter to a more sheltered spot. Most perennials require some cold in the winter to flower the next year, so find a spot that is still

Hens and chicks

cold, but sheltered. An unheated garage or enclosed porch is a good place; even your garden shed will offer your plants more protection than they would get sitting in the great outdoors, exposed to the elements on all sides. You may also want to wrap more tender perennials with insulating material for extra protection from the cold.

If you haven't got the room or access to these spaces, consider your basement window wells. They are sheltered, below ground and have a nearby source of some heat from the window. Wait until your pots have frozen. Layer straw at the bottom of the well, sit your pots on the straw, and then cover them with more straw. Waiting until the pots freeze prevents rot and can keep pesky mice from easily eating the succulent treats you are conveniently leaving out for them. If mice are a problem, you may want to consider sprinkling some commercial mouse bait around the pots. If you have pets or small children around or don't want to use poisons, a layer of Styrofoam insulation under and on top of the pots will also provide protection, without being quite so appealing to small rodents.

The pots themselves can be winter-proofed before you plant your perennials. Place a layer of Styrofoam insulation (packing peanuts) at the bottom of the pot and around the inside of the planter before adding your soil and plants. Make sure excess water can still drain freely from the container. Commercial planter insulating materials are available at garden centres. Insulating containers is particularly useful for high-rise dwellers with balcony gardens. This insulation will also protect the roots from heat buildup in the summer.

Finally, planters can be buried in the garden for the winter. Find an open space in a flowerbed, dig a hole deep enough to allow you to sink the planter up to its rim. It'll be messy in spring when you dig it up. It also requires that enough empty space be available in the garden to fit your planter or planters.

Perennials for Planters
Artemisia
Cranesbill
Daylily
Goat's Beard
Hosta
Lady's Mantle
Lamium
Penstemon
Pinks
Potentilla
Saxifrage
Sedum
Snow-in-Summer
Speedwell

Lady's mantle

Caring for Perennials

MANY PERENNIALS REQUIRE LITTLE CARE, BUT ALL WILL BENEFIT from a few maintenance basics. Weeding, pruning, deadheading and staking are just a few of the chores that, when done on a regular basis, keep major work to a minimum.

Weeding is an important task.

Weeding

Controlling weeds is one of the most important things you will have to do in your garden. Weeds compete with your perennials for light, nutrients and space. Weeds can also harbour pests and diseases. Try to prevent weeds from germinating. If they do germinate, pull them out while they are still small and before they have a chance to flower, set seed and start a whole new generation of problems.

Weeds can be pulled out by hand or with a hoe. Quickly scuffing across the soil surface with the hoe will pull out small weeds and sever larger ones from their roots. A layer of mulch is an excellent way to suppress weeds.

Mulching

Mulches are important gardening tools. They prevent weed seeds from germinating by blocking out the light. Soil temperatures remain more consistent and more moisture is retained under a layer of mulch. Mulch also prevents soil erosion during heavy rain or strong winds. Organic mulches can consist of things like compost, bark chips, shredded leaves or grass clippings. Organic mulches are desirable because they improve the soil and add nutrients as they break down.

In spring, spread a couple inches of mulch over your perennial beds around your plants. Keep the area immediately around the crown or stem of your plants clear. Mulch that is too close to your plants can trap moisture and prevent good air

circulation, encouraging disease. If the layer of mulch disappears into the soil over summer, you should replenish it.

A fresh layer of mulch, up to 10 cm (4") thick, can be laid once the ground freezes in fall, to protect the plants over winter. This layer is particularly important if you can't depend on snow to cover your garden in the winter, as is the case in much of central and southern Saskatchewan and Manitoba. You can cover the plants with dry material like chopped straw, pine needles or shredded leaves. Keep in mind that as the ground freezes, so may your pile of potential mulch. One solution is to cover most of the bed with mulch, leaving only the plants exposed, before the ground freezes. Put the extra mulch needed to cover the plants in a large plastic bag or in a wheelbarrow, and put it somewhere where it will take longer to freeze, perhaps in a garage or garden shed. Once the ground is completely frozen, you will have a supply of mulch that you can use to cover the plants.

In late winter or early spring, once the weather starts to warm up, pull the mulch layer off the plants and see if they have started growing. If they have, you can pull the mulch back, but keep it nearby in case you need to put it back on to protect the tender new growth from a late frost. Once your plants are well on their way and you are no longer worried about frost, you can remove the protective mulch completely. Compost the old mulch and apply a new spring and summer mulch.

Applying bark chip mulch

Removing whole spent flowering stem

Pinching off spent bloom, or deadheading

Deadheading

Deadheading—the removal of flowers once they are finished blooming—serves several purposes. It keeps plants looking tidy, prevents them from spreading seeds (and therefore seedlings) throughout the garden, often prolongs blooming and helps prevent pest and disease problems.

Deadheading is not necessary for every plant. Some plants have seedheads that are left in place to provide interest in the garden over winter. Other plants are short-lived, and by leaving some of the seedheads in place, you encourage future generations to replace the old plants. Hollyhock is one example of a short-lived perennial that reseeds. In some cases, the self-sown seedlings do not possess the attractive features of the parent plant. Deadheading may be required in these cases.

Perennials with Interesting Seedheads

Astilbe
Clematis
Crocus
False Solomon's Seal
Goat's Beard
Meadowsweet
Poppy
Purple Coneflower
Russian Sage
Sedum 'Autumn Joy'

Clematis

Corydalis

Perennials that Self-seed
Bleeding Heart (variable seedlings)
Corydalis
Foxglove
Lady's Mantle
Lupine
Pinks

Deadhead flowers by pinching them off with your fingers or by snipping them off with hand pruners. Bushy plants that have many tiny flowers, particularly ones that have a short bloom period like basket-of-gold, can be more aggressively pruned back with garden shears once they are finished flowering. In some cases, as with creeping phlox, shearing will promote new growth and possibly blooms later in the season.

Perennials to Shear Back After Blooming
Creeping Phlox
Bellflower
Cranesbill
Lamium
Potentilla
Snow-in-Summer
Thyme

Pruning

Many perennials will benefit from a bit of grooming. Resilient health, plentiful blooming and more compact growth are the signs of a well-groomed garden. Pinching, thinning and disbudding plants before they flower will enhance the beauty of a perennial garden. The methods for pruning are simple, but some experimentation is required to get the right effect in your own garden.

Thin clump-forming perennials like coneflower or bee balm early in the year when shoots have just emerged. These plants develop a dense clump of stems that allows very little air or light into the centre of the plant. Remove half of the shoots when they first emerge. This removal will increase air circulation and prevent diseases such as powdery mildew. The increased light encourages more compact growth and more flowers. Throughout the growing season, thin any growth that is weak, diseased or growing in the wrong direction.

Trimming or pinching perennials is a simple procedure, but timing it correctly and achieving just the right look can be tricky. Early in the year, before the flower buds have appeared, trim the plant to encourage new side shoots. Remove the tip and some stems just above a leaf or pair of leaves. Go stem by stem, but if you have a lot of plants, you can trim off the tops with your hedge shears to one-third of the height you expect the plants to reach. The growth that begins to emerge can be pinched again. Beautiful layered effects can be achieved by staggering the trimming times by a week or two.

Bee Balm

Perennials to Prune Early in the Season

Artemisia
Bergamot
Purple Coneflower
Sedum 'Autumn Joy'

Give plants enough time to set buds and flower. Continual pinching encourages very dense growth but also delays flowering. Most spring-flowering plants cannot be pinched back or they will not flower. Early-summer or mid-summer bloomers should be pinched only once, as early in the season as possible. Late-summer and fall bloomers can be pinched several times but should be left alone past June. Don't pinch the plant if flower buds have formed—it may not have enough energy or time left in the year to develop a new set of buds. Experimentation and keeping detailed notes will improve your pinching skills.

Disbudding, the final grooming stage, is the removal of some flower buds to encourage the remaining ones to produce larger flowers. This technique is popular with peony growers.

Staking

Staking, the use of poles or wires to hold plants erect, can often be avoided by astute thinning and pinching, but a few plants will always need a bit of support to look their best in your garden. Three types of stakes go with the different growth habits that need support. Plants that develop tall spikes, like hollyhock, delphinium and some foxgloves,

Artemisia

require each spike to be staked individually. A strong, narrow pole such as a bamboo stick can be pushed into the ground early in the year and the spike tied to the stake as it grows. A forked branch can also be used to support single-stem plants.

Many plants, such as peony, get a bit top-heavy as they grow and tend to flop over once they reach a certain height. A wire hoop, sometimes called a peony ring, is the most unobtrusive way to hold up such a plant. When the plant is young, the legs of the peony ring are pushed into the ground around it, and as the plant grows up, it is supported by the wire ring. At the same time the bushy growth hides the ring. Wire tomato cages can also be used.

Other plants, like coreopsis, form a floppy tangle of stems. These plants can be given a bit of support with twiggy branches that are

Peony

inserted into the ground around the young plants, which then grow up into the twigs.

Some people consider stakes to be unsightly no matter how hidden they are. You can do a couple of things to reduce the need for staking. Don't assume a plant will do better in a richer soil than is recommended. Very rich soil causes many plants to produce weak, leggy growth that is prone to falling over. Also, a plant that likes full sun will be stretched out and leggy if grown in the shade. Plants can give each other some support in the border. Mix in plants that have a more stable structure between the plants that need support. A plant may still fall over slightly, but only as far as its neighbour will allow. Many plants are available in compact varieties that don't require staking.

Spiral stakes

Watering

Watering is another basic of perennial care. Many perennials need little supplemental watering if they have been planted in their preferred conditions and are given a moisture-retaining mulch. The rule of watering is to water thoroughly and infrequently. When you do water, make sure the water penetrates several inches into the soil.

Fertilizing

If you prepare your beds well and add new compost to them each spring, you should not need to add extra fertilizer. If you have a limited amount of compost, you can mix a slow-release fertilizer into the soil around your perennials in the spring. Some plants, such as delphinium, are heavy feeders that need additional supplements throughout the growing season.

Many organic and chemical fertilizers are available at garden centres. Be sure to use the recommended quantity because too much fertilizer will do more harm than good. Roots can be burned by fertilizer that is applied in high concentrations. Problems are more likely to be caused by chemical fertilizers because they are more concentrated than organic fertilizers.

Delphinium is a heavy feeder.

Propagating Perennials

LEARNING TO PROPAGATE YOUR OWN PERENNIALS IS AN INTERESTING and challenging aspect of gardening that can save you money, but it also takes time and space. Seeds, cuttings and divisions are the three methods of increasing your perennial population, and benefits and problems are associated with each method.

Shade cloth over cold frame (below)

Seeds

Starting perennials from seed is a great way to propagate a large number of plants at a relatively low cost. Seeds can be purchased, or collected from your own or a friend's perennial garden. Propagating from seed does have its limitations. Some cultivars and varieties don't pass on their desirable traits to their offspring. Other perennials take a very long time to germinate, if they germinate at all, and an even longer time to grow to flowering size. However, many perennials grow easily from seed and flower within a year or two of being transplanted into the garden. Although starting perennials from seed can be difficult, the satisfaction of watching tiny seedlings grow into mature plants makes it worth the effort.

Specific propagation information is given for each plant in this book, but a few basic rules for starting all seeds should be followed. Some seeds can be started directly in the garden, but it is easier to control temperature and moisture levels and to provide a sterile environment if you start the seeds indoors. Seeds can be started in pots or, if you need a lot of plants, flats. Use a sterile soil mix intended for starting seeds. The soil will generally need to be kept moist but not soggy. Most seeds germinate in moderately warm temperatures of about 14–21°C (57°–70°F).

Many seed-starting supplies are available at garden centres. Some supplies are useful, but many are not necessary. Seed-tray dividers are useful. These dividers, often called plug trays, are made of plastic and prevent the roots from tangling with the roots of the other plants and from being disturbed when seedlings are transplanted. Heating coils or pads can be useful. Placed under the pots or flats, they keep the soil at a constant temperature.

All seedlings are susceptible to a problem called 'damping off,' which is caused by soil-borne fungal organisms. An afflicted seedling looks as though someone has pinched the stem at soil level, causing the plant to topple over. The pinched area blackens and the seedling dies. Sterile soil mix, air circulation and evenly moist

Filling cell packs

Using folded paper to plant small seeds
Spray bottle provides gentle mist

Prepared seed tray

soil will help prevent this problem. Products to prevent damping off are also available at your local garden centre.

Fill your pot or seed tray with the soil mix and firm it down slightly—not too firmly or the soil will not drain. Wet the soil before planting your seeds, or they may wash into clumps if the soil is watered after the seeds are planted. Large seeds can be planted individually and spaced out in pots or trays. If you have divided inserts for your trays, you can plant one or two seeds per section. Small seeds may have to be sprinkled over the soil mix a bit

Cinnamon powder is a natural fungicide and has been shown to be particularly effective against damping-off. In addition, weak chamomile tea (after it has cooled) is another natural fungicide.

more randomly. Fold a sheet of paper in half and place the small seeds in the crease. Gently tapping the underside of the fold will bounce or roll the seeds off the paper in a more controlled manner. Some seeds are so tiny that they look like dust. These seeds can be mixed with a small quantity of very fine sand and spread on the soil surface. These tiny seeds may not need to be covered with any more soil. Medium-sized seeds can be lightly covered and large seeds can be pressed into the soil and then lightly covered. Do not cover seeds that need to be exposed to light to germinate. Water the seeds using a very fine spray if the soil starts to dry out. A hand-held spray bottle will moisten the soil without disturbing the seeds.

Plant only one type of seed in the pot or flat. Each species has a different rate of germination and the germinated seedlings will require different conditions than the seeds that have yet to germinate. To keep the environment moist, you can place pots inside clear plastic bags. Change the bag or turn it inside out once the condensation starts to build up and drip. Plastic bags can be held up with stakes or wires poked in around the edges of the pot. Many seed trays come with clear plastic covers that can be placed over the flats to keep the moisture in. Covers can be removed once the seeds have germinated.

Seeds generally do not require a lot of light to germinate, so pots or trays can be kept in a warm, out-of-the-way place. Once the seeds have germinated, they can be placed in a bright location but out of direct sun. Plants should be transplanted to individual pots once they have three or four true leaves. True leaves are the ones that look like mature leaves. (The first one or two leaves are actually part of the seed.) Plants in trays can be left until neighbouring leaves start to touch each other. At this point, the plants will be competing for light and should be transplanted to individual pots.

Corydalis

Young seedlings do not need to be fertilized. Fertilizer will cause seedlings to produce soft, spindly growth that is susceptible to attack by insects and diseases. The seed itself provides all the nutrition the seedling will need. A fertilizer, diluted to one-quarter or one-half strength, can be used once seedlings have four or five true leaves.

Seeds have protective devices that prevent them from germinating when conditions are not favourable or from all germinating at once. In the wild, staggered germination periods improve the chances of survival. Many seeds will easily grow as soon as they are planted, but others need to have their defences lowered before they will germinate. Some seeds also produce poisonous chemicals in their seed coats to deter insects.

Perennials to Start from Seed

Columbine
Corydalis
Delphinium
Pinks
Foxglove
Lady's Mantle
Lupine

Seeds can be tricked into thinking the conditions are right for sprouting. Some thick-coated seeds can be soaked for a day or two in a glass of water to promote germination. Doing so mimics the end of the dry season and the beginning of the rainy season, which is when the plant would germinate in its natural environment. The water softens the seed coat and in some cases washes

Soaking seeds speeds germination.

away the chemicals that have been preventing germination. Lupine, for example, has seeds that need to be soaked before germinating.

Other thick-coated seeds need to have their seed coats scratched to allow moisture to penetrate the seed coat and prompt germination. In nature, birds scratch the seeds with gravel in their craws and acid in their stomachs. Nick the seeds with a knife or gently rub them between two sheets of sandpaper. Leave the seeds in a dry place for a day or so after scratching them before planting them. The seeds will have a chance to get ready for germination before they are exposed to water. Lupine and anemone have seeds that need their thick coats scratched.

Plants from northern climates often have seeds that wait until spring before they germinate. These seeds must be given a period of cold weather, which mimics winter, before they will germinate. One method of cold treatment is to plant the seeds in a pot or tray and place them in the refrigerator for up to two months. Check the container regularly and don't allow them to dry out. This method is fairly simple,

Flax grows easily from seed.

but not very practical if your refrigerator is crowded. Bergenia and windflower seeds respond to cold treatment.

A less space-consuming method is to mix the seeds with some moistened sand, peat or sphagnum moss. Place the mix in a sealable sandwich bag and pop it in the refrigerator for up to two months, again being sure the sand or moss doesn't dry out. The seeds can then be planted in the pot or tray. Spread the seeds and the moist sand or moss onto the prepared surface and press it down gently.

A cold frame is a wonderful tool for the gardener. It can be used to protect tender plants over the winter, to start vegetable seeds early in the

Scarifying seeds with sandpaper

Preparing seeds for cold treatment

spring, to harden plants off before moving them to the garden, to protect fall-germinating seedlings and young cuttings or divisions and to start seeds that need a cold treatment. This mini-greenhouse structure is built so that ground level on the inside of the cold frame is lower than on the outside. The angled, hinged lid is fitted with glass. The soil around the outside of the cold frame insulates the plants inside. The lid lets light in, collects some heat during the day and prevents rain from damaging tender plants. If the interior gets too hot, raise the lid for ventilation.

A hot frame or hotbed is a cold frame that has been modified by the addition of insulation and heat. A typical hot frame has heating coils or a heating cable in the floor to prevent the soil from freezing or to maintain a constant soil temperature for germinating seeds or rooting cuttings. Another way to create one is to set up a cold frame over a deep bed of horse manure about 61 cm (2') deep. The decomposition of the manure through the winter releases heat, which will keep the plants inside the frame warm. Keep plants in pots to prevent the roots from being burned by the manure.

Cuttings

Cuttings are an excellent way to propagate varieties and cultivars that you really like but that don't come true from seed or don't produce seed at all. Each cutting will grow into a reproduction of the parent plant. Cuttings are taken from the stems of some perennials and the roots of others.

Removing lower leaves

Dipping in rooting hormone

Firming cutting into soil

Newly planted cuttings

Healthy roots

Alternative plastic cold frame

Stem Cuttings

Stem cuttings are generally taken in the spring and early summer. During this time, plants go through a flush of fresh, new growth, either before or after flowering. Avoid taking cuttings from plants that are in flower. Plants that are in flower, or that are about to flower, are busy trying to reproduce; plants that are busy growing, by contrast, are already full of the right hormones to promote quick root growth. If you do take cuttings from plants that are flowering, be sure to remove the flowers and the buds to divert the plant's energy back into growing.

Large numbers of cuttings don't often result in as many plants. Cuttings need to be kept in a warm, humid place to root, which makes them very prone to fungal diseases. Providing proper sanitation and encouraging quick rooting will increase the survival rate of your cuttings.

Debate exists over what the size of a cutting should be. Some gardeners claim that a smaller cutting, 2–5 cm

Perennials to Propagate from Stem Cuttings

Artemisia
Bellflower
Bleeding Heart
Euphorbia
Penstemon
Pinks
Potentilla
Sedum 'Autumn Joy'
Snow-in-Summer
Thyme

(1–2") long, is more likely to root and root more quickly. Other gardeners claim that a larger cutting, 10–15 cm (4–6"), long develops more roots and becomes established more quickly once planted in the garden. You may wish to try different sizes to see what works best for you.

The size of a cutting is determined by the number of leaf nodes it has. You will want at least three or four nodes on a cutting. The node is where the leaf joins the stem, and it is from here that the new roots will grow. The base of the cutting will be just below a node. Strip the leaves gently from the first and second nodes, and plant them below the soil. The new plants will grow from the nodes above the soil. The leaves can be left in place on the cutting above ground. If there is a lot of space between nodes, your cutting will be longer than recommended. Some plants have almost no space at all between nodes. Cut these plants to the recommended length and gently remove the leaves from the lower half of the cutting. Plants with several nodes close together often root quickly and abundantly.

Always use a sharp, sterile knife to make the cuttings. Cuts should be made straight across the stem. Once you have stripped the leaves, you can dip the end of the cutting into a rooting hormone powder intended

Thyme

for softwood cuttings. Sprinkle the powder onto a piece of paper and dip the cuttings into it. Discard any extra powder left on the paper to prevent the spread of disease. Tap or blow the extra powder off the cutting. Cuttings caked with rooting hormone are more likely to rot rather than root, and they do not root any faster than those that are lightly dusted. Your cuttings are now prepared for planting.

The sooner you plant your cuttings the better. The less water the cuttings lose, the less likely they are to wilt and the more quickly they will root. Cuttings can be planted in a similar manner to seeds. Use sterile soil mix intended for seeds or cuttings in pots or trays that can be covered with plastic to keep in the humidity. Other mixes you can use to root cuttings are sterilized sand, perlite, vermiculite or a combination

Pinks

Phlox

Keep the cuttings in a warm place, about 18–21° C (65–70° F), in bright, indirect light. A couple of holes poked in the bag will allow for some ventilation. Turn the bag inside out when condensation becomes heavy. Keep the soil mix moist. A hand-held mister will gently moisten the soil mix without disturbing the cuttings.

Most cuttings will require from one to four weeks to root. After two weeks, give the cutting a gentle tug. You will feel resistance if roots have formed. If the cutting feels as though it can be pulled out of the soil mix, then gently push it back down and leave it for longer. New growth is also a good sign that your cutting has rooted. Some gardeners simply leave the cuttings alone until they can see roots through the holes in the bottoms of the pots. Uncover the cuttings once they have developed roots.

Apply a foliar feed when the cuttings are showing new leaf growth. Plants quickly absorb nutrients

Daylily

of the three. Firm the soil mix down and moisten it before you start planting. Poke a hole in the surface of the soil mix with a pencil or similar object, tuck the cutting in and gently firm the soil mix around it. Make sure the lowest leaves do not touch the soil mix and that the cuttings are spaced far enough apart that adjoining leaves do not touch each other. Pots can be placed inside plastic bags. Push stakes or wires into the soil around the edge of the pot so that the plastic will be held off the leaves. The rigid plastic lids that are available for trays may not be high enough to fit over the cuttings, in which case you will have to use stakes and a plastic bag to cover the tray.

through the leaves; therefore, you can avoid stressing the newly formed roots. Your local garden centre should have foliar feeds and information about applying them. Use your hand-held mister to apply foliar feeds.

Once your cuttings are rooted and have had a chance to establish themselves, they can be potted up individually. If you rooted several cuttings in one pot or tray, you may find that the roots have tangled together. If gentle pulling doesn't separate them, take the entire tangled clump and try rinsing some of the soil away. You should be able to free the roots enough to separate the plants.

Pot the young plants in a sterile potting soil. They can be moved into a sheltered area of the garden or a cold frame and grown in pots until they are large enough to plant in the garden. The plants may need some protection over the first winter. Keep them in the cold frame if they are still in pots. Give them an extra layer of mulch if they have been planted out.

Basal Cuttings

Basal cuttings involve removing the new growth from the main clump and rooting it in the same manner as stem cuttings. Many plants send up new shoots or plantlets around their bases. Often, the plantlets will already have a few roots growing. The young plants develop quickly and may even grow to flowering size the first summer. You may have to cut back some of the top growth of the shoot because the tiny developing roots won't be able to support a lot of top growth. Treat these cuttings in the same way you would a stem cutting. Use a sterile knife to cut out the shoot. Sterile soil mix and humid conditions are preferred. Pot plants individually or place them in soft soil in the garden until new growth appears and roots have developed.

Perennials to Start from Basal Cuttings

- Bellflower
- Bergamot
- Cranesbill
- Daylily
- Delphinium
- Euphorbia
- Hens and Chicks
- Lamium
- Lupine
- Phlox
- Sedum

Lamium

Euphorbia

Root Cuttings

Root cuttings can also be taken from some plants. Dandelions are well known for this trait: even the smallest piece of root left in the ground can sprout a new plant, foiling every attempt to eradicate them from lawns and flowerbeds. Some perennials have this ability as well. The main difference between starting root cuttings and stem cuttings is that root cuttings must be kept fairly dry because they can rot very easily.

Cuttings can be taken from the fleshy roots of certain perennials that do not propagate well from stem cuttings. These cuttings should be taken in early or mid-spring when the ground is just starting to warm up and the roots are just about to break dormancy. At this

time, the roots of the perennials are full of nutrients, which the plants stored the previous summer and fall, and hormones are initiating growth. You may have to moisten the soil around the plant so that you can loosen it enough to get to the roots.

Keep the roots slightly moist, but not wet, while you are rooting them, and keep track of which end is up. Roots must be planted in a vertical, not horizontal, position on the soil, and roots need to be kept in the orientation they held when attached to the parent plant. People use different tricks to recognize the top from the bottom of the roots. One method is to cut straight across the tops and diagonally across the bottoms.

You do not want very young or very old roots. Very young roots are usually white and quite soft; very old roots are tough and woody. The roots you should use will be tan coloured and still fleshy. To prepare your root, cut out the section you will be using with a sterile knife. Cut the root into pieces that are 2.5–5 cm (1–2") long. Remove any side roots before planting the sections in pots or planting trays. You can use the same type of soil mix the seeds and stem cuttings were started in. Poke the pieces vertically into the soil and leave a tiny bit of the end poking up out of the soil. Remember to keep the pieces the right way up.

Keep the pots or trays in a warm place out of direct sunlight. Avoid over-watering them. They will send up new shoots once they have rooted, and they can be planted in the same manner as the stem cuttings (see p. 52).

Rhizomes

Rhizomes are the easiest root cuttings with which to propagate plants. Rhizomes are thick, fleshy roots that grow horizontally along the ground, or just under the soil. Periodically, they send up new shoots from along the length of the rhizome, thus spreading the plant. Take rhizome cuttings when the plant is growing vigorously (usually in the late spring or early summer).

Dig up a section of rhizome. If you look closely, you will see that it seems to be growing in sections. The places where these sections join are called nodes. From these nodes, feeder roots (smaller, stringy roots) extend downwards and new plants sprout upwards. You may even see that small plants are already sprouting. The rhizome should be cut into pieces. Each piece should have at least one of these nodes in it.

Fill a pot or planting tray to about 2.5 cm (1") from the top of the container with perlite, vermiculite or seeding soil mix. Moisten the soil mix and let the excess water drain away. Lay the rhizome pieces flat on the top of the mix and almost cover them with more of the soil mix. If you leave a small bit of the top exposed to the light, it will encourage the shoots to sprout. The soil mix does not have to be kept wet. Let it dry out a bit between mistings to prevent rot. Once your cuttings have established themselves, they can be potted individually and grown in the same manner as stem cuttings (see p. 52).

Perennials to Propagate from Rhizomes

- Bellflower
- Bergenia
- Cranesbill
- Iris

Bellflower

Iris

Division

Division is quite possibly the easiest way to propagate perennials. As most perennials grow, they form larger and larger clumps. Dividing this clump once it gets big will rejuvenate the plant, keep its size in check and provide you with more plants. If a plant you really want is expensive, consider buying only one because within a few years you may have more than you can handle.

Digging up perennials for division (above & centre)

Clump of stems, roots & crowns (below)

How often a perennial needs dividing or can be divided will vary. Some perennials, like astilbe, need dividing almost every year to keep them vigorous, while others, like peony, should never be divided because they dislike having their roots disturbed. Each perennial entry in the book gives recommendations for division. Watch for signs that a perennial should be divided:

- the centre of the plant has died out
- the plant no longer flowers as profusely as it did in previous years
- the plant encroaches on the growing space of other plants sharing the bed.

Begin by digging up the entire clump and knocking any large clods of soil away from the rootball. The clump can then be split into several pieces. A small plant with fibrous roots can be torn into sections by hand. A large plant can be pried apart with a pair of garden forks inserted back to back into the clump. Plants with thicker tuberous or rhizomatous roots can be cut into sections with a sharp, sterile knife. In all cases, cut away any old sections that have died out and replant only the newer, more vigorous sections.

Once your original clump is divided into sections, replant one or two of them into the original location. Take this opportunity to work organic matter into the soil where the perennial was growing before replanting it. The other sections can be moved to new spots in the garden or potted up and given away as gifts to gardening friends and neighbours. Get the sections back into the ground as quickly as possible to prevent the exposed roots from drying out. Plan where you are going to plant your divisions and have the spots prepared before you start digging up. Plant your perennial divisions in pots if you aren't sure where to put them all. Water new transplants thoroughly and keep them well watered until they have re-established themselves.

Pulling a clump apart

The larger the sections of the division, the more quickly the plant will re-establish itself and grow to blooming size again. For example, a perennial divided into four sections will bloom sooner than one divided into 10 sections. Very small divisions may benefit from being planted in pots until they are bigger and better able to fend for themselves in the border.

Newly planted divisions will need extra care and attention when they are first planted. They will need regular watering and, for the first few days, shade from direct sunlight. A light covering of burlap or damp newspaper should shelter them enough for this short period. Divisions that were planted in pots should be moved to a shaded location.

Cutting apart and dividing tuberous perennials

There is some debate about the best time to divide perennials. Some gardeners prefer to divide perennials when plants are dormant, while others believe that perennials establish themselves more quickly if they are divided during a vigorous growth period. You may wish to experiment with dividing at different times of the year to see what works best. If you divide perennials

while they are growing, you will need to cut back one-third to one-half of the growth so as not to stress the roots while they are repairing the damage done to them.

Problems & Pests

PERENNIAL GARDENS ARE BOTH AN ASSET AND A LIABILITY WHEN it comes to pests and diseases. Perennial beds often contain a mixture of different plant species. Because many insects and diseases attack only one species of plant, mixed beds make it difficult for pests and diseases to find their preferred hosts and establish a population. At the same time, because the plants are in the same spot for many years, the problems can become permanent. Luckily, beneficial insects, birds and other pest-devouring organisms can also develop permanent populations to help keep pests and diseases under control.

For many years pest control meant spraying or dusting. The goal was to try to eliminate every pest in the garden. A more moderate approach is advocated today. The goal is now to maintain problems at levels at which only negligible damage is done. Synthetic pesticides should be used only as a last resort. They can cause more harm than good. They endanger the gardener and his or her family, and they kill the good organisms as well as the bad ones, leaving the garden open to even worse attacks.

Managing pests organically involves four steps. The cultural controls are the most important. The physical controls come next, followed by the biological controls. The chemical controls or synthetic pesticides should only be used when the first three possibilities have been exhausted.

Cultural controls are the regular gardening techniques you use in the day-to-day care of your garden.

Growing perennials in the conditions they prefer and keeping your soil healthy with plenty of organic matter are just two of the cultural controls you can use to keep pests manageable in your garden. Choose resistant varieties of perennials that are not prone to problems. Space perennials so that they have good air circulation around them and are not stressed from competing for light, nutrients and room. Remove plants from the garden if they are constantly decimated by the same pests every year. Remove and destroy diseased foliage and prevent the spread of disease by keeping your gardening tools clean and by tidying up fallen leaves and dead plant matter at the end of the growing season.

Physical controls are generally used to combat insect problems. These include doing things like picking the insects off the perennials by hand, which is not as daunting a solution as it seems if you catch the problem when it is just beginning. Other physical controls are barriers that stop the insects from getting to the plant or traps that either catch or confuse the insect. The physical control of diseases can generally only be accomplished by removing of the infected perennial parts to prevent the spread of the problem.

Biological controls make use of natural predators, including birds, snakes, frogs, spiders, lady beetles and certain bacteria. Encourage these creatures to take up permanent residence in your garden. A birdbath and birdfeeder will encourage birds to enjoy your yard and feed on a wide variety of insect pests. Many beneficial insects are probably already living in your garden, and they can be encouraged to stay with alternate food sources. Many beneficial insects also eat the nectar from flowers. The flowers of nectar plants like sea holly are popular with some predatory insects.

In a perennial garden you should rarely have to resort to chemicals, but if it does become necessary, some organic options are available. Organic sprays are no less dangerous than chemical ones, but they will break down into harmless compounds because they come from natural sources. The main drawback to using any chemicals is that they may also kill the beneficial insects you have been trying to attract to your garden. Organic chemicals should be available at local garden centres and should be applied at the rates and for the pests recommended on the packages. Proper and early identification of problems is vital for finding a quick solution.

If you're compelled to use a synthetic pesticide, it is imperative that you follow the directions and cover yourself with appropriate protective gear.

Whereas cultural, physical, biological and chemical controls are all possible defences against insects, disease must be controlled culturally. Prevention is often the only hope. Often a healthy, unaffected plant is much less vulnerable than one that is weak owing to disease, pest infestation or a number of other factors. Once a plant has been infected, it should probably be destroyed to prevent the spread of the disease.

Glossary of Pests & Diseases

PESTS

Aphids

Cluster along stems, on buds and on leaves. Tiny, pear-shaped, winged or wingless; green, black, brown, red or grey. Suck sap from plants, causing distorted or stunted growth; sticky honeydew forms on the surfaces and encourages sooty mold.

What to Do: Squish small colonies by hand; dislodge with brisk water spray; spray serious infestations with insecticidal soap; many predatory insects and birds feed on them.

Beetles & Weevils

Some are beneficial, e.g., lady beetles; others, e.g., June beetles, eat plants. Larvae: see Borers, Grubs. Many types and sizes; usually round with hard, shell-like outer wings covering membraneous inner wings. Leave wide range of chewing damage; cause small or large holes in or around margins of leaves; entire leaf or areas between leaf veins is consumed; may also chew holes in flowers.

What to Do: Pick the beetles off at night and drop them into an old coffee can half filled with soapy water (soap prevents them from floating); spread an old sheet under plants and shake off beetles to collect and dispose of them.

Borers

Larvae of some moths and beetles burrow into plant stems, leaves and/or roots. Worm-like; vary in size and get bigger as they bore through plants. Burrow and weaken stems to cause breakage; leaves wilt; may see tunnels in leaves, stems or roots; rhizomes may be hollowed out entirely or in part; common problem in iris plants, except Siberian iris, which is resistant to borers.

What to Do: Remove and destroy affected parts; try squishing borers within leaves; may need to dig up and destroy infected roots and rhizomes.

Bugs (True Bugs)

Many are beneficial; a few are pests. Small, up to 1 cm ($\frac{1}{2}$") long; green, brown, black or brightly coloured and patterned. Pierce plants to suck out sap; toxins may be injected that deform plants; sunken areas are left where pierced; leaves rip as they grow; leaves, buds and new growth may

Green aphids

be dwarfed and deformed.

What to Do: Remove debris and weeds from around plants in fall to destroy overwintering sites; pick off by hand and drop into soapy water; spray with insecticidal soap.

Cutworms

Larvae of some moths. About 2.5 cm (1") long, plump, smooth-skinned caterpillars; curl up when poked or disturbed. Usually only affects young plants and seedlings, which may be completely consumed or chewed off at ground level.

What to Do: Create barriers from old toilet tissue rolls to make collars around plant bases; push tubes at least halfway into ground.

Grubs

Larvae of different beetles; problematic in lawns and may feed on perennial roots. Commonly found below soil level, usually curled in a C-shape. Body is white or grey and head may be white, grey, brown or reddish. Eat roots, causing plant to wilt despite regular

Japanese beetles

watering. Entire plant may pull out of the ground with only a gentle tug in severe cases.

What to Do: While digging around your plants, toss any grubs you find onto a stone path or patio for birds to find and devour; control populations by applying parasitic nematodes or milky disease spores to infested soil (ask at your local garden centre).

Leafminers

Larvae of some flies. Tiny, yellow or green, stubby maggots. Tunnel within leaves leaving winding trails; tunneled areas are a lighter colour than rest of leaf; unsightly rather than health risk to plants.

What to Do: Remove and destroy infected foliage; remove debris from area in fall to destroy overwintering sites; attract parasitic wasps with nectar plants like sea holly.

Slugs & Snails

Slugs lack shells; snails have a spiral shell; smooth, grey, green, black, beige, yellow or

Slug

spotted. Leave large, ragged holes in leaves and silvery slime trails on and around plants.

What to Do: Attach strips of copper to wood around raised beds or smaller boards inserted around susceptible groups of plants. Slugs and snails will get shocked if they try to cross copper surfaces; pick them off by hand in the evening; spread wood ash or diatomaceous earth (available from garden centres) on ground around plants to pierce their soft bodies and cause them to dehydrate.

Spider Mites
Almost invisible to the naked eye; relatives of spiders without their insect-eating habits. Tiny, eight-legged, red, yellow or green; may spin webs. Usually found on undersides of plant leaves. Suck juice out of leaves; may see fine webbing on leaves and stems; may see mites moving on leaf undersides; leaves become discoloured and speckled, then turn brown and shrivel up.

What to Do: Wash them off with a strong spray of water daily until all signs of infestation are gone; predatory mites are available through garden centres for ornamental plants, or spray plants with insecticidal soap.

Thrips
Difficult to see; may be visible if you disturb them by blowing gently on an infested flower. Tiny, slender, narrow, fringed wings; yellow, black or brown. Suck juice out of plant cells, particularly flowers and buds, causing mottled petals and leaves, dying buds and distorted and stunted growth.

What to Do: Remove and destroy infected plant parts; encourage native predatory insects with nectar plants like asters, daisies or sea holly; spray severe infestations with insecticidal soap.

Whiteflies
Flying insects that flutter up into the air when the plant is disturbed. Tiny, moth-like, white; live on undersides of plant leaves. Suck juice out of plant leaves, causing yellowed leaves and weakened plants; leave sticky honeydew on leaves, which encourages sooty mold.

What to Do: Destroy weeds where insects may live; attract native predatory beetles and parasitic wasps with nectar plants like sea holly or purple coneflower; spray severe cases with insecticidal soap.

DISEASES
Anthracnose
Fungus. Yellow or brown spots on leaves; sunken lesions and blisters on stems; can kill plant.

What to Do: Choose resistant varieties and cultivars; remove and destroy infected plant parts; thin out stems to improve air circulation; avoid handling wet foliage; keep soil well drained; clean up and destroy material from infected plants at end of growing season.

Aster Yellows
Transmitted by insects called leafhoppers. Stunted or deformed growth; leaves yellowed and deformed; flowers dwarfed and greenish; can kill plant.

What to Do: Control insects with insecticidal soap; remove and destroy infected plants; destroy any local weeds sharing these symptoms.

Blight
Fungal or bacterial diseases, many types; e.g., leaf blight, snow blight, tip blight. Leaves, stems and flowers blacken, rot and die.

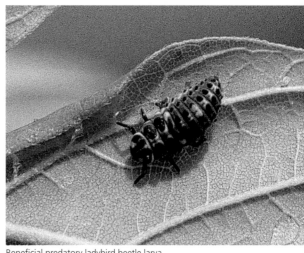

Beneficial predatory ladybird beetle larva

What to Do: Thin stems to improve air circulation; keep mulch away from base of plants; remove debris from garden at end of growing season. Remove and destroy infected plant parts.

Mildew on leaves

Grey Mould
(***Botrytis* Blight**)
Fungal disease. Leaves, stems and flowers blacken, rot and die.

What to Do: Remove and destroy any infected plant parts; thin stems to

Caterpillars eat flowers.

may be yellow, white or grey. *Powdery mildew:* white or grey powdery coating on leaf surfaces that doesn't brush off.

What to Do: Choose resistant cultivars; space plants well; thin stems to encourage air circulation; remove and destroy infected leaves or other parts; tidy any debris in fall.

Nematodes

Tiny, worm-like organisms that give plants disease symptoms. One type infects foliage and stems; the other type infects the roots. *Foliar:* yellow spots that turn brown on leaves; leaves shrivel and wither; problem starts on lowest leaves and works up the plant. *Root knot:* plant is stunted and may wilt; yellow spots on leaves; roots have tiny bumps or knots.

What to Do: Remove infected plants, mulch soil and clean up debris in fall. Don't touch wet foliage; add organic matter and parasitic nematodes to soil. Not usually a problem throughout Saskatchewan and Manitoba where the ground freezes too deeply for pests to overwinter.

improve air circulation, keep mulch away from the base of plant, particularly in spring, when plant starts to sprout; remove debris from garden at the end of growing season.

Leaf Spot

Two common types: one caused by bacteria and the other by fungi. *Bacterial:* small, brown or purple speckles grow to encompass entire leaves; leaves may drop. *Fungal:* black, brown or yellow spots cause leaves to wither.

What to Do: Controls are similar for both types of leaf spot, though the bacterial infection is more severe. Remove and destroy infected plant parts; remove entire plant with bacterial infection and sterilize tools; avoid wetting foliage or touching wet foliage; remove debris at end of growing season.

Mildew

Two types: both are caused by fungus, but they have slightly different symptoms. *Downy mildew:* yellow spots on upper sides of leaves and downy fuzz on the undersides; fuzz

Rot

Several different fungi that affect different parts of the plant. *Crown rot:* affects base of plant, causing stems to blacken and fall over, and leaves to yellow and wilt; can kill plant. *Root rot:* leaves yellow and plant wilts; digging up plant will show roots rotted away.

What to Do: Keep soil well drained; don't damage plant if you are digging around it; keep mulches away from plant base; destroy infected plants.

Mosaic virus

Rust

Fungus. Pale spots on upper leaf surfaces; orange, fuzzy or dusty spots on leaf undersides.

What to Do: Destroy infected plant parts; choose rust-resistant varieties and cultivars; avoid handling wet leaves; provide plant with good air circulation; clear up garden debris at end of season.

Sooty Mould

Fungus. Thin, black film forms on leaf surfaces, reducing the amount of light getting to leaf surfaces.

What to Do: Wipe mould off leaf surfaces; control insects like aphids and whiteflies (honeydew left on leaves forms mould).

Viruses

Plant may be stunted and leaves and flowers distorted, streaked or discoloured. Viral diseases in plants cannot be controlled.

What to Do: Destroy infected plants; control insects like aphids, leafhoppers and whiteflies that spread disease.

Wilt

If watering hasn't helped, consider these two fungi. *Fusarium wilt:* plant wilts, leaves turn yellow then die; symptoms generally appear first on one part of the plant before spreading to other parts. *Verticillium wilt:* plant wilts, leaves curl up at the edges, leaves turn yellow then drop off; plant may die.

What to Do: Both wilts are difficult to control. Choose resistant varieties and cultivars; clean up debris at end of growing season; destroy infected plants; solarize soil before replanting (may help if you've lost an entire bed of plants to these fungi).

Pest Control Alternatives

The following treatments for pests and diseases allow the gardener some measure of control without resorting to harmful chemical fungicides and pesticides.

Ant Control

Mix 700 ml (3 c.) water, 250 ml (1 c.) white sugar and 20 ml (4 tsp.) liquid boric acid in a pot. Bring this mix just to a boil and remove it from the heat source. Let the mix cool. Pour small amounts of the cooled mix into bottlecaps or other very small containers and place them around the ant-infested area. You can also try setting out a mixture of equal parts powdered borax and icing sugar (no water).

Antitranspirants

These products were developed to reduce water transpiration, or loss of water, in plants. The waxy polymers surround fungal spores, preventing the spread of spores to nearby leaves and stems. When applied according to label directions, these products are environmentally friendly. Available from garden centres.

Baking Soda & Citrus Oil

This mixture treats both leaf spot and powdery mildew. In a spray bottle, mix 20 ml (4 tsp.) baking soda, 15 ml (1 tbsp.) citrus oil and 4 *l* (1 gal.) water. Spray the foliage lightly, including the undersides. Do not pour or spray this mix directly onto soil.

Baking Soda & Horticultural Oil

Research has confirmed the effectiveness of this mixture against powdery mildew. Mix 20 ml (4 tsp.) baking

Predatory ground beetle

soda, 15 ml (1 tbsp.) horticultural oil in 4 *l* (1 gal.) water. Fill a spray bottle and spray the foliage lightly, including the undersides. Do not pour or spray this mix directly onto soil.

Coffee Grounds Spray

Boil 1 kg (2 lb.) used coffee grounds in 11 *l* (3 gal.) water for about 10 minutes. Allow to cool; strain the grounds out. Apply as a spray to reduce problems with whiteflies.

Compost Tea

Mix 500 g–1 kg (1–2 lb.) compost in 19 *l* (5 gal.) of water. Let sit for four to seven days. Dilute the mix until it resembles weak tea. Use during normal watering or apply as a foliar spray to prevent or treat fungal diseases.

Fish Emulsion/Seaweed (Kelp)

These products are usually used as foliar nutrient feeds but also appear to work against fungal diseases either by preventing the fungus from spreading to noninfected areas or by changing the growing conditions for the fungus.

Garlic Spray

This spray is an effective, organic means of controlling aphids, leafhoppers, whiteflies and some fungi and nematodes. Soak 90 ml (6 tbsp.) finely minced garlic in 10 ml (2 tsp.) mineral oil for at least 24 hours. Add 500 ml (2 c.) of water and 7.5 ml (1½ tsp.) of liquid dish soap. Stir and strain into a glass container for storage. Combine 15–30 ml (1–2 tbsp.) of this concentrate with 500 ml (2 c.)

water to make a spray. Test the spray on a couple of leaves and check after two days for any damage. If no damage, spray infested plants thoroughly, ensuring good coverage of the foliage.

Horticultural Oil

Mix 75 ml (5 tbsp.) horticultural oil per 4 *l* (1 gal.) of water and apply as a spray for a variety of insect and fungal problems.

Insecticidal Soap

Mix 5 ml (1 tsp.) of mild dish detergent or pure soap (biodegradable options are available) with 1 *l* (1 qt.) of water in a clean spray bottle. Spray the surfaces of insect-infested plants and rinse well within an hour of spraying to avoid foliage discoloration.

Neem Oil

Neem oil is derived from the neem tree (native to India) and is used as an insecticide, miticide and fungicide. Most effective when used preventively. Apply when conditions are favourable for disease development. Neem is virtually harmless to most beneficial insects and microorganisms.

Sulfur & Lime-Sulfur

These products are good as preventive measures for fungal diseases. You can purchase ready-made products or wettable powders that you mix yourself. Do not spray when the temperature is expected to be 32° C (90° F) or higher, or you may damage your plants.

About This Guide

THE PERENNIALS IN THIS BOOK ARE ORGANIZED ALPHABETICALLY by their most familiar common names, which in some cases are the proper botanical names. If you are familiar only with the common name for a plant, you will be able to find it easily in the book. The botanical name is always listed in italics under the common name, and readers are strongly encouraged to learn and use these botanical names when buying or researching plants. Whereas the common name for a plant may be different from one province to another, a plant's botanical name defines exactly what it is everywhere on the planet.

Clearly indicated at the beginning of each entry are height and spread ranges, flower colours, bloom periods and the hardiness zone range for the entire genus; individual species within a genus that may have different zone ranges are identified in the Recommended section of each entry. The Quick Reference Chart at the back of the book summarizes the different features and requirements of all the perennials.

Each entry gives clear instructions and tips for seeding, planting and growing the perennial, and it recommends some of our favourite species and varieties. Keep in mind that often many more hybrids, cultivars and varieties are available than we have space to mention. Check with local greenhouses or garden centres when making your selection. That said, we present plenty of wonderful perennials in this book to provide you with many seasons of gardening pleasure.

Pests or diseases that commonly affect perennials are also listed for each entry. Consult the 'Problems & Pests' section of the introduction (p. 58) for information on how to solve these problems.

Finally, we have kept jargon to a minimum, but check the glossary on p. 342 for any unfamiliar terms.

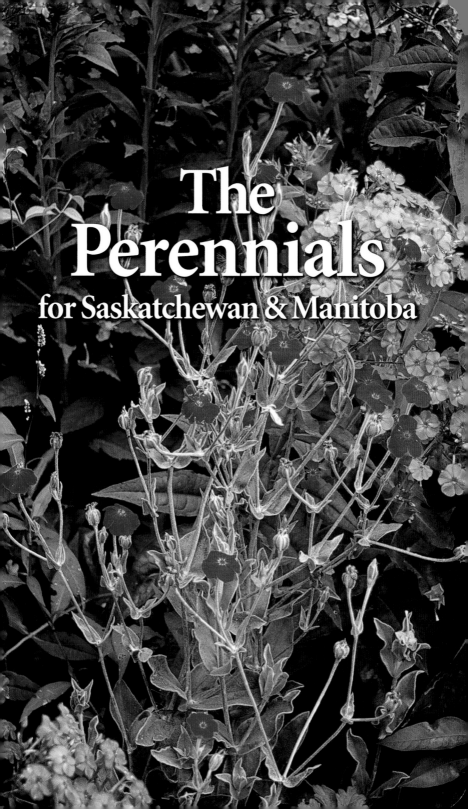

The
Perennials
for Saskatchewan & Manitoba

Arabis
Wall Rockcress
Rock Cress
Arabis

Height: 5–20 cm (2–8") **Spread:** 20–60 cm (8–24") **Flower colour:** white, pink; foliage **Blooms:** mid- to late spring **Zones:** 3–8

AFTER A LONG WINTER, IT IS ALWAYS NICE TO SEE GREEN EMERGING through the thin layer of snow in early spring. Arabis provides a carpet of green and an early blast of bloom long before most other perennials even attempt to flower, which makes it pretty special in my books. Arabis is a popular perennial, not only for its early blooming capabilities, but because it can grow in small increments of soil, on slopes and tucked between the rocks of stone walls. Many a summer at my farmhouse saw arabis spilling over an embankment. Visitors would often come to my door just to ask what that lovely plant was, and they left with a new appreciation for nothing other than arabis.

Planting

Seeding: Start in container in early spring; seeds require light for germination

Planting out: Any time during growing season

Spacing: 20–45 cm (8–18") apart

Growing

Arabis prefers to grow in **full sun**. The soil should be **average** or **poor, well drained** and **alkaline**. Mix plenty of lime into the soil to increase the pH if necessary. This plant will do best in a climate that doesn't have extremely hot summer weather. Stem cuttings taken from the new growth may be started in summer. Divide in early fall every two or three years.

Tips

Use arabis in a rock garden, along a border or on a rock wall. It may also be used as a groundcover on an exposed slope or as a companion plant with small bulbs.

Cut the plant back after flowering to keep it neat and compact. Don't plant arabis where it may overwhelm plants that are slower growing.

Recommended

A. alpina **subsp.** *caucasica* (*caucasica*) forms a low mound of small rosettes of foliage and bears white flowers in early spring. It grows 20 cm (8") tall and 30–60 cm (12–24") wide. **'Compinkie'** has pink flowers. **'Snow Cap'** ('Schneehaube') produces abundant white flowers.

A. procurrens forms a low mat of foliage. It bears small, white flowers

A. procurrens 'Variegata'

in spring and early summer. It grows 5–7 cm (2–3") tall and 20–40 cm (8–16") wide. This species is more shade tolerant than *A. caucasica*. **'Variegata'** (variegated rock cress) has white-edged foliage. (Zones 4–8)

Problems & Pests

White rust, downy mildew and rust are possible. Aphids are occasionally a problem along with *Arabis* midge, which causes deformed shoots that should be removed and destroyed.

A. caucasica

Artemisia
Wormwood, Sage
Artemisia

Height: 15 cm –1.8 m (6"–6') **Spread:** 30–91 cm (12–36")
Flower colour: white or yellow, generally inconspicuous; foliage plant
Blooms: late summer **Zones:** 1–8

THE GENUS *ARTEMISIA* IS VERY DIVERSE AND KNOWN FOR ITS
textured, silvery foliage. Many of its species have been used medicinally and for flavouring liqueurs and meats. Some are essential forage for grazing animals in certain native
habitats throughout North America. Artemisia is
often confused with sage. While these two plants do
share a number of physical characteristics and a strong, pun-
gent scent, they are
otherwise very different, and
sage belongs to a different genus.
Generations of gardeners from
many cultures have proven that
it's difficult to go wrong with any
artemisia selection because of this
plant's drought tolerance, hardiness, habit and sheer beauty.

*There are almost 300 species
of artemisia in the world.*

Planting

Seeding: Not recommended

Planting out: Spring, summer or fall

Spacing: 30–91 cm (12–36")

Growing

Artemisia grows best in **full sun**. The soil should be of **average to high fertility** and **well drained**. It dislikes wet, humid conditions. Artemisia plants respond well to pruning in late spring. If you prune before May, frost may kill any new growth. Whenever artemisia begins to look straggly, it may be cut back hard to encourage new growth and maintain a neater form. Some species can become invasive. Division can be done every one to two years when plants appear to be thinning in the centres.

Tips

Artemisia can be used in rock gardens and borders. The silver grey

A. v. ORIENTAL LIMELIGHT (above)

A. stelleriana 'Silver Brocade' (below)

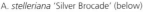

A. *ludoviciana* 'Valerie Finnis'

foliage contrasts well with brightly coloured flowers when used in mixed beds.

If you want to control the spreading habit of an artemisia, plant it in a bottomless container. Sunk into the ground, the container is hidden, and it will prevent the plant from spreading beyond the container's edges.

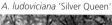

A. *ludoviciana* 'Silver Queen'

With the bottom missing, good drainage can also be maintained.

Recommended

A. absinthium (common wormwood) is a clump-forming, woody-based perennial. It has aromatic, hairy, grey foliage and bears inconspicuous yellow flowers in late summer. It grows 60–91 cm (24–36") tall and spreads about 61 cm (24"). **'Lambrook Silver'** is approximately two-thirds the size of the species with attractive silvery grey foliage. (Zones 3–7)

A. lactiflora (white mugwort) is an upright, clump-forming perennial, and one of the few artemisias that bears showy flowers. It grows 1.2–1.8 m (4–6') tall and spreads 60–91 cm (24–36"). The foliage is dark green or grey-green. Attractive, creamy white flowers are borne from late summer to mid-fall. **'Guizho'** is a newer cultivar that showcases fern-like, blackish green foliage,

supported by auburn stems. Creamy white, fragrant flowers are striking against the dark leaves. (Zones 3–8)

A. ludoviciana (white sage, western mugwort) is an upright, clump-forming perennial. It grows 61 cm–1.2 m (24"–4') tall and spreads 61 cm (24"). The foliage is silvery white and the flowers are inconspicuous. The species is not grown as often as the cultivars. **'Silver King'** is compact and very hardy. It has very hairy, silvery-white foliage and grows about 61 cm (24") tall. **'Silver Queen'** has deeply divided, silvery foliage and grows 60–75 cm (24–30") tall. It can be invasive. **'Valerie Finnis'** is a good choice for hot, dry areas. It has very wide, silvery leaves, is less invasive than the species and combines beautifully with many other perennials. (Zones 4–8)

A. schmidtiana (silvermound) is a low, dense, mound-forming perennial. It grows 30–61 cm (12–24") tall and spreads 30–45 cm (12–18"). The foliage is feathery, hairy and silvery grey. **'Nana'** (dwarf silvermound) is very compact and grows only half the size of the species. It will take on a scragglier appearance if grown in a location with too much shade or moisture. Apply a fertilizer with a low percentage of nitrogen to promote a thicker, mounding growth habit.

A. stelleriana **'Silver Brocade'** is a low-growing, creeping perennial that is sometimes mistaken for the annual dusty miller. Soft, silver foliage covers the woody base, and it grows 15 cm (6") tall and 45–60 cm

A. ludoviciana 'Silver King'

(18–24") wide. Tall, white stems appear in mid- to late summer supporting insignificant yellow flowerheads high above the fancy foliage. (Zones 2–8)

A. vulgaris **'ORIENTAL LIMELIGHT'** bears marbled, off-white, lacy foliage on tall stems. It grows 90 cm–1.2 m (3–4') tall and 75–90 cm (30–36") wide. (Zones 3–8)

Problems & Pests

Rust, downy mildew and fungal problems are possible.

A. schmidtiana 'Nana'

Astilbe

Astilbe

Height: 25 cm–1.2 m (10"–4') **Spread:** 20–91 cm (8–36") **Flower colour:** white, pink, purple, peach, red; foliage **Blooms:** early, mid- or late summer depending on the cultivar **Zones:** 3–8

I HAVE DEVELOPED A GREAT RESPECT FOR PERENNIALS that exhibit versatility. Astilbe is one of those perennials that not only looks great in the garden, but also is a long-lasting cut flower. In arrangements, the flower plumes dry beautifully all by themselves, especially when you neglect to refill the vase. The fine, lacy foliage, which is very attractive in itself, is surpassed only by the graceful, show-stopping plumes of ivory white to deep burgundy and every shade of purple, red and pink you can imagine. Although this shade-loving perennial requires more moisture than most, it is well worth every drop. The ideal location will reward you with an abundance of flowers for cutting and arrangements all summer long.

The origins of the word 'astilbe' are not flattering. In Greek, a means 'not', and stilbos means 'brilliant or glittering' in reference to the obscure pink or white flowers of some early wild species.

Planting

Seeding: Not recommended; seedlings do not come true to type

Planting out: Spring

Spacing: 20–91 cm (8–36") apart

Growing

Astilbe enjoys **light** or **partial shade** and tolerates full shade, though it flowers less in deep shade. The soil should be **fertile**, **humus rich**, **acidic**, **moist** and **well drained**. Astilbe likes to grow near water sources, such as ponds and streams, but dislikes standing in water. Apply mulch in summer to keep the roots cool and moist. Divide every three years in spring or fall to maintain plant vigour.

Tips

Astilbe can be grown along the edges of bog gardens or ponds and in woodland gardens and shaded borders.

The root crown of an astilbe tends to lift out of the soil as the plant grows bigger. Solve this problem by applying a top dressing of rich soil as mulch when the plant starts lifting or by digging up the entire plant and replanting it deeper into the soil.

Astilbe flowers fade to various shades of brown. The flowers may be removed once flowering is finished, or they may be left in place. Astilbes self-seed easily, and the flowerheads look interesting and natural in the garden well into fall.

Recommended

A. x *arendsii* (astilbe, false spirea) grows 45 cm –1.2 m (18"–4') tall and spreads 45–91 cm (18–36"). There are many cultivars available from this hybrid group. The following are a few popular ones. **'Avalanche'** bears white flowers in late summer. **'Bressingham Beauty'** bears bright pink flowers in mid-summer. **'Cattleya'** bears reddish pink flowers

A. x *arendsii* cultivars

in mid-summer. **'Fanal'** bears red flowers in early summer and has deep bronze foliage. Finally, **'Weisse Gloria'** bears creamy white flowers in mid- to late summer.

A. chinensis (Chinese astilbe) is a dense, vigorous perennial that is more tolerant of dry soil than other astilbe species. It grows about 61 cm (24") tall and spreads 45 cm (18"). It bears fluffy white, pink or purple flowers in late summer. **'Pumila'** is more commonly found than the species. This plant forms a low groundcover with dark pink flowers. It grows 25 cm (10") tall and spreads 20 cm (8"). **'Superba'** is a tall form with lavender purple flowers produced in a long, narrow spike. *A. chinensis* cultivars usually bloom later in the season than other astilbes, thereby extending the flowering season well into early autumn.

A. x *arendsii* cultivar

A. chinensis 'Pumila'

A. japonica (Japanese astilbe) is a compact, clump-forming perennial. The species is rarely grown in favour of the cultivars. **'Deutschland'** grows 50 cm (20") tall and spreads 30 cm (12"). It bears white flowers in late spring. **'Peach Blossom'** is less dramatic but just as effective, with peach-coloured, fragrant blooms and glossy leaves. This variety is an early bloomer, maturing to a 50 cm (20") height and spread.

Problems & Pests

A variety of pests can attack on occasion, including powdery mildew, bacterial leaf spot and fungal leaf spot.

In late summer, transplant seedlings found near the parent plant for plumes of colour throughout the garden.

A. x *arendsii* cultivar

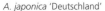
A. *japonica* 'Deutschland'

Baptisia
False Indigo
Wild Indigo
Baptisia

Height: 91 cm–1.2 m (3–4') **Spread:** 91 cm (36") **Flower colour:** blue, purple, yellow; foliage **Blooms:** mid-summer **Zones:** 2–8

THIS IS ONE 'WILDFLOWER' THAT IS SURE TO EVOKE A COMMENT or two from passersby. Its mounds of attractive, olive green foliage remain intact well after summer, adorning beds and borders well into our winter season. Its deep blue flowers persist well into summer and are followed by the most interesting black seedpods that also look good in winter. Baptisia is quite hardy and reliable but a little slow to grow. The rewards far outweigh the wait, though. This plant has an unwarranted reputation for being fussy because it does not like being divided. On the plus side, it can remain in one location, undisturbed, for years and is anything but invasive.

The curly seedpods are attractive in dried arrangements when still attached to the stems.

Planting

Seeding: Sow ripe seed indoors or in a cold frame in late winter; cultivars will not come true to type when propagated from seed

Planting out: Spring

Spacing: 1 m (3')

Growing

Baptisia prefers **full sun** and will tolerate partial shade. It will grow successfully in any **well-drained** soil. It is extremely drought resistant, long lived and dislikes being moved because of its long tap root. Make sure to plant it in a suitable location, so it won't have to be moved later. Divide, only if necessary, during its dormancy in late winter. Keep in mind that it may have a difficult time re-establishing.

Tips

Baptisia works well in herb or wildflower gardens, meadows, mixed borders or cottage gardens. It's a suitable specimen plant and useful when naturalizing. This may be the plant for those who have had no success growing lupines. Overall the look of the two plants is similar, although baptisia is less fussy. It thrives in informal borders and exposed sites and on hillsides and dry sunny embankments.

Recommended

B. australis grows 91 cm–1.2 m (3–4') tall and 91 cm (36") wide. This native prairie wildflower is both tall and colourful. Deep blue, short spikes emerge in mid-summer. Curly black seedpods emerge in fall

B. australis (above & below)

after flowering is done. Dense, bushy foliage enhances the tall flower stems, reminiscent of their cousin the lupine.

'Purple Smoke' bears deep lavender, 1.2 m (4') tall flower spikes. The stems change to a charcoal-green with age. Tufts of dense, finger-like foliage surround the tall, wiry stems.

Problems & Pests

Powdery mildew, leaf spot and rust can be troublesome.

Bellflower

Campanula

Height: 10–91 cm (4–36") **Spread:** 15–91 cm (6–36") **Flower colour:** blue, white, purple, pink **Blooms:** spring, summer **Zones:** 2–8

SOMETIMES A PERENNIAL WILL OFFER SUCH AN ARRAY OF SPECIES, cultivars and hybrids that it can be difficult to decide which ones to try. Bellflower creates this dilemma for many gardeners. Bellflower has a wide variety of favourable features, but one of the best is a blooming cycle so long, it never seems to end. For those who desire consistent colour in their perennial borders, bellflower is one of the best plants I can recommend. Carpathian bellflower is a perfect example. Its foliage is totally covered with attractive blooming 'bells' for most of the growing season.

Planting

Seeding: Not recommended. Direct sow in spring or fall; germination can be erratic

Planting out: Spring or fall

Spacing: 15–91 cm (6–36")

Growing

Bellflowers grow well in **full sun**, **partial shade** or **light shade**. The soil should be of **average to high fertility** and **well drained**. Bellflowers appreciate summer mulch to keep their roots cool, and winter mulch is beneficial when snow cover is inconsistent.

Bellflowers respond well to deadheading to prolong the bloom cycle. Use scissors to cut back one-third of the plant at a time, allowing other sections to continue blooming. As the pruned section starts to bud, cut back other sections for continued blooming. It is important to divide bellflowers every few years in early spring or late summer to keep plants vigorous and to prevent them from becoming invasive.

C. persicifolia

Bellflower can be propagated by basal, new-growth or rhizome cuttings.

C. carpatica

C. *persicifolia* cultivar (above)

C. *cochleariifolia* cultivar (below)

Tips

Low, spreading and trailing bellflowers can be used in rock gardens and on rock walls. Upright and mounding bellflowers can be used in borders and cottage gardens. You can also edge beds with the low-growing varieties.

Recommended

C. **'Birch Hybrid'** is a low-growing, spreading perennial that will trail over the edge of troughs, pots or walls if given the chance. It bears light blue to mauve flowers in summer and grows 10–15 cm (4–6") tall and 30 cm (12") wide. (Zones 4–8)

C. carpatica (Carpathian bellflower, Carpathian harebell) is a spreading, mounding perennial. It grows 25–30 cm (10–12") tall, spreads 30–61 cm (12–24") and bears blue, white or purple flowers in summer. **'Blue Clips'** is a smaller, compact plant with large blue flowers. **'Bressingham White'** is a compact plant with large white flowers. **'Jewel'** grows low to the ground, bearing deep blue flowers. It grows 10–20 cm (4–8") tall. **'Kent Belle'** is a stately new hybrid with large, deep violet blue bells on arching stems.

C. cochleariifolia (fairy thimble, creeping bellflower) is a creeping, mat-forming perennial that is ideal for edging, in rock or alpine gardens or cascading down a rock wall. It can withstand a step or two, along a pathway or between stepping stones. It bears tiny, nodding, bell-shaped flowers in blue or white atop a tightly packed clump of miniature leaves. This hardy, tough miniature grows 10 cm (4") tall and 15–30 cm (6–12") wide. **'Blue Tit'** bears deep blue flowers.

C. glomerata (clustered bellflower) is a reliably hardy, heavy bloomer. It produces large clusters of violet, lavender, blue or white, bell-shaped flowers in mid-summer. It grows about 25–45 cm (10–18") tall and wide. **'Acaulis'** is a dwarf form that grows to 20 cm (8") tall and is suitable for edging and rock gardens. **'Superba'** vigorously produces deep purple flowers and grows to 61 cm (24") tall and wide.

C. carpatica

C. persicifolia (peach-leaved bellflower) is an upright perennial. It grows about 91 cm (36") tall and spreads about 30 cm (12"). It bears white, blue or purple flowers from early summer to mid-summer.

Over 300 species of Campanula are found throughout the Northern Hemisphere, in habitats ranging from high rocky crags to boggy meadows.

C. poscharskyana (Serbian bellflower) is a trailing perennial. It grows 15–30 cm (6–12") tall and spreads 60–91 cm (24–36"). It bears light purple flowers in summer and early fall.

C. persicifolia

C. 'Dickson's Gold' has unique gold foliage and loose clusters of baby blue flowers. It works best in a rock garden setting, partially shaded from the hot sun. It grows 15 cm (6") tall and almost twice as wide. (Zones 4–8)

Problems & Pests

Minor problems with vine weevils, spider mites, aphids, powdery mildew, slugs, rust and fungal leaf spot are possible.

Bergamot
Bee Balm
Monarda

Height: 61 cm–1.2 m (2–4') **Spread:** 30–75 cm (12–30") **Flower colour:** red, pink, purple and cream **Blooms:** summer **Zones:** 3–8

I HAVE ALWAYS LOVED BERGAMOT, WHETHER IN MY TEA OR IN the garden. My first experience was with native bergamot, *Monarda fistulosa*, and the love affair has continued since that time. I once saw an aspen grove whose understorey was alive with these beautiful and fragrant rose purple flowers. The flamboyant blooms coupled with that unique bergamot fragrance was indeed a heady experience. Powdery mildew, a common affliction of bergamot, is now much less of a problem with the advent of newer cultivated varieties along with the tried and true 'Marshall's Delight' or 'Gardenview Scarlet.' Once you try growing one, you'll be hooked for life.

The fragrant leaves can be used in teas and potpourris.

Planting

Seeding: Start seeds outdoors in a cold frame or indoors in early spring

Planting out: Spring or fall

Spacing: 30–61 cm (12–24") apart

Growing

Bergamot grows well in **full sun**, **partial shade** or **full shade**. The soil should be of **average fertility**, **humus rich**, **moist** and **well drained**. Divide every two or three years in spring before new growth emerges.

Tips

Use bergamot beside a stream or pond, or in a lightly shaded, well-watered border.

Bergamot will attract bees, butterflies and hummingbirds to your garden. Avoid using pesticides that can seriously harm or kill these creatures, especially if you plan to ingest this, or any plant, in your garden.

The fresh or dried leaves may be used to make a refreshing, minty,

M. didyma cultivars (above & below)

As the name suggests, bee balm is extremely attractive to bees, hummingbirds and other pollinators. This plant also serves as a nectar source for butterflies.

citrus-scented tea. Put a handful of fresh leaves in a teapot, pour boiling water over the leaves and let steep for at least five minutes. Sweeten the tea with honey to suit your own taste.

Recommended

M. didyma is a bushy, mounding plant that forms a thick clump of stems. It grows 61 cm–1.2 cm (2–4') tall and spreads 30–61 cm (12–24"). Red or pink flowers are borne in late summer. **'Gardenview Scarlet'** bears large scarlet flowers and is resistant to powdery mildew. **'Marshall's Delight'** doesn't come true to type from seed and must be propagated by cuttings or divisions. It is very resistant to powdery mildew and bears pink flowers. **'Panorama'** is a group of hybrids with flowers in scarlet, pink or salmon. **'Petite Delight'** is the first in a series of dwarf varieties. It grows 30–46 cm

M. didyma cultivar
'Petite Delight'

(12–18") tall and bears purple-pink flowers. **'Raspberry Wine'** bears red wine-coloured flowers. **'Rosy Purple'** reaches 91 cm–1.2 m (3–4') heights and has deep purplish red flowers, and **'Violet Queen'** is equally as tall and bears deep purple flowers.

Problems & Pests

Powdery mildew is the worst problem, but rust, leaf spot and leaf hoppers can cause trouble. To help prevent powdery mildew, thin the stems in spring. If mildew strikes after flowering, cut the plants back to 15 cm (6") to increase air circulation. Don't allow the plant to dry out for extended periods.

M. didyma

This plant is named after the Spanish botanist and physician Nicholas Monardes (1493–1588).

'Marshall's Delight'

Bergenia

Bergenia

Height: 30–61 cm (12–24") **Spread:** 45–61 cm (18–24") **Flower colour:** red, purple, dark to light pink, white; foliage **Blooms:** early spring **Zones:** 2–8

BERGENIA PRODUCES BOLD FOLIAGE THAT IS SPECTACULAR IN autumn, when it takes on a bronze tint. Two plantings come to mind whenever people ask me about bergenia. I once had the opportunity to see a garden in northern Saskatchewan whose keeper was well into her 80s. Her garden encompassed an eight by ten foot area filled with nothing other than a stunning grouping of bergenia in full bloom. Another outstanding memory of bergenia was a grouping of the healthiest specimens I've ever seen, growing under a towering spruce tree that must have been almost 100 years old. Most gardeners will experience comparative results in just about any setting, with or without the adverse conditions. Bergenia is a true prairie winner.

Planting

Seeding: Seed may not come true to type; fresh, ripe seeds should be sown uncovered and soil kept at 20–21˚ C (69–70˚ F)

Planting out: Spring

Spacing: 45–61 cm (18–24")

Growing

Bergenias grow well in **full sun** or **partial shade**. The soil should be of **average to rich fertility** and **well drained**. A moist soil is preferable, but plants are drought tolerant once established.

Propagating by seed can be somewhat risky. You may not get what you hope for. A more certain way to get more of the plants you have is to propagate them with root cuttings. Bergenias spread just below the surface by rhizomes, which may be cut off in pieces and grown separately as long as a leaf shoot is attached to the section. Divide every two to three years when the clump begins to die out in the middle.

B. cordifolia (below)

B. cordifolia cultivar

B. c. 'Bressingham White'

Tips

These versatile, low-growing, spreading plants can be used as groundcovers, to edge borders and pathways, in rock gardens and in mass plantings under trees and shrubs.

Once flowering is complete, in early spring, bergenias still make a beautiful addition to the garden with their thick, leathery, glossy leaves. A bergenia plant provides a soothing background for other flowers with its expanse of green. As well, many varieties turn attractive colours of bronze and purple in fall and winter.

Recommended

B. cordifolia (heart-leaved bergenia) grows about 61 cm (24"), with an equal or greater spread. Its flowers are a deep shade of pink and the foliage turns bronze or purple in fall and winter. **'Bressingham Ruby'** provides winter colour with maroon

foliage and pinky-red flowers in early spring. It grows slightly larger than the white Bressingham selection, reaching 35 cm (14") tall. **'Bressingham White'** grows about 30 cm (12") tall and has white flowers. **'Purpurea'** has magenta purple flowers and red-tinged foliage.

B. **'Evening Glow'** ('Abdënglut') grows about 30 cm (12") tall and spreads 45–61 cm (18–24") wide. The flowers are a deep magenta-crimson. The foliage turns red and maroon in the winter. (Zones 3–8)

B. x *schmidtii* is a compact plant that grows 30 cm (12") tall and spreads 61 cm (24"). The flowers are pink. (Zones 4–8)

B. **'Winter Fairy Tale'** ('Wintermärchen') grows 30–45 cm (12–18") tall and spreads 45–61 cm (18–24"). The flowers are pinkish red and the dark green leaves are touched with red in winter. (Zones 4–8)

Problems & Pests

Rare problems with slugs, fungal leaf spot, root rot, weevils, caterpillars and foliar nematodes are possible.

Another common name for this plant is elephant ears because of its large, leathery leaves.

Bishop's Hat
Epimedium

Height: 20–45 cm (8–18") **Spread:** 30–45 cm (12–18") **Flower colour:** red, pink, purple, white, yellow; foliage **Blooms:** spring, summer **Zones:** 4–8

ALTHOUGH I HAVE MANAGED TO LOSE MY BISHOP'S HAT A number of times to extreme winters, I have always replanted it. Its finest attribute is the distinctly different foliage that only gets better as the summer cools into autumn. It is always well behaved, with a slow, spreading habit that complements shrubby and perennial neighbours alike throughout the growing season. Bishop's hat is a great addition to shady, dry areas where it is difficult to find anything else that will thrive. This spreading groundcover is best suited to locations where you can view the bronzy foliage before it packs it in for another winter, such as under a shade tree or beside your favourite garden bench.

Bishop's hat leaves often turn from green to shades of bronze in cooler weather.

Planting

Seeding: Sow ripe seed indoors or in a cold frame in early spring

Planting out: Spring

Spacing: 20–30 cm (8–12")

Growing

Bishop's hat prefers **partial sun** in an area well protected from cold, dry winds. The soil should be **rich, moist** and **well drained**. Most varieties are fairly drought tolerant. The oldest foliage and flowers should be sheared back in late winter or early spring, before the new flower buds emerge. This will provide the plant with enough energy to produce the best display of foliage and blooms. A thick mulch should be applied in mid- to late fall, whether snow coverage is reliable or not. The mulch will provide a protective barrier while maintaining an adequate moisture level in the soil. Divide in fall after flowering, but only when necessary.

Tips

Bishop's hat can be trained as a climbing vine or left without support to serve as a groundcover. It works well around the bases of trees and shrubs, under a shady canopy, in a woodland setting or on the side of a sheltered wall. Make sure to plant it in a location where the beautiful foliage and flowers are easily seen, especially in autumn.

Recommended

E. x *grandiflorum* 'Lilafee' is a very compact variety. It vigorously produces purple-tinged young leaves

E. x *rubrum*

and deep purple flowers. It grows 20–25 cm (8–10") tall.

E. x *rubrum* (red barrenwort) is the most common form of bishop's hat available. A little less vigorous than others, it possesses a spreading habit as well. The clumps of foliage are touched with a reddish green that intensifies with age. Wiry stems support pink and yellow bicoloured flowers, reminscent of *Aquilegia* (columbine). Its mature size is 30 cm (12") tall and wide.

E. x *versicolour* 'Sulphureum' grows to 20–30 cm (8–12") tall and wide in a clumping form. It has 5–11 copper red leaflets per leaf and bears yellow flowers with long spurs.

E. x *youngianum* stays lower to the ground, growing 20–30 cm (8–12") tall and wide. Medium green leaflets are borne on red-tinted stems; white or pale pink flowers emerge in spring, sometimes with spurs. 'Niveum' bears white flowers with colourful young foliage. 'Roseum' has soft pink to purple flowers with variable foliage.

Problems & Pests

Vine weevil and mosaic virus can become a problem.

Bitterroot

Lewisia

Height: 15–20 cm (6–8") **Spread:** 15 cm (6") **Flower colour:** pink, salmon, orange, yellow, white; foliage **Blooms:** spring, summer **Zones:** 3–8

BITTERROOT HAS THE DISTINCT HONOUR OF BEING ONE OF THE most challenging yet most rewarding perennials that I have ever grown. It is very susceptible to rot, so achieving the right combination of soil and location has required a fair bit of trial and error. The secret is to plant it on a fairly good slope to encourage efficient drainage, and to place a mulch of gravel around the crown. This combination will result in a spectacular show of brightly coloured flower sprays above a succulent, evergreen rosette.

The genus was named after the explorer and plant collector Meriwether Lewis (1774–1838).

Planting

Seeding: Sow seed indoors or in a cold frame in early spring or late fall

Planting out: Spring, fall

Spacing: 15 cm (6")

Growing

Bitterroot requires **light shade** in a **sheltered area**. The soil should be of **average fertility to organically rich**, **neutral to acidic** and **sharply drained**. Offsets can be removed and replanted in early summer. A thin layer of tiny gravel should be placed around the base, allowing the foliage to be slightly elevated above ground. Apply a thick, airy layer of mulch over top for protection from winter exposure.

Tips

Bitterroot is best planted in a location that offers excellent drainage. It is ideal for alpine, rock and trough gardens, and its delicate appearance will attract the attention of onlookers when planted along a pathway or tucked into a rock wall. Plant it in a sheltered location if using it in mixed beds and borders.

Recommended

L. cotyledon forms a tight, flat rosette of evergreen leaves with wavy edges and rounded tips. Reddish stems emerge from the clump, topped with clusters of daisy-like solid or striped flowers in shades of salmon, orange and yellow with tiny yellow centres. The stripe follows the outside edge of each petal. This species is the largest of the entire genus.

Problems & Pests

Root rot, rust, snails, slugs, aphids and mealy bugs may become problems occasionally.

L. cotyledon variety (below)

Bleeding Heart

Dicentra

Height: 30 cm–1.2 m (1–4') **Spread:** 45–91 cm (18–36") **Flower colour:** pink, white, red, purple; foliage **Blooms:** spring, summer **Zones:** 2–8

FROM THE ORIGINAL BLEEDING HEART TO THE COVETED FERN LEAF selections we all grow now, this plant is truly a traditional favourite. Children continue to be fascinated by the classic, heart-shaped blooms. I remember as a little girl being thrilled by the 'little hearts' in my grandmother's garden. It was not long ago that my grandmother gave a clump of her plant to both my mother and me. What a thrill to plant memories of my childhood into my own garden. As a mother and a gardener, I have watched my own children's fascination with this 'heart of the garden' with great joy.

Planting

Seeding: Start freshly ripened seed in a cold frame; plants self-seed in the garden

Planting out: Spring

Spacing: 45–91 cm (18–36") apart

Growing

Bleeding hearts prefer **light shade** but tolerate full sun or full shade. The soil should be **moist and humus rich**. Though these plants prefer to remain evenly moist, they are quite drought tolerant, particularly if the weather doesn't get hot. Very dry summer conditions will cause the plant to die back, but it will revive in fall or the following spring.

It is most important for bleeding hearts to remain moist while in flower in order to prolong the flowering period. Constant summer moisture will keep the flowers coming until mid-summer. Common bleeding heart and fringed bleeding heart rarely need dividing. Western bleeding heart can be divided every three years or so.

D. spectabilis

Enjoy these showy blooms in the garden because they don't work well as cut flowers.

D. eximia

D. formosa

D. eximia

D. spectabilis

Tips

Bleeding hearts can be naturalized in a woodland garden or grown in a border or rock garden. They make excellent early-season specimen plants. They do well near a pond or stream.

Recommended

D. eximia (fringed bleeding heart) forms a loosely mounded clump of lacy, fern-like foliage. It grows 38–61 cm (15–24") tall and spreads about 45 cm (18"). The pink or white flowers are borne mostly in spring, but they may be produced sporadically over summer. Hot, dry weather will cause the plant to go dormant during summer. **'Alba'** bears creamy white flowers with light green foliage. **'King of Hearts'** is a compact variety that grows no taller than 8" with rosy pink flowers. **'Stuart Boothman'** remains smaller than the species, approximately 30 cm (12") tall, with an equal or greater spread. Dark pink flowers are produced over a long period from spring to mid-summer amid blue-grey foliage. (Zones 3–8)

D. formosa (western bleeding heart) is a low-growing, wide-spreading plant. It grows about 45 cm (18") tall and spreads 60–91 cm (24–36"). The pink flowers fade to white as they mature. This plant is likely to self-seed, and it can become

invasive. This is the most drought tolerant of the bleeding hearts and the most likely to continue flowering all summer. **'Adrian Bloom'** forms a compact clump of dark grey-green foliage. It grows about 30 cm (12") tall and spreads about 45 cm (18"). Bright red flowers are produced in late spring but continue to appear intermittently all summer. **'Luxuriant'** is a low-growing hybrid with blue-green foliage and red-pink flowers. It grows about 30 cm (12") tall and spreads about 45 cm (18"). Flowers appear in spring and early summer. **Var.** *alba* has white flowers.

D. spectabilis (common bleeding heart) forms a large, elegant mound. It reaches 1.2 m (4') in height and spreads about 45 cm (18"). It bears late-spring and early-summer flowers. The inner petals are white while the outer petals are pink. This species is likely to die back in the summer heat, and it prefers dappled shade. **'Alba'** has entirely white flowers. **'Gold Heart'** has yellow-green, lacy foliage, dark reddish stems and contrasting pink and white flowers.

Problems & Pests

Slugs, downy mildew, *Verticillium* wilt, viruses, rust and fungal leaf spot can cause occasional problems.

D. formosa

These delicate plants are the perfect addition to a moist woodland garden. Plant them next to a shaded pond or stream.

D. spectablis 'Alba'

Buttercup
Ranunculus
Ranunculus

Height: 5–91 cm (2–36") **Spread:** 30–91 cm (12–36") **Flower colour:** yellow, white **Blooms:** summer to fall **Zones:** 3–8

BUTTERCUP VARIETIES DO NOT SEEM TO BE GROWN WITH GREAT frequency in Saskatchewan or Manitoba. Perhaps it's because they thrive in both sunshine and moisture, a combination not always available in unison on the prairies. They are, however, very adaptable to a wide range of conditions even if they do ultimately prefer wet feet. If you are new to growing buttercup, start with *R. acris* var. *flore-pleno* because it forms a very attractive carpet of the cutest heart-shaped leaves that are covered with glowing yellow double flowers.

Most buttercups prefer to grow in moist or bog-like locations. The botanical name is reflective of this tendency, meaning 'frog' in Latin.

Planting

Seeding: Not recommended; germination is erratic

Planting out: Spring

Spacing: 30–91 cm (12–36")

Growing

Buttercup prefers **full sun to partial shade**. The soil should be **evenly moist** but **well drained** and in a cool location. Divide in spring or fall when necessary. Water thoroughly before and during the flowering cycle, but allow it to dry out slightly once the cycle is complete.

R. acris var. flore-pleno

Tips

Buttercup is grown for its colourful flowers and ornate foliage. It deserves an area where it can be seen easily and won't be lost among larger perennials and shrubs. The taller varieties are ideal for mixed borders while the creepers are better suited to rock gardens, along stone walls and border edges.

Recommended

R. acris (tall buttercup, yellow bachelor's button, meadow buttercup) is a clump-forming perennial that produces wiry stems carrying deeply lobed leaves. Bright yellow flowers emerge through the foliage atop tall stems in mid-summer. The species is difficult to find. However, **Var.** *flore-pleno* is more common and grows 61 cm (24") tall. It bears double, rosette-like, bright yellow blossoms.

R. ficaria (celandine buttercup, lesser celandine, pilewort) bears single, cup-shaped blossoms in bright yellow shades that appear in spring. It grows only 5 cm (2") tall but spreads 30–45 cm (12–18") wide. The glossy green leaves are marked with hints of silver and gold. **'Albus'** produces single, creamy white flowers. **'Brazen Hussy'** bears bright yellow flowers atop purple-black foliage and **'Double Mud'** has pastel yellow flowers with brown markings resembling mud stains. (Zones 4–8)

R. repens (creeping buttercup) is a vigorous spreader, reaching 15–30 cm (6–12") heights and 61–91 cm (24–36") widths. The tightly packed leaves create a fresh green mat of foliage underneath showy flowers. **'Buttered Popcorn'** has single yellow flowers and bright, chartreuse variegated, ornate foliage. (Zones 4–8)

Problems & Pests

Powdery mildew, slugs, aphids and spider mites can all become problematic.

Chrysanthemum
Fall Garden Mum, Hybrid Garden Mum
Chrysanthemum

Height: 61 cm (24") **Spread:** 60–91 cm (24–36") **Flower colour:** orange, yellow, pink, red, purple, white **Blooms:** late summer and fall **Zones:** 3–9

FOR SUCCESS WITH CHRYSANTHEMUMS ON THE PRAIRIES, IT IS indeed necessary to choose carefully. Photoperiodism is the physiological mechanism that regulates whether or not a plant will flower. The chrysanthemum is a classic short day plant, which means that it will perceive long nights as the trigger to initiate and develop flowers. That is fine in warmer climates, but on the prairies, when our short days are short enough to trigger blooming, we almost always will have a killing frost. This can have a rather negative effect on the bloom. Thankfully we have the Morden Series, which is the only fall garden mum that will bloom early enough to beat the killing frost in regions with short seasons.

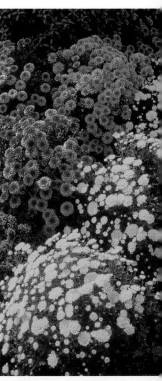

Planting

Seeding: Not recommended

Planting out: Spring, summer or fall

Spacing: 45–61 cm (18–24")

Growing

Chrysanthemum grows best in **full sun**. The soil should be **fertile, moist** and **well drained**. Divide in spring or fall every two years to keep the plant vigorous and to prevent it from thinning out in the centre. Pinch plants back in early summer to encourage bushy growth. You can deadhead in late fall or early winter, but leave the stems intact to protect the crown of the plant. The earlier in the season you can plant a chrysanthemum, the better. Early planting improves its chances of surviving the winter.

Tips

This plant provides a blaze of colour in the late-season garden, often flowering until the first hard

frost. Group them in borders or use them as specimen plants near the house or in large planters. Some gardeners purchase chrysanthemums as flowering plants in late summer and put them in the spots where summer annuals have faded.

Chrysanthemums can be moved to a more prominent spot once they start to colour. The plants are so adaptable that they continue growing as if nothing happened.

Recommended

C. x *morifolium* 'Morden' series was developed in Canada and is reliably hardy to Zone 3. **'Morden Canary'** bears double yellow blossoms and grows to 50 cm (20") tall while **'Morden Candy'** bears double pink flowers at the same height. **'Morden Delight'** produces bronze red flowers and grows to 61 cm (24") tall.

'**Morden Everest**' bears double white flowers at a 40 cm (15") height and '**Morden Fiesta**' has double purple flowers to the same height. '**Morden Gaiety**' bears double orange-bronze flowers and '**Morden Garnet**' has double red flowers; both grow to 50 cm (20") tall.

Problems & Pests

Aphids can be a true menace to these plants. Insecticidal soap can be used to treat the problem, but it should be washed off within an hour because it discolours the foliage when the sun hits it. Though these problems are not as common, also watch for spider mites, white-flies, leaf miners, leaf spot, powdery mildew, rust, aster yellows, blight, borers and rot.

Cimicifuga
Bugbane
Cimicifuga

Height: 1.2–2.2 m (4–7') **Spread:** 61 cm (24") **Flower colour:** white; foliage
Blooms: late summer **Zones:** 3–8

I RESERVE WORDS LIKE AWESOME FOR REALLY SPECTACULAR trees; however, cimicifuga is one herbaceous perennial that is truly awesome. I like to compare it to a giant astilbe with attitude. *C. ramosa* 'Atropurpurea' is made up of a few cultivated varieties that are extremely hardy on the Canadian prairies. They bloom late in the season, require little care once established, and many have a delightful fragrance. My favourite are the newest 'black-leaved' types, such as 'Brunette,' which has deep bronzy purple, lacy clumps of foliage and pale pink, fragrant, bottlebrush-like flower spikes. The flowers are most stunning when touched by the early morning light. What better treat, while enjoying the day's first cup of coffee in your favourite chair every morning?

Planting
Seeding: Sow ripe seed indoors or in a cold frame, in early spring

Planting out: Spring, summer

Spacing: 60–75 cm (24–30")

Growing

Cimicifuga prefers **partial shade to full sun**. The soil should be **rich in organic matter** and **moist**. Divide in spring when necessary. Staking may be required, owing to the overall mature size, but only in exposed locations. Mulching in fall will provide a protective barrier for insulation and moisture maintenance in areas where snow coverage is less reliable. Rhizome divisions should be planted in the autumn, but be careful not to damage or disturb the root any more than necessary.

Tips

Cimicifuga looks attractive among other plants when included in a mixed bed or border. It is also useful in shade gardens, woodland or naturalized settings, as a specimen or in a moist border.

Recommended

C. racemosa (black cohosh, black snakeroot) grows to 1.2–2.2 m (4–7') tall and 61 cm (24") wide. Tall, white-flowered spikes emerge through dark bronzy green, deeply lobed leaves. The flowers are scented, and some people find the fragrance pleasant while others find it offensive. Fruit capsules emerge after the spent flowers in the fall.

C. ramosa '**Atropurpurea**' (purple-leaf bugbane) is one of two cultivars that are becoming increasingly popular throughout the prairies. The cultivars are more readily available than the species. '**Atropurpurea**' produces a clump of exotic, dark purple, lacy foliage. Tall spikes of creamy white flowers on dark wiry stems poke through the clump, reaching 1.5–2.1m (5–7') tall. '**Brunette**' bears even darker foliage, dark purple with an almost black tinge. Pale pink, lanky spikes are borne late summer. (Zones 4–8)

Problems & Pests

Rust is possible, but problems are infrequent to rare.

C. racemosa

Both the common name and genus refer to the insecticidal properties that this plant possesses. 'Cimex' is Latin for insect while 'fugare' means to flee.

'Brunette'

Clematis

Clematis

Height: 61 cm–5 m (2–16.5') **Spread:** 45 cm–91 cm (18–36") **Flower colour:** blue, pink, red, purple, white, yellow **Blooms:** spring, summer **Zones:** 1–8

FROM THE VIGOROUS CLIMBERS TO THE BEAUTIFUL UPRIGHT, shrub-like varieties, there is sure to be at least one clematis for every gardener. I find that *C. recta* is the most useful clematis for my needs. It is unequalled in its ability to disguise ugly garden additions like septic tank covers. Plant this variety beside whatever you want to hide, and as it sprawls, place a brick on a board on top of the stems. Because this clematis has a natural tendency to grow upright, now growth will quickly and effectively grow over your unsightly problem. If you need to access whatever you're hiding, flip the clematis back. When you're done, replace the stems and weights and presto, instant screen! With a little imagination, and this perennial climber, you'll soon be viewing lush growth and hundreds of blossoms rather than that utility box, air conditioner or septic tank.

Planting

Seeding: Sow seed in a cold frame in early spring; cultivars will not come true to type

Planting out: Spring, summer

Spacing: 91 cm (36") minimum, depends on the width of the climbing apparatus.

Growing

Clematis prefers **full sun to partial shade** and **fertile**, **organically rich**, **moist** and **well-drained** soil. The term to remember when choosing a location for a clematis is 'hot head; cool feet.' The portion of the plant that is above ground requires at least half a day of sun, while the roots need to remain cool. The roots can be kept cool by covering the base with a thick layer of mulch and planting a perennial or shrub nearby to shade the ground at the base of the vine.

Tips

As long as the sunlight is adequate, vines will grow just about anywhere that support is provided. Clematis will twine its way up a trellis,

C. x jackmanii

C. x jackmanii cultivar

C. *'Prairie Traveler's Joy' was given this name because it was often discovered in the hedgerows along roadsides, by travellers.*

C. recta

an arbor, fencing, netting, an obelisk, or even on or up an adjacent tree or shrub. It fits into a cottage garden or any informal setting. Clematis is a little like a chameleon in that it will conform to its environment, whether twirling up a classical column in front of a royal-looking rose, or spreading out as a groundcover in a natural setting.

Before pruning your clematis, figure out which of the following three groups it is from. **Group A** bears flowers in early spring and only on old growth (produced the previous year). Prune Group A plants by removing weak and dead stems once the flowering cycle is complete. **Group B** is split into two sub-groups. Group B1 varieties flower on old wood, producing a heavy flush of flowers from May to June on the previous season's growth followed by a smaller flush of blooms in the fall on new growth. Group B2 blooms simultaneously on the current season's and previous season's growth, from June to September. The B groups should be lightly pruned in late February or March by removing weak or dead wood; the remaining stems should be carefully arranged. **Group C** varieties bloom from early summer to fall and only on new wood (the current year's growth). This group should be cut back to two

strong sets of buds on each stem in late February or March, as close to ground level as possible.

Recommended

C. heracleifolia '**Davidiana**' (blue bush clematis) is a little different from the taller, vining species. This species is closer in habit to a vigorous shrub that dies back in fall, and is smaller than most clematis species. It may still require support, though. It bears clusters of open, blue flowers with yellow button centres in late summer, and grows 91 cm (36") tall and 61 cm (24") wide. The flowers are produced on the current year's growth. Prune this variety down to a 30 cm (12") height in fall. (Zones 3–8)

C. integrifolia (solitary clematis) is more of a spreading clump than a climber. Nodding, purplish blue, outward-facing flowers are borne on the tips of 61–91 cm (24–36") dark stems. Fluffy seedheads form once the flowers have finished. This species is suitable for many purposes, as a groundcover or specimen, or allowed to wind its way through an adjacent rose bush. This species blooms on the current year's growth. It should be cut back to a 30 cm (12") height in fall. (Zones 2–8)

C. x *jackmanii* is very likely the most popular clematis available on the prairies. Its enormous purple flowers with bright yellow centres emerge prolifically on twining vines from summer to fall, and it can grow 4–5 m (13–15') tall in one season. One of the reasons it is so prevalent on the prairies is because of its ability to tolerate our winters with little difficulty. It blooms on the current year's growth, so prune it back to a 30 cm (12") height in the fall. (Zones 3–8)

C. x '**Prairie Traveler's Joy**' is a climber, reaching 4–5 m (13–15') in height. Extremely vigorous, drought tolerant and hardy, this hybrid is useful as a groundcover as well as a climber. It bears star-shaped, white flowers that bloom all summer followed by fluffy seedheads. It may need a hard prune every couple of years to rejuvenate it.

The fuzzy seedheads of some species gave rise to the alternative common name 'old man's beard.'

C. integrifolia

C. integrifolia (above)

C. recta '**Purpurea**' (ground clematis) is a short, herbaceous climber. It bears deep red-purple leaves and fragrant, starry white flowers. Silver seedheads follow the spent flowers in fall. Its mature size is 91 cm–1.2 m (3–4') tall and 45–61 cm (18–24") wide. (Zones 2–8)

C. tangutica (golden clematis) vigorously produces stems covered in small, yellow, bell-shaped flowers throughout the summer. The foliage is dense and ornate. Fluffy seedheads are formed in the fall after flowering. It is much more tolerant of poor conditions compared to other clematis species, and is easily trained as a climbing vine, growing 5 m (15') tall. It may require a hard prune every year or two to rejuvenate. (Zones 2–8)

Problems & Pests

Mildew, earwigs, slugs, aphids, caterpillars, oil beetles, spider mites and
Clematis wilt require different levels
of control. Clematis wilt can be very
problematic. For the best chance of
recovery, it's best to recognize the
symptoms and catch the problem
early. It is important to remove and
destroy the affected stems. Make sure
to trim 2–5 cm (1–2") below the
infected area, in order to remove all
of the infection. New growth should
begin to emerge readily. If it persists,
spray with a fungicide.

*C. 'Prairie Traveler's Joy' was
associated with the devil and
witchcraft because it was thought
to choke out other plants.
Ironically, it was also thought to
be connected with God and the
Virgin Mary, owing to its white,
feathery fruits.*

C. x jackmanii

C. tangutica

Columbine

Aquilegia

Height: 15–91 cm (6–36") **Spread:** 30–61 cm (12–24") **Flower colour:** red, yellow, pink, purple, blue, white; colour of spurs often differs from that of the petals; foliage **Blooms:** spring, summer **Zones:** 2–8

COLUMBINE HAS A CERTAIN CHARM. IT IS NATIVE TO MOST temperate areas of the world; its flowers come in a wonderful range of lively colours; and its foliage is light, delicate and lacy. The pendent, spurred flowers occur on stalks above the leaves and always appear to dance in the breeze. Some say that the flowers resemble fancy little hats, hence one of its many common names—granny's bonnet. Although quite showy, columbine varieties are often small and can easily be lost if mixed together with most traditional perennials in a border. Plant columbine towards the front or along the edge of the border to display this old–fashioned beauty so that everyone can enjoy it.

Planting

Seeding: Direct sow in spring

Planting out: Spring

Spacing: About 30–61 cm (12–24") apart

Growing

Columbines grow well in **full sun** or **partial shade** and in **fertile**, **moist** and **well-drained** soil, though it adapts well to most soil conditions. Columbine is known to self-seed, and is considered vigorous but not invasive. The young seedlings can be transplanted to other locations. Division is not required but can be done to propagate desirable plants. They may take a while to recover because they dislike having their roots disturbed.

Tips

Use columbines in a rock garden, a formal or casual border or in a naturalized or woodland garden.

Each year a few new plants may turn up near the parent plant. If you have a variety of columbines planted near each other, you may even wind up

Columbines are short-lived perennials that seed freely throughout the garden, and establish themselves in unexpected, and often charming, locations.

A. x *hybrida* 'McKana Giants'

A. x hybrida 'McKana Giants'

A. x hybrida 'McKana Giants'

A. vulgaris 'Nora Barlow'

with a new cultivar. Columbines crossbreed easily, resulting in many hybrid forms. The wide variety of flower colours is the most interesting result. The new seedlings may not be identical to the parents, and there is some likelihood that they will revert to the original species.

Recommended

A. canadensis (wild columbine, Canada columbine) is native to most of eastern North America. It grows up to 61 cm (24") tall and spreads about 30 cm (12"). Yellow flowers with red spurs are borne in spring and summer.

A. flabellata (fan columbine) is a vigorously growing plant with blue-tinged leaves and soft bluish purple flowers that emerge in summer. **'Cameo Mix'** offers a variety of bicoloured blossoms atop silvery green foliage, ranging from creamy white to soft salmon. The average mature size of this mix is 15 cm (6").

A. x hybrida (*A.* x *cultorum*, hybrid columbine) forms mounds of delicate foliage. Many groups of hybrids have been developed for their showy flowers of various colours. When the exact parentage of a plant is uncertain, it is grouped under this heading. **'Double Pleat'** (double pleat hybrids) grow 75–80 cm (30–32") tall. They bear double flowers in combinations of blue and white or pink and white. **'Dragonfly'** (dragonfly hybrids) is a series of compact plants that reach only 61 cm (24") in height and 30 cm (12") in width; flowers come in a range of colours. **'McKana Giants'** (McKana hybrids) are popular and bear flowers in yellow, pink, red, purple, mauve and white. They grow up to 91 cm (36") tall. **'Ruby Port'** bears deep wine red, double flowers. **'Sunlight White'** is quite large, growing 91 cm (36") tall and bearing double, spurless, white flowers with the occasional streak of lime. Both 'Ruby Port' and 'Sunlight White' are frequently used as cut flowers. (Zones 3–8)

A. **'Royal Purple'** is reminiscent of a double clematis bloom and features deep, dark purple, spurless flowers with bright yellow stamens and contrasting foliage. It grows only 61 cm (24") tall at maturity. This columbine is a newer double introduction that may be hard to find, but it's well worth it. (Zones 3–8)

A. viridiflora grows to 30–35 cm (12–14") tall, and has fragrant, unusually coloured flowers featuring chartreuse spurs grasping onto chocolate-purple flowers, which in turn enclose bright yellow-green stamens. (Zones 4–8)

A. vulgaris (European or common columbine) comes in a variety of colours and grows about 91 cm (36") tall and 45 cm (18") wide. It has been used to develop a number of hybrids and cultivars. **'Magpie'** (William Guiness) is a unique combination of dark purple and white, reaching 61 cm (24") in height. **'Nora Barlow'** is a popular cultivar with double flowers in white, pink and green-tinged red. (Zones 2–8)

A. x hybrida 'Double Pleat'

Problems & Pests

Mildew and rust can be troublesome during dry weather. Fungal leaf spot, crown and root rot, aphids, caterpillars and leaf miners can be problematic too.

If you wish to keep a particular form, you must preserve it carefully through frequent division or root cuttings.

A. canadensis

Coral Bells
Alum Root
Heuchera

Height: 30 cm–1.2 m (1–4') **Spread:** 30–45 cm (12–18") **Flower colour:** red, pink, white, yellow, purple, green; foliage **Blooms:** spring, summer **Zones:** 3–8

A BALANCED GARDEN DESIGN INCLUDES PLANTS THAT ARE attractive without flowers. Coral bells fall beautifully into this category. This plant's diverse foliage shapes, sizes and colours offer endless possible uses. With a great selection of new cultivars available, coral bells is likely to be one of the most widely used perennials in years to come. The fancy-leaved varieties have spectacular foliage in shades of purple, red, amber, copper and almost black, and let's not forget the new, somewhat garish, varieties with mottled vein patterns in metallic shades. The newer cultivars produce more flowers as well, with clouds of tiny flowers strung along tall stems, making this plant attractive to busy little hummingbirds.

Planting

Seeding: Species, but not cultivars, may be started from seed in spring indoors to extend the season, or directly sown outdoors

Planting out: Spring, fall

Spacing: 30–45 cm (12–18") apart

Growing

Coral bells grow best in **light** or **partial shade.** Foliage colours can bleach out in full sun, and plants become leggy in full shade. The soil should be of **average to rich fertility, humus rich, neutral to alkaline, moist** and **well drained.** Good air circulation is essential. If the soil is acidic, apply horticultural lime to the soil each year.

The spent flowers should be removed to prolong the blooming period. Every two or three years, coral bells should be dug up to remove the oldest, woodiest roots and stems. Coral bells may be divided at this time, if desired, then replanted with the crown just above soil level. Cultivars may be propagated by division in spring or fall.

H. brizioides 'Firefly'

These delicate woodland plants will enhance your garden with their bright colours, attractive foliage and airy sprays of flowers.

H. sanguinea

H. micrantha var. *diversifolia* 'Palace Purple'
H. micrantha 'Chocolate Ruffles'

Tips

Use coral bells as edging plants, clustered in woodland gardens or as groundcovers in low-traffic areas. Combine different foliage types for an interesting display.

Coral bells have a strange habit of pushing themselves up out of the soil. Mulch in fall if the plants begin heaving from the ground.

Recommended

Most of the cultivars listed are hybrids developed from crosses between the various species. They are grouped with one of their acknowledged parents in the following list.

H. americana is a mound-forming plant. The heart-shaped foliage is marbled and veined in bronze when it is young and matures to deep green. The plant grows about 45 cm (18") tall and spreads 30 cm (12"). The flowers are brownish green, produced in early summer. Cultivars have been developed for their attractive and variable foliage. **'Chocolate Veil'** has dark chocolatey purple leaves with silvery patches between the veins. Its flowers are greenish purple. **'Pewter Veil'** has silvery-purple leaves with dark grey veining. Its flowers are white flushed with pink. **'Stormy Seas'** displays a combination of colours within the foliage, shades of lavender, charcoal and hints of pewter and silver. Tall stems of creamy white flowers are borne in late spring. **'Velvet Night'** produces the darkest leaves to date. Large, near-black leaves are tinged with a metallic purple-grey.

H. x *brizioides* is a group of mound-forming hybrids, developed through extensive cross-breeding of the various species for their attractive flowers. They grow 30–75 cm (12–30") tall and spread 30–45 cm (12–18"). **'Firefly'** has fragrant, bright pinkish red flowers. **'June Bride'** has large, white flowers. **'Raspberry Regal'** is a larger plant, growing up to 1.2 m (4') tall. The foliage is strongly marbled and the flowers are bright red.

H. micrantha is a mounding, clump-forming plant. It grows up to 91 cm (36") tall. The foliage is grey-green and the flowers are white. The species is not common in gardens, but there are many cultivars that are very common. **'Bressing-ham Hybrids'** are compact hybrids that can be started from seed. Flowers will be pink or red. **'Chocolate Ruffles'** has ruffled, glossy, brown foliage with purple undersides that give the leaves a bronzed appearance. **'Pewter Moon'** has light pink flowers and silvery leaves with bronzy purple veins. **Var.** *diversifolia* **'Palace Purple'** is one of the best-known cultivars of all the coral bells. This compact cultivar has deep purple foliage and white blooms. It grows 45–50 cm (18–20") tall. It can be started from seed, but only some of the seedlings will be true to type. (Zones 4–8)

H. sanguinea is the hardiest species. It forms a low-growing mat of foliage. It grows 30–45 cm (12–18") tall, with an equal spread. The dark green foliage is marbled with silver. The red, pink or white flowers are borne in summer. **'Coral Cloud'** has pinkish red flowers and glossy, crinkled leaves. **'Frosty'** has red flowers and silver-variegated foliage. **'Northern Fire'** has red flowers and leaves mottled with silver. **'White Cloud'** produces silvery-white mottled green foliage. In late spring, white flowers emerge, reaching 45 cm (18") in height.

Problems & Pests
Healthy coral bells have very few problems. In stressed situations, they can be afflicted with foliar nematodes, powdery mildew, rust or leaf spot.

H. americana cultivar

Cut flowers can be used in arrangements.

H. micrantha cultivar

Corydalis
Corydalis

Height: 8–18" **Spread:** 8–12" or more **Flower colour:** yellow, cream, blue; foliage **Blooms:** spring, summer **Zones:** 3–8

CORYDALIS IS SOMETIMES MISTAKEN FOR A FERN-LEAVED bleeding heart, but only until the exotic, tubular flowers begin to emerge throughout the summer months in rich shades of purple, blue and yellow. Yellow corydalis, *C. lutea*, has a decidedly lovely habit of self-seeding in the most unlikely places. I have found it growing in the oddest places that you would never dream could support the growth of a plant. Unlike some plants that have a habit of self-sowing, this one is very easily removed when small. Corydalis is a great addition to an alpine garden or a rockery because it is small and has a long blooming cycle, gracing the garden with the most interesting blossoms for months on end.

Planting

Seeding: Direct sow fresh seed in early fall; germination can be erratic

Planting out: Spring

Spacing: 12"

Growing

Corydalis grows well in **light** or **partial shade** with morning sun. The soil should be of **average to rich fertility**, **humus rich** and **well drained**. Plants will die back in the hottest part of summer. Trim the faded foliage, and new leaves will sprout as the weather cools in late summer and fall. These plants self-seed and can be propagated by transplanting the tiny seedlings. Division can be done in spring or early summer, but corydalis resents having its roots disturbed.

Tips

Corydalis is admired for its delicate flowers and attractive, ferny foliage. Use it in woodland or rock gardens, in borders, on rock walls and along paths. Let it naturalize in unused or underused areas.

Recommended

C. flexuosa (blue corydalis) is an erect plant with blue spring flowers. It grows 12" tall and spreads 8" or more. Keep this plant well watered during hot weather. **'Gold Panda'** produces green foliage that changes to a shade of chartreuse with age, and bears cobalt blue flowers. **'Purple Leaf'** is a compact variety that produces bronze-coloured leaves with violet blue flowers. (Zones 4–7)

C. lutea

C. lutea (yellow corydalis) is a mound-forming perennial that bears yellow flowers from late spring often to early fall. It grows 12–18" tall and spreads 12" or more. This is the hardiest species; it is also the most vigorous and can become invasive. Most gardeners don't mind the ferny-leaved plants turning up here and there, however.

C. ochroleuca (white corydalis) bears cream to white flowers in late spring and summer and is very similar to *C. lutea* in habit. It grows about 12" tall, with an equal spread. (Zones 5–8)

Problems & Pests

Rare problems with downy mildew and rust are possible.

Cranesbill

Geranium

Height: 15–91 cm (6–36") **Spread:** 30–91 cm (12–36") **Flower colour:**
white, red, pink, purple or blue; foliage **Blooms:** summer **Zones:** 2–8

THE PERENNIAL CRANESBILL IS A RELATIVE OF THE ANNUAL
geranium (*Pelargonium*), and both are available in a huge range of heights
and colours that are sure to suit your garden needs. Cranesbill tends to grow
into a mound or mat of lush, scented and ornate foliage. If the foliage is
looking a little tired after the flowers have finished, give it a hard pruning to
encourage a rejuvenating flush of new foliage. It will then remain attractive
for the remainder of the growing season. In fact, hard pruning is a good
technique to use with most of your early-summer blooming perennials if
they start looking a little spent.

Planting

Seeding: Species are easy to start from seed in early fall or spring. Cultivars and hybrids may not come true to type.

Planting out: Spring or fall

Spacing: 30–91 cm (12–36") apart

Growing

Cranesbill prefers to grow in **partial** or **light shade** but will **tolerate full** Soil of **average fertility** and with **good drainage** is preferred, but most conditions are tolerated, except waterlogged soil. This plant dislikes hot weather. Shear back spent blooms for a second set of flowers. Prune back foliage in late summer, if it is looking ratty, to rejuvenate. Divisions should be done in spring.

Tips

This long-flowering plant is great in the border to fill in the spaces between shrubs and other larger plants and to keep the weeds down.

G. pratense

G. x oxonianum

G. *sanguineum* cultivar
G. *sanguineum* var. *striatum*

It can be included in rock gardens and woodland gardens and mass planted as a groundcover.

Recommended

G. '**Johnson's Blue**' forms a spreading mat of foliage. It grows 30–45 cm (12–18") tall and spreads about 75 cm (30"). Bright blue flowers are borne over a long period in summer.

G. macrorrhizum (bigroot geranium, scented cranesbill) forms a spreading mound. It grows 30–50 cm (12–20") tall and spreads 40–61 cm (16–24"). Flowers in variable shades of pink are borne in spring and early summer. '**Album**' bears white flowers in summer on compact plants. '**Bevan's Variety**' bears magenta flowers.

G. x *oxonianum* is a vigorous, mound-forming plant with attractive evergreen foliage. It bears pink flowers from spring to fall. It grows up to 75 cm (30") tall and spreads about 61 cm (24"). '**A.T. Johnson**' bears many silvery-pink flowers. '**Wargrave Pink**' is a very vigorous cultivar. It grows 61 cm (24") tall and spreads to 91 cm (36"), bearing salmon pink flowers. (Zones 3–8)

G. pratense (meadow cranesbill) forms an upright clump, growing 61–91 cm (24–36") tall and spreads to 61 cm (24"). Clusters of white, blue or light purple flowers are borne for a short period in early summer. It self-seeds freely. '**Mrs. Kendall Clarke**' bears rose pink flowers with blue-grey veining. '**Plenum Violaceum**' bears purple double flowers for a longer period than the species because it sets no seed. (Zones 3–8)

G. sanguineum (bloody cranesbill, bloodred cranesbill) forms a dense, mounding clump. It grows 15–30 cm (6–12") tall and spreads 30–61 cm (12–24"). Bright magenta flowers are borne mostly in early summer and sporadically until fall. **'Album'** has white flowers and a more open habit than other cultivars. **'Alpenglow'** has bright rosy red flowers and dense foliage. **'Elsbeth'** has light pink flowers with dark pink veins. The foliage turns bright red in fall. **'Shepherd's Warning'** is a dwarf plant that grows 15 cm (6") tall with rosy pink flowers. **Var. *striatum*** is heat and drought tolerant. It has pale pink blooms with blood red veins. (Zones 3–8)

Problems & Pests
Rare problems with leaf spot and rust can occur.

G. pratense 'Plenum Violaceum'

G. 'Johnson's Blue'

Crocus
Pasque Flower
Pulsatilla

Height: 15–30 cm (6–12") **Spread:** 10–30 cm (4–12") **Flower colour:** purple, blue, red, white; foliage **Blooms:** early to mid-spring **Zones:** 2–8

NOTHING ON THE PRAIRIES REPRESENTS SPRING LIKE THE CROCUS. Every spring for as long as I can remember, I have taken my children out 'crocus hunting' as our spring ritual. These traditions tend to get passed on from generation to generation, and it is my hope that we will retain enough native prairie habitat that this will continue with my grandchildren and theirs. Thankfully we have the ability to grow the commonly found hybrid to enjoy just outside our door. Just another tradition worth passing on to all fellow prairie gardeners.

P. patens is native to the prairies, usually found blooming through the snow in early spring.

Planting

Seeding: Sow seed as soon as it is ripe and when soil temperature is about 21° C (70° F); best sown in fall

Planting out: Spring

Spacing: 10–30 cm (4–12") apart

Growing

Crocus grows well in **full sun** or **partial shade**. The soil should be **fertile** and **very well drained**. Poorly drained, wet soil can quickly kill this plant. Crocus resents being disturbed in any way. Plant it while it is very small and don't divide it.

Propagate crocus by taking root cuttings in early spring. You may have to soak the soil around the plant to loosen it enough to get to the roots. Dig carefully to expose a root, then remove it and replant it. Take a look at the 'Propagation' section in the introduction (p. 54) for more information about starting root cuttings.

Tips

Crocus is ideal for rock gardens, borders, gravelly banks or alpine trough gardens. It can be grown in a variety of pots or planters and moved to a sheltered spot, perhaps in a corner of the garage, or an enclosed but unheated porch, during the winter for protection. Make sure the pots are moved into the light once the plant begins to show signs of growth.

Recommended

P. patens (Easter pasque flower) is a clump-forming perennial. The hairy leaves are heart-shaped and finely divided. Cup-shaped, violet blue or

P. patens (above); *P. vulgaris* (below)

yellowish white flowers emerge in early spring. It grows to 15 cm (6") tall and 10 cm (4") wide. (Zones 3–8)

P. vulgaris (anemone pulsatilla) forms a mounded clump of lacy foliage. Flowers in shades of blue, purple or occasionally white are borne in early spring, before the foliage emerges. The seedheads are very fluffy and provide interest when the flowers are gone. **'Alba'** has white flowers. **'Papageno'** has large, semi-double flowers, available in a mix of shades, and each petal has a fringed edged. **'Rubra'** has bright purple-red flowers.

Problems & Pests

Tender, young growth can be attractive to slugs.

Cupid's Dart
Catananche

Height: 45–91 cm (18–36") **Spread:** 30 cm (12") **Flower colour:** blue, purple, white **Blooms:** mid-summer to fall **Zones:** 3–8

CUPID'S DART IS A CHARMINGLY SHORT-LIVED BUT SELF-SEEDING perennial. My first introduction to cupid's dart was when I was just becoming interested in wildflower-type gardens that form as a result of self-seeding. Areas left to self-seed are always fascinating, always changing and never without activity. Plants prone to self-seeding seem to do so in areas that are best suited to their needs. Maintenance requirements are few and as simple as taking your favourite hoe out early in the growing season for thinning purposes. Once you can recognize one plant from another, remove a good number of plants to guarantee a superb showing of blooms.

Planting

Seeding: Directly sow in garden once the warm spring ground allows. Soil temperature should be 21° C (70° F).

Planting out: Spring

Spacing: 30 cm (12") apart

Growing

Cupid's dart prefers **full sun** but **tolerates partial shade**. The soil should be **sandy**, **humus rich** and **well drained**. Cupid's dart dislikes wet soil, so find a spot where the ground is well drained and dries up quickly in spring. This fast-growing perennial will flower the first year from seed, and it can be grown as an annual. Divide every year or so to keep the plant vigorous.

Tips

Use in borders, in mass plantings, on dry banks and in cottage gardens, rock gardens and planters.

The cut flowers can be used in fresh and dried arrangements.

Recommended

C. caerulea is a short-lived, clump-forming perennial with narrow grass-like foliage. It grows 45–91 cm (18–36") tall and spreads 30 cm (12"). Blue or purple-blue flowers are borne from mid-summer to frost. **'Alba'** produces solid silvery-white flowers and **'Bicolor'** has white flowers with purple centres. **'Blue Giant'** has silver-tinted foliage and medium blue blooms. **'Major'** bears deep lavender flowers with dark purple-blue centres, while **'Perry's White'** has white flowers with creamy centres.

'Bicolor'

Problems & Pests

Powdery mildew can occur, but it is unlikely to be serious.

C. caerulea

Daylily
Hemerocallis

Height: 75 cm–1.2 m (2½–4') **Spread:** 61 cm–1.2 m (2–4') **Flower colour:** every colour except blue and pure white; foliage **Blooms:** spring, summer **Zones:** 2–8

IN MY OPINION, NOTHING CAN BEAT THE DAYLILY. EXTENSIVE breeding has ensured that the daylily is a top-ranking garden perennial. Although each daylily bloom lasts for only one day, you can easily select varieties that will bloom at different times to prolong the blooming cycle for months. They are useful massed as a groundcover or mixed into perennial borders and containers. I find myself drawn to bicoloured daylily varieties. Their dual-coloured flowers are very easy to co-ordinate with like or contrasting colours in the perennial border. 'Moonlight Masquerade' is a perfect example of a bicoloured variety that blends flawlessly from one grouping of colour to another. Most other varieties will as well, offering you endless possibilities.

Planting

Seeding: Not recommended; hybrids and cultivars don't come true to type from seed

Planting out: Spring

Spacing: 60 cm–1.2 m (2–4')

Growing

Daylilies will grow in any light from **full sun** to **full shade**. The deeper the shade, the fewer flowers produced. The soil should be **fertile**, **moist** and **well drained**, but these plants adapt to most conditions and are hard to kill once they are established. Deadhead small varieties to keep them blooming for as long as possible. Feed your daylilies in spring and mid-summer to produce the best display of blooms. In order to keep plants vigorous, propagate by division every two to three years. They can be left alone indefinitely, but blooming and overall growth may be reduced.

Taken from the Greek words for day, 'hemera' *and beauty,* 'kallos,' *the genus and the common name indicate that this plant's lovely blooms last only one day.*

H. fulva 'Kwanso Variegata'

H. fulva cultivar

H. 'Luxury Lace' (above)

Tips

Plant daylilies alone or grouped in borders, on banks and in ditches to control erosion. Naturalize them in woodland or meadow gardens. Small varieties are nice in planters.

Purple-flowered daylilies can stain fingers and clothes when you are deadheading them; use caution.

Recommended

Daylily comes in a seemingly infinite number of forms, sizes and colours and in a wide variety of species, cultivars and hybrids. What follows are just a few suggestions from each colour group. See your local garden centre or browse through a variety of mail-order catalogues for a larger selection.

H. **'Chicago Jewel'** grows to 62 cm (25") tall, producing ruffled, deep purple flowers surrounding creamy throats. Blooming takes place late spring to early summer.

H. citrina (citron daylily) is an evening-blooming, fragrant species. Large, yellow flowers tower over top mounds of strap-like, dark green leaves. Considered non-invasive, this species will grow 90 cm–1.2 m (3–4') tall and 61 cm (24") wide.

H. fulva will spread slowly, to a width of 1.5 m (4'). It bears rusty orange flowers on tall, rigid stems. The dark bluish green foliage can reach lengths of 30–91 cm (12–36"). **'Kwanso'** bears double, orangy brown flowers and spreads to 91 cm (36"). This plant is more suited to difficult areas owing to its aggressive nature. It is useful under and in between trees or steep slopes, where no other plant seems to thrive. It will mature to a height of 75 cm–1.2 m (2½–4') and a width of 61–91 cm (24–36"). **'Kwanso Variegata'** bears flowers similar to the cultivar 'Kwanso,' but the foliage is striped with white margins.

H. **'Luxury Lace'** is a repeat bloomer, which is becoming more common as new cultivars are developed. The flowers are lavender-pink with a ruffle along the petal edge. Blooming begins in midseason, maturing to 80 cm (32") tall.

Problems & Pests

Generally these plants are pest free. Rare problems with rust, *Hemerocallis* gall midge, aphids, spider mites, thrips and slugs are possibilities.

Delphinium

Delphinium

Height: 20 cm–1.8 m (8"–6') **Spread:** 30–91 cm (12–36") **Flower colour:** blue, purple, pink, yellow, white solids, bicolours; foliage **Blooms:** late spring, early summer **Zones:** 2–8

WHEN I THINK OF TRADITIONAL, English-style borders, delphinium always comes to mind. From the short, dwarf selections to the tall, statuesque varieties, prairie gardeners can grow them all. Many who visit our gardens at the University of Saskatchewan are envious of our ability to grow the delphinium, as it is impossible to grow in climates with hot, humid summers. One thing to keep in mind is the bigger the delphinium, the more fertilizer it will take to look truly spectacular. The most recent breeding breakthrough is new hybrids that produce the spectacular spikes of the tall varieties on truly dwarf plants. What will they think of next?

All parts of delphinium are poisonous, so avoid planting in locations where children and pets will have easy access.

Planting

Seeding: Seeds started directly in the garden in spring will produce flowers the following year; seedlings may not be true to type

Planting out: Spring or fall; plant with crown at soil level to avoid crown rot

Spacing: 30–91 cm (12–36") apart

Growing

Grow in a **full sun** location that is protected from strong winds. The soil should be **fertile, moist** and **humus rich** with **excellent drainage**. Delphiniums benefit from well-composted manure mixed into the soil. To encourage a second flush of smaller blooms, remove the first flower spikes once they begin to fade and before they begin to set seed. Cut them off just above the foliage. New shoots will begin to grow and the old foliage will fade back. The old growth may then be cut right back, allowing new growth to fill in. These heavy feeders require fertilizer twice a year, in spring and summer. Delphiniums require division every spring to maintain their vigour.

Tips

Delphiniums are classic cottage garden plants. Plant taller varieties at the back of the border where they make a magnificent, multi-coloured backdrop for warmer foreground flowers such as peonies, poppies and black-eyed Susans.

Taller varieties require staking while shorter types don't. Plant tall delphiniums in a sheltered location

D. x *elatum* hybrid (above & below)

D. x *belladonna* hybrid
D. x *elatum* 'Magic Fountain Hybrids'

and stake the flower stalks to prevent or minimize wind damage. Each flower spike will need to be individually staked as soon as it reaches 30 cm (12") in height. You could use an upside-down wire basket to support a clump.

Recommended

D.* x *belladonna (belladonna hybrids) bears blue, white or mauve flowers in open, loose, branched spikes. It grows 91 cm–1.2 m (3–4') tall and spreads 30–45 cm (12–18"). Many cultivars are derived from this species, including **'Blue Bees,'** which has pale blue flowers with white centres. **'Wendy'** has dark purple-blue flowers.

D.* x *elatum (elatum hybrids) bear densely held flowers of blue, purple, white, pink or yellow on tall spikes. They are divided into three height categories. Dwarfs grow up to 1.5 m (5'), mediums grow 1.7 m (5 1/2') and talls grow 2 m (6'). All spread up to 91 cm (36"). **'Blue Dawn'** has blue flowers with dark blue centres. **'Magic Fountain Hybrids'** offer colours ranging from bright whites to lavenders and blues. This series shouldn't require staking because of its short and compact growth habit. Single and double flowers emerge atop mounds of deeply divided, maple-like leaves. **'Sungleam'** produces small, semi-double, creamy flowers with deep yellow centres. **'Turkish Delight'** has pink flowers with white centres.

D. grandiflorum (Chinese) bears flowers of blue, purple or white in loose, branched clusters. It grows 20–50 cm (8–20") tall and spreads up to 30 cm (12"). **'Album'** has white flowers. **'Blue Butterfly'** bears bright blue flowers on compact, short-lived plants.

Problems & Pests

Slugs, aphids, powdery mildew and delphinium moth caterpillar can be problematic. Watch for curled leaves and deformities in the newest growth. Failing to recognize signs that the caterpillar is present will result in leaf deformities and plants that bloom poorly or not at all. Eradicate the caterpillars by removing the newest growth and all affected parts, or cut back to the ground once the plants have reached an 18" height, to encourage new, healthy growth.

These are plants so gorgeous in bloom that you can build a garden or plan a party around their flowering.

D. x elatum hybrids (above & below)

Elephant Ears
Ligularia
Ligularia

Height: 40 cm–1.8 m (16"–6') **Spread:** 61 cm–1.5 cm (2–5') **Flower colour:** yellow, orange; ornamental foliage **Blooms:** summer, sometimes early fall **Zones:** 2–8

ELEPHANT EARS IS AN IMPRESSIVE, SHADE-LOVING PERENNIAL to say the least. That such a grand plant can thrive in a shady area is amazing, but thrive it does. There simply is no substitute for this stellar species. If you happen to put elephant ears in an area that is exposed to hot afternoon sun, the massive leaves will wilt until shade returns. There's no need to worry, though; this plant will magically perk up in the evening with no obvious harm done. Consistent moisture and shade are key to prevent this wilting.

Planting

Seeding: Not recommended

Planting out: Spring

Spacing: 60 cm–1.5 m (2–5')

Growing

Elephant ears should be grown in **light shade** or **partial shade** with protection from the afternoon sun. The soil should be of **average fertility**, **humus rich** and **moist**. Division is rarely, if ever, required but can be done in spring or fall to propagate a desirable cultivar.

Tips

Use elephant ears alongside a pond or stream. It can also be used in a well-watered border or naturalized in a moist meadow or woodland garden. The foliage can wilt in hot sun, even if the soil is moist.

L. dentata

L. wilsoniana

L. dentata

L. stenocephala 'The Rocket'

The leaves will revive at night, but this won't help how horrible they look during the day. To prevent this, plant elephant ears in a cool, shaded place in the garden.

Recommended

L. dentata (bigleaf ligularia, golden groundsel) forms a clump of rounded, heart-shaped leaves. It grows 91 cm–1.5 m (36"–5') tall and spreads 91 cm–1.2 m (3–4'). In summer and early fall, it bears clusters of orange-yellow flowers above the foliage. **'Britt-Marie Crawford'** (black groundsel) is a new cultivar that produces rounded, dark purple leaves with serrated edges. Daisy-like, golden orange flowers emerge in late summer. This is the darkest ligularia to date, and it grows 40 cm (16") tall and wide with 3.75 m (45") tall flowers. **'Desdemona'** and **'Othello'** are two similar cultivars. They have orange flowers and purple-green foliage. They come fairly true to type when grown from seed. (Zones 3–8)

L. przewalskii (Shevalski's ligularia) also forms a clump but has deeply incised leaves. It grows 1.2–1.8 m (4–6') tall and spreads 61 cm–1.2 m (24"–4'). In mid- and late summer, it produces yellow flowers on long purple spikes. (Zones 4–8)

L. stenocephala (narrow-spiked ligularia) has toothed rather than incised foliage and bears bright yellow flowers on dark purple-green spikes. It grows 91 cm–1.5 m (3–5') in height and width. This species is closely related to the previous one, and **'The Rocket'** may be a hybrid of the two. This cultivar has heart-shaped leaves with ragged-toothed margins. The leaf veins are dark, becoming purple at the leaf base. (Zones 3–8)

L. wilsoniana (giant groundsel) is similar in appearance to 'The Rocket' but is extremely hardy and blooms earlier in the season. Tall spikes of yellow, densely packed flowers rise above large, rounded, green leaves. It grows 1.5–1.8 m (5–6') tall when placed in the right location.

Problems & Pests

Elephant ears has no serious problems, but slugs can damage young foliage.

L. dentata

L. stenocephala 'The Rocket'

Euphorbia
Spurge
Euphorbia

Height: 30–91 cm (12–36") **Spread:** 30–61 cm (12–24") **Flower colour:** yellow, green; foliage **Blooms:** spring to mid-summer **Zones:** 2–8

EUPHORBIA IS A GENUS THAT ENCOMPASSES A LARGE ARRAY OF plants, including the well-known poinsettia. On a recent garden tour in England, I found myself enamoured by the qualities euphorbia had to offer, although at first I didn't know what I was looking at. I was enjoying an upright lime green specimen that appeared to have tiny diamonds inset on every bract. It was truly remarkable so innocently shining in the sun. On closer inspection, it turned out to be none other than a species of euphorbia. Often it's little discoveries like these that are the most welcome.

Planting

Seeding: Use fresh seed for best germination rates; start seed in cold frame in spring

Planting out: Spring or fall

Spacing: 45–61 cm (18–24")

Growing

Euphorbia grows well in **full sun** and **light shade**. The soil should be of **average fertility, moist, humus rich** and **well drained**. Euphorbia plants are drought tolerant and can be invasive in too fertile a soil. Propagate euphorbia by stem cuttings; they may also self-seed in the garden. Division is rarely required. Euphorbias dislike being disturbed once established.

Tips

Use euphorbia in a mixed or herbaceous border, rock garden or lightly shaded woodland garden.

E. polychroma

E. griffithii 'Fireglow'

You may wish to wear gloves when handling this plant because some people find the milky sap irritates their skin.

If you are cutting the stems for propagation, dip the cut ends in hot water before planting to stop the sticky white sap from running.

Recommended

E. dulcis is a compact, upright plant that grows about 30 cm (12") tall, with an equal spread. The spring flowers and bracts are yellow-green. The dark bronze-green leaves turn red and orange in the fall.

E. griffithii is a mounding perennial resembling a low-growing shrub. It grows 50–91 cm (20–36") tall and 61 cm (24") wide. The cultivars are more readily available, including **'Fireglow,'** one of the more popular and hardy types. It bears orangy yellow bracts in early summer.

E. polychroma (above & below)

E. polychroma (*E. epithimoides*)
is a mounding, clump-forming
perennial. It grows 30–61 cm
(12–24") tall and spreads 45–61 cm
(18–24"). Yellow bracts surround
the long-lasting, inconspicuous
flowers. The foliage turns shades of
purple, red or orange in fall. There
are several cultivars, though the
species is more commonly available. **'Candy'** has yellow bracts and
flowers, but the leaves and stems
are tinged with purple. **'Emerald
Jade'** is a compact plant that grows
to 35 cm (14") in height. The bracts
are yellow, but the flowers are
bright green.

Problems & Pests

Aphids, spider mites and nematodes
are possible, as well as fungal root
rot in poorly drained, wet soil.

E. dulcis

E. griffithii 'Fireglow'

Evening Primrose
Sundrops
Oenothera

Height: 15–91 cm (6–36") **Spread:** 15–45 cm (6–18") **Flower colour:** yellow, pink, white **Blooms:** spring, summer **Zones:** 3–8

THERE IS NO OTHER PERENNIAL IN THE GARDEN THAT CAN substitute for the evening primrose. All of the selections that we grow today originate from native North American wildflowers. This past summer I had countless samples of our native evening primrose (*O. biennis*) come into my office for identification. People were thrilled by this showy, fairy-like, yellow flower that magically opens up in the evening and closes back up by morning. If you plant any of the night-blooming evening primroses you will attract the most interesting nocturnal insects, such as the sphinx moth. Conversely, sundrops open during the day, offering diversity like no other.

Planting
Seeding: Start in cold frame in mid-spring

Planting out: Spring

Spacing: 15–45 cm (6–18") apart

Growing

Evening primrose prefers **full sun**. The soil should be of **poor to average fertility** and be **very well drained**. This perennial self-seeds easily and can become invasive in very fertile soil. It's not bothered by hot, humid weather. Divide in spring.

Tips

Use this plant in the front of a border and to edge borders and pathways. Evening primroses will brighten a gravelly bank or rock garden.

Evening primrose can be a bit invasive, self-seeding in unexpected places in the garden.

Recommended

O. fruticosa (sundrops, evening primrose) grows 45–91 cm (18–36") tall and spreads 30–45 cm (12–18"). It bears bright yellow flowers in summer. The foliage of this plant turns red after a light frost. **'Summer Solstice'** ('Sonnenwende') is a smaller, compact plant. It bears larger flowers for a long period from early summer to early fall. The foliage turns red in summer and burgundy in fall.

O. macrocarpa (Ozark sundrops, Missouri primrose, fluttermills) produces tall, lanky stems with large, crepe-like, bright yellow blooms. Its sprawling tendency is best suited to rock gardens. This cultivar tolerates drought, poor soils and hot sun. It grows 15–30 cm (6–12") tall and wide.

O. speciosa (showy evening primrose) is a tall, upright, spreading plant. It grows 15–61 cm (6–24") tall and spreads 30–45 cm (12–18"). The flowers are pink or white. **'Pinkie'** is a night-blooming plant, with white flowers that mature to pink with darker pink veins. (Zones 4–8)

Problems & Pests

Rare problems with downy mildew, powdery mildew, leaf gall, rust and leaf spot. Plants may develop root rot in poorly drained soil.

O. speciosa cultivar

Evening primrose is also known as evening star because of the phosphorescent light it emits at night.

O. speciosa

False Solomon's Seal

Smilacina

Height: 20–91 cm (8–36") **Spread:** 61 cm (24") **Flower colour:** white; foliage **Blooms:** mid- to late spring **Zones:** 3–8

FALSE SOLOMON'S SEAL, AS THE NAME SUGGESTS, IS DIFFERENT from Solomon's seal (*Polygonatum commutatum*) in appearance, but it shares that plant's preference for a shady, woodland environment. The two would certainly make great neighbours in the right location. Without the flowers, the leaves and stems could almost be mistaken for those of the toad lily (*Tricyrtis*)—of the monster variety, that is. False Solomon's seal is currently a stranger to the prairie landscape, but for no reason other than its anonymity. Its fully hardy to our climate, and its ornamental value is second to none. All it needs is the proper introduction. So let me introduce you to false Solomon's seal, sure to be a favourite in years to come.

Planting

Seeding: Not recommended

Planting out: Spring or fall

Spacing: 61 cm (24") apart

Growing

False Solomon's seal grows well in **light** or **full shade**. The soil should be of **average fertility**, **humus rich**, **acidic**, **moist** and **well drained**. Cultivate peat moss into the soil to provide a little acidity. Humus-rich conditions can be beneficial as well. Divide in spring.

Tips

Use in an open woodland or natural garden. In a shaded border, it can be combined with hostas and other shade-loving perennials.

Recommended

S. racemosa (false solomon's seal, false spikehead, *Maianthemum racemosum*) forms a spreading clump of upright, arching stems 91 cm (36") tall and 61 cm (24") wide. Short spikes of white flowers emerge in spring. Berries are borne once the flowers are finished and ripen well into winter. (Zones 4–8)

S. stellata (star-flowered lily of the valley, starflower) forms into a clump that matures to 20–61 cm (8–24") tall and 61 cm (24") wide. Medium green foliage complements the whitish green flowers. Dark red or blue berries follow after the spent flowers in fall.

Problems & Pests

Rust and leaf spot are possible but rarely serious.

S. racemosa (above & below)

The berries are covered in tiny red dots that slowly blend, enveloping the reddish yellow flesh throughout the ripening process.

Flax

Linum

Height: 10–61 cm (4–24") **Spread:** 30 cm (12") **Flower colour:** blue, red
Blooms: spring to fall **Zones:** 2–8

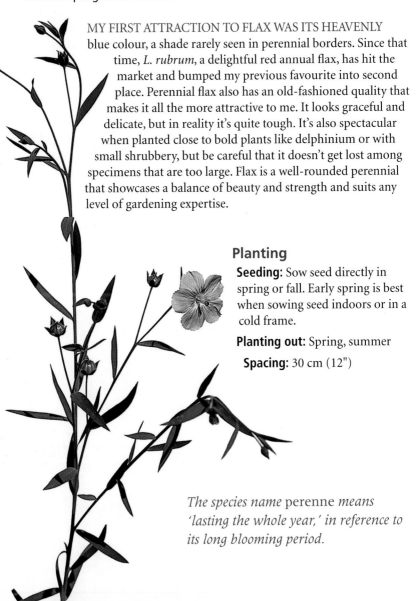

MY FIRST ATTRACTION TO FLAX WAS ITS HEAVENLY
blue colour, a shade rarely seen in perennial borders. Since that
time, *L. rubrum*, a delightful red annual flax, has hit the
market and bumped my previous favourite into second
place. Perennial flax also has an old-fashioned quality that
makes it all the more attractive to me. It looks graceful and
delicate, but in reality it's quite tough. It's also spectacular
when planted close to bold plants like delphinium or with
small shrubbery, but be careful that it doesn't get lost among
specimens that are too large. Flax is a well-rounded perennial
that showcases a balance of beauty and strength and suits any
level of gardening expertise.

Planting

Seeding: Sow seed directly in
spring or fall. Early spring is best
when sowing seed indoors or in a
cold frame.

Planting out: Spring, summer

Spacing: 30 cm (12")

The species name perenne *means
'lasting the whole year,' in reference to
its long blooming period.*

Growing

Flax prefers **full to partial sun**. The soil should be **light**, of **average fertility**, **organically rich** and **very well drained**. Do not plant it in a location that is consistently wet owing to late melting snow. Make sure to provide excellent winter drainage. Though very drought tolerant, it's considered short-lived, but it self-seeds readily. Yearly propagation may be necessary to ensure longevity. Propagate by allowing it to seed itself, directly sowing the seed or dividing plants in spring or fall.

Tips

Flax works well in wild, woodland or meadow settings. The delicate blue flowers are charming in cottage gardens, mixed beds and borders. It is commonly used in herb or medicinal gardens as well.

A yearly shearing encourages a new flush of growth and rejuvenation.

Recommended

L. perenne is a clump-forming, airy perennial that reaches 10–61 cm (4–24") in height and 30 cm (12") in width. Slender stems emerge from mounds of blue-green, narrow leaves. The stems are tipped with panicles of tiny, flat, blue flowers with yellow centres. **'Nanum'** bears tiny, blue flowers on a very compact plant. **'Sapphire'** is an upright clump with a tendency to arch. Pale blue flowers are borne from spring through summer.

L. perenne (above & below)

Problems & Pests

Stem rot, rust, wilt, anthracnose, damping off, slugs, snails and aphids can all cause different levels of damage.

Flax fibre has been used for thousands of years to make cloth.

Fleece-Flower

Persicaria

Height: 15 cm–1.2 m (6"–4') **Spread:** 30 cm–1.4 m (12"–5') **Flower colour:** red, pink, white; foliage **Blooms:** summer **Zones:** 3–8

FLEECE-FLOWER GOT OFF TO A RATHER POOR START AS A GROUP of herbaceous ornamentals. It was known early on as a weedy, invasive genus and quickly, but undeservedly, gained a bad name. Most of the common names alone discourage gardeners from growing anything from this genus, so it's not a big surprise that people didn't take the time to get to know this versatile performer. A great many fleece-flower varieties are neither invasive nor weedy. In fact, *Persicaria* is quite often part of garden designers' 'never fail to impress' bag of tricks. As a result, this plant is experiencing a boost in popularity. If you're willing to try something new, give at least one of the many varieties a try. You won't be disappointed.

Planting

Seeding: Sow seed indoors or in a cold frame in early spring

Planting out: Spring, summer

Spacing: 30–61 cm (12–24")

P. affinis is small enough to plant in an alpine or rock garden and low enough to act as a groundcover.

Growing

Fleece-flower prefers **full sun to partial shade**. The soil should be **moist** and **well drained**. *P. bistorta* is more tolerant of drier soils. Propagate by division in spring or fall.

Tips

Fleece-flower works well in traditional settings, including mixed beds and borders, cottage gardens or as a groundcover. Integrate fleece-flower into woodland, meadow or wild settings for naturalizing.

Contact with all parts may irritate the skin. The sap may cause mild stomach upset if ingested.

Recommended

P. affinis **'Dimity'** (Himalayan knotweed) is an evergreen, mat-forming perennial that grows 15–20 cm (6–8") tall and 30–61 cm (12–24") wide. The leathery foliage turns a bronzy red colour in the fall. Short spikes of red flowers are held above the foliage, fading to pink with age.

P. bistorta (bistort, snakeweed) bears large, vivid pink or white spikes reaching 75 cm (30") tall. Dense, wavy foliage grows rapidly. **'Superba'** grows a little taller with a similar spread of 61 cm (24") and bears pink flowers.

P. microcephala **'Red Dragon'** is a vigorous, clump-forming perennial. It produces red stems covered in leaves that are deep burgundy with a plum or mint-coloured chevron and a metallic sheen. The foliage becomes greener later in the season,

P. affinis

accented by a red leaf margin and a red chevron. White, insignificant flowers emerge in summer. This cultivar grows 61 cm (24") tall and 76 cm–1 m (30–40") wide. (Zones 4–8 with added winter protection)

Problems & Pests

Aphids, slugs and snails are the only predators.

Fleece-flower has a bad reputation of being very invasive; the varieties listed here are vigorous but not invasive.

P. microcephala 'Red Dragon'

Forget-Me-Not
Myosotis

Height: 15–30 cm (6–12") **Spread:** 15–30 cm (6–12") **Flower colour:** blue, pink, white **Blooms:** spring, summer **Zones:** 3–8

FEW OTHER PLANTS IN THE GARDEN BEAR TRUE, SKY BLUE blossoms the way forget-me-not does. It is always a welcome sight to see these blue flowers mixed in among brightly coloured, spring-flowering bulbs after a long, bleak winter. Forget-me-not is a vigorous self-seeder, but it's easily kept in check by removing the seedlings that appear later in the growing season. Forget-me-not has also earned its place in folklore with other 'love flower' candidates because its name is said to have originated from an old romantic tale of true love. Whether you consider yourself a romantic or not, this flower offers early season colour and will thrive under tree canopies where little else will grow.

Planting

Seeding: Sow seed indoors or in a cold frame in early spring. *M. scorpiodes* can be directly sown in a wet location or the muddy perimeter around a pond or water feature.

Planting out: Spring, summer

Spacing: 15–20 cm (6–8")

M. sylvatica (above & below)

Growing

Forget-me-not prefers **full sun** with a little midday or **partial shade**. The soil should be of **poor to average fertility**, **moist** but **well drained**. Divide when dormant and make sure to propagate regularly to ensure longevity. Forget-me-not self-seeds freely, so it will propagate naturally. If you don't want it coming up everywhere, deadhead regularly.

Tips

The smaller *Myosotis* species are suitable for rock and alpine gardens, but deadhead so they don't take over slower growing plants. *M. scorpioides* is best planted around a water feature or pond. *M. sylvatica* works well in mixed beds and borders, meadows, wildflower or cottage gardens or as edging.

Recommended

M. alpestris (alpine forget-me-not) forms a tight, low-growing clump of foliage. It grows 10–15 cm (4–6") tall and bears clusters of dainty, purple-blue, pink or white flowers in late spring and early summer.

M. scorpioides (water or true forget-me-not) is a marginal aquatic perennial with a slow, creeping habit that grows 15–30 cm (6–12")

tall and wide. Narrow, mid-green leaves cover semi-upright, angular stems. Tiny, flat, bright blue flowers with white, yellow or pink eyes peek out through the foliage. **'Spring Carpet'** has a slightly smaller habit and bears bright blue flowers. This species is particularly short-lived and self-seeds freely.

M. sylvatica (woodland forget-me-not) is a self-seeding biennial that grows 15–25 cm (6–9") tall and 15 cm (6") wide. It bears flowers in shades of blue, pink and white, ideal for adding colour to a dull corner.

Problems & Pests

Snails, slugs, powdery and downy mildew, rust and grey mould can all become problematic.

Foxglove
Digitalis

Height: 61 cm–1.5 m (2–5') **Spread:** 30–61 cm (12–24") **Flower colour:** pink, purple, yellow, maroon, red, white **Blooms:** summer **Zones:** 2–8

ALTHOUGH WE CAN GROW BEAUTIFUL FOXGLOVES here in Canada, there's something to be said for those in England, where foxglove is grown everywhere with great abandon. After a recent foray across the pond, I began to consider incorporating the common foxglove back into my gardens after a long absence. Foxglove can be challenging to grow on the prairies, but this plant, with its extraordinary flowers, is one of my all-time favourites, regardless of where in the world it's growing.

Planting

Seeding: Directly sow in garden or start indoors in early spring; flowers are unlikely the first year

Planting out: Spring

Spacing: 30–61 cm (12–24") apart

The extremely poisonous nature of foxglove has been known to cause rashes, headaches and nausea simply from touching the plant.

Growing

Foxglove grows well in **partial** or **light shade**. The soil should be **fertile**, **humus rich**, **moist** and **acidic**. This plant adapts to most soils that are neither too wet nor too dry. You may wish to deadhead once flowering has finished, but it is a good idea to leave some spikes in place to spread seeds for new plants. Division is unnecessary because foxglove will not live long enough to be divided. It continues to occupy your garden by virtue of its ability to self-seed.

Tips

Foxgloves is another must-have for the cottage garden or for those people interested in heritage plants. It makes an excellent vertical accent along the back of a border. It is also an interesting addition to a woodland garden. Some staking may be required if the plants are in a windy location. Remove the tallest spike, and the side shoots will bloom on shorter stalks that may not need staking.

If too many foxgloves are growing, then you may wish to thin them out or transplant some to another location—perhaps into a friend's garden.

D. purpurea 'Apricot Beauty'

D. purpurea

The hybrid varieties become less vigorous with time and self-sown seedlings may not come true to type. Sprinkle new seed in your foxglove bed each spring to ensure a steady show from the lovely flowers.

Recommended

D. grandiflora, one of the hardier foxgloves, has short, wind-proof flower spikes. Its pale yellow flowers are suitable for cutting. Considered long-lived, with a reliable repeat blooming cycle, it grows 61–91 cm (24–36") tall and 30 cm (12") wide.

D. x *mertonensis* (strawberry fox-glove) is a true perennial, unlike most foxglove cultivars, which are generally biennials. It bears rose pink flowers and grows 91 cm–1.2 m (3–4') tall. (Zones 4–8)

D. purpurea 'Alba'
D. grandiflora

D. purpurea forms a rosette of foliage from which tall flowering spikes emerge, growing 61 cm–1.5 m (2 –5') tall. Flowers come in a wide range of colours. Inside each bell-shaped flower are spots in contrasting colours. **'Alba'** bears white flowers. **'Apricot Beauty'** bears apricot pink flowers. **Excelsior Hybrids** bear dense spikes of flowers in several colours. **Foxy Hybrids** are considered dwarf by foxglove standards, but easily reach 91 cm (36") in height. They are available in a range of colours. (Zones 4–8)

Problems & Pests

Anthracnose, fungal leaf spot, powdery, mildew, root rot, stem rot, aphids, Japanese beetles and mealybugs are possible problems for foxgloves.

D. purpurea (above & below)

Foxglove derives its common name from the shape of the flowers, which resembles the fingers of a glove.

Gaillardia
Blanket Flower
Gaillardia

Height: 30–91 cm (12–36") **Spread:** 30–61 cm (12–24") **Flower colour:** combinations of red, orange and yellow **Blooms:** early summer to early fall **Zones:** 3–9

GAILLARDIA IS ANOTHER FINE EXAMPLE OF A DAISY-LIKE SELECTION for your garden that is sure to provide bright, sunny colour for an extended period of time. It is ideal for any sunny location, as it is very tolerant of the drought-like conditions experienced in many parts of the prairies over the past few years. All blanket flower varieties are attractive, but 'Goblin' is especially striking when planted at the base of Asiatic lilies that echo a similar colour. To add to an already lengthy blooming cycle, remove the faded flowers every couple of weeks and flowering will last well into fall. The warmly coloured petals will complement the turning leaves and fiery colours of autumn.

Planting

Seeding: Start seeds indoors or in the garden in early spring; leave uncovered because the seeds need light to germinate

Planting out: Spring

Spacing: 45 cm (18")

Growing

Blanket flower grows best in **full sun**. The soil should be **fertile, light** and **well drained**. Poor soils are tolerated, but plants will not overwinter in heavy, wet soil. Deadheading encourages the plants to bloom all summer. Cut the plants back to within 15 cm (6") of the ground in late summer to encourage new growth and promote the longevity of these often short-lived plants.

Tips

Blanket flower is a North American prairie plant that looks at home in a cottage garden, a wildflower garden or a meadow planting. It is also attractive when planted in clumps of three or four in a mixed or herbaceous border. Because it is drought tolerant, it is ideal for neglected and rarely watered parts of the garden. Dwarf varieties make good container plantings.

Recommended

G. x *grandiflora* is a bushy, upright plant 61–91 cm (24–36") tall and 30–61 cm (12–24") in spread. It bears daisy-like flowers all summer and into early fall. The petals have yellow tips and red bases. **'Burgundy'** is 61–91 cm (24–36") tall with wine red flowers. **'Kobold'**

G. x *grandiflora* (above & below)

('Goblin') is a compact cultivar that grows only 30 cm (12") tall. The flowers are variegated red and yellow, like those of the species.

Problems & Pests

Powdery mildew, downy mildew, leaf spot, rust, aster yellows and leafhoppers are possible, but rarely cause much trouble.

Gentian

Gentiana

Height: 10–61 cm (4–24") **Spread:** 15–30 cm (6–12") **Flower colour:** blue and white, white, blue, purple **Blooms:** mid- to late summer **Zones:** 2–8

GENTIANS ARE FOUND ALL OVER THE WORLD EXCEPT AFRICA. They generally grow in cool, temperate climates or in mountainous regions. Gentians are famous for their true blue flowers, a relatively rare colour in flowering perennials. My personal favourite is *G. acaulis,* or spring gentian. It is native to the European Alps and makes a stunning addition to the spring garden, but it can be a bit challenging for a beginner to grow. To ensure its success, keep the roots cool and moist. Alpine garden settings, rock gardens and even trough gardens are the best growing environments for most gentians, but it's worth experimenting in your beds and borders as well. You just never know what you might discover.

Planting

Seeding: Sow seed indoors or in a cold frame in early spring or fall

Planting out: Spring

Spacing: 15–30 cm (6–12")

Growing

Gentian prefers **full sun to partial shade** in locations with cool and damp summers, and partial sun in locations with dry and hot summers. The soil should be **light, sandy** or **gritty, humus rich, moist** and **well drained**. To propagate, plant offsets in spring, or divide the rootball every three years or so.

Tips

Alpine, trough and rock gardens possess the perfect cultural requirements for a gentian. It's small enough to work as edging in mixed beds and borders that require a late blast of colour.

Recommended

G. acaulis (spring gentian, trumpet gentian) is a low-growing, spreading alpine plant. It produces large, upward-facing flowers in deep blue shades. It's best suited to rock gardens. Plant in a cool and moist location and protect from hot sun. It grows 10–15 cm (4–6") tall and 25–30 cm (10–12") wide.

G. clausa (closed gentian) is an erect, dense, mound-forming perennial that reaches 30–61 cm (12–24") heights and spreads of 15 cm (6"). Dark green leaves form a mass under the urn-shaped, white or dark blue flowers with white stripes. (Zones 3–8)

G. cruciata (cross gentian) is a clump-forming perennial. It bears small, bell-shaped, dark blue flowers atop leathery, mid-green leaves. It grows to 20–41 cm tall (8–16") and 25–30 cm (10–12") wide. (Zones 3–7)

G. septemfida (crested gentian) grows 20 cm (8") tall with a similar spread. Oval leaves grow in pairs on short stems, bearing clusters of purplish blue, urn-shaped blooms with white throats.

Problems & Pests

Gentians are rarely affected by insects or disease; however, rust, leaf spot, slugs and snails have been known to cause a little damage.

Globe Thistle

Echinops

Height: 91 cm–1.8 m (36"–5') **Spread:** 61–91 cm (24–36") **Flower colour:** blue, purple, grey; foliage **Blooms:** summer **Zones:** 2–8

THISTLES IN THE GARDEN HAVE LARGELY been frowned upon throughout the ages. The very word brings weeds to the minds of some, or worse, prickly weeds that are extremely hard to eradicate. Some find it hard to believe that gardeners would intentionally grow a thistle plant; however, once they try growing the cultivated varieties, they are sure to change their tune and give it nothing but praise.

Globe thistle is an outstanding specimen both in the garden and as a cut flower, fresh or dried. It has a vigorous but non-invasive growth habit and will not take over your garden. It will thrive in very hot areas as long as your soil is adequate. After the flowers have emerged, you'll soon be graced with an increase in your butterfly population as well.

Planting

Seeding: Directly sow seed in mid-spring

Planting out: Spring, summer

Spacing: 61–91 cm (24–36")

Bees and butterflies are in love with globe thistle.

Growing

Globe thistle prefers **full sun** but tolerates partial sun. Its preference is **average to moist**, **well-drained** soil; however, it tolerates just about any soil condition, as long as it is receiving adequate sunlight. The flower stems may require staking if planted in very rich soil. Deadhead spent flowers before they set seed to prevent them from sprouting up everywhere. Division can be done in spring or fall, but this may be difficult owing to the large taproot.

Tips

Globe thistle is a sun worshipper and loves to be planted towards the back of a hot, sunny mixed border. It is also suitable for xeriscaping, massing, wild garden settings, as a specimen or for cutting and everlasting gardens.

Recommended

E. ritro grows tall, producing coarse, deeply cut, grey-green foliage with prickly, jagged edges. Spiky, globular, bluish purple flowers float above the dense foliage on erect, grey stems. The species can reach 91 cm–1.2 m (3–4') heights and 61 cm (24") spreads. **'Vietch's Blue'** bears smaller flowers in a paler shade of blue.

E. sphaerocephalus vigorously produces clumps of jagged, rough leaves in shades of grey-green. Tall, stiff, grey stems emerge with spherical, metallic grey flowers. It grows 1.2–1.5 m (4–5') tall and 61–91 cm (24–36") wide. This species is tolerant of open, windy exposures, extreme heat and drought. **'Arctic Glow'** is much smaller, maturing to 91 cm (36") tall on stiff reddish stems. Overall the foliage is similar in appearance to the species, but the flowers are white, glowing, spiky globes. (Zones 3–8)

Problems & Pests

Globe thistle is generally problem free, but watch out for aphids.

E. ritro (above & below)

Goat's Beard

Aruncus

Height: 15 cm–1.8 m (6"–6') **Spread:** 30–45 cm (12–18") **Flower colour:** cream, white; foliage **Blooms:** early to mid-summer **Zones:** 2–8

ELEGANT, FEATHERY, IVORY PLUMES PAIRED WITH LACY FOLIAGE are just what the landscape designer ordered. I am very fond of plants with greatly contrasting foliage and blooms. Goat's beard is similar to astilbe in many ways but airier in form. It is ideal as an understorey perennial, planted beneath tree canopies in a woodland setting. Goat's beard will lend an element of class to a garden setting begging for sophistication. The ivory flower plumes coupled with rich green, lacy foliage will transform your garden from cottage to classic in no time.

Planting

Seeding: Use fresh seed. Keep soil moist and conditions humid. The soil temperature should be 21–24° C (70–75° F).

Planting out: Spring or fall

Spacing: 30–45 cm (12–18") apart

Growing

Goat's beard prefers to grow in **partial to full shade.** If planted in deep shade, the plant will have fewer blooms. It will also tolerate full sun as long as the soil is kept evenly moist. The soil should be **rich** and **moist**, with **plenty of humus** mixed in. Goat's beard tends to self-seed, but removing the spent flowers maintains the attractive appearance of the plant and encourages a longer blooming period. Division should be done in spring or fall. Goat's beard

A. dioicus (above & below)

Goat's beard looks a bit like astilbe and is often grouped with this smaller plant to create an interesting contrast in size.

may be quite difficult to divide because it develops a thick root mass. Use a sharp knife to cut the root mass into pieces.

Tips

This plant looks very natural growing along the edge of woodland or in an open forest. It may be used at the back of a border or alongside a stream or pond.

Goat's beard has both female and male plants, both bearing flowers. The male flowers are full and fuzzy while the female flowers are pendulous.

If you want to start some new plants from seed, allow the seedheads to ripen before removing them. Keep in mind that you will need to have both male and female plants to produce seeds that will sprout. Don't save male flowerheads because they will not produce seeds.

A. dioicus

A. aethusifolius

Recommended

A. aethusifolius (dwarf Korean goat's beard) forms a low-growing, compact mound. It grows 15–40 cm (6–16") tall and spreads up to 30 cm (12"). Branched spikes of loosely held, cream flowers are produced in early summer. This plant looks similar to astilbe and is sometimes sold by that name.

A. dioicus forms a large, bushy, shrub-like perennial. It grows 91 cm–1.8 m (3–6') tall, with an equal spread. Large plumes of cream white flowers are borne from early to mid-summer. There are several cultivars, though they can be hard to find. **'Kneiffii'** is a dainty cultivar with finely divided leaves and arching stems with nodding plumes. It grows about 91 cm (36") tall and spreads 45 cm (18"). **'Zweiweltkind'** ('Child of Two Worlds') is a compact plant with drooping, white flowers. **Var. astilbioides** is a dwarf variety that grows only 61 cm (24") tall.

A. aethusifolius

Problems & Pests

Occasional problems with fly larvae are possible.

A. dioicus

Goutweed
Snow on the Mountain
Aegopodium

Height: 30 cm (12") **Spread:** indefinite **Flower colour:** white, but inconspicuous; grown for foliage **Blooms:** summer **Zones:** 1–8

SOMETIMES THERE ARE PLANTS THAT SHOULD ONLY BE GROWN surrounded by concrete, and goutweed is one such plant. Don't get me wrong—goutweed is attractive and extremely useful when used in the correct location. It can be problematic, however, when paired with less vigorous plants and in areas where its aggressiveness can become a nuisance, including your lawn. A good trick to curb goutweed's invasive nature is to use it as a specimen by planting it in a bottomless plastic pot and burying the pot to its edge in your garden. This barrier will ensure that it remains where you plant it. If you want it to use goutweed as a groundcover, choose a location surrounded by hardscaping, such as sidewalks, or plant it where it can spread freely. Goutweed's versatility knows no bounds, as it will grow where everything else has failed.

Planting

Seeding: Not recommended

Planting out: Spring, summer, fall

Spacing: 30–61 cm (12–24")

Growing

Goutweed grows well in any light conditions from **full sun to full shade**. Soil of **poor fertility** is recommended to curb invasiveness, but any **well-drained** soil is fine. This plant is drought tolerant. Division is rarely required, but you will have to dig up any parts of the plant that venture into undesired areas.

Tips

Though this groundcover plant can be used almost anywhere, it is best to plant it either where it has lots of room to spread or where it is restricted from spreading. Good places include steep banks that are difficult to mow, in the dry shade under a tree where nothing else will grow, in planters or where a natural barrier exists, such as the area between a house and a walkway or driveway.

If the foliage starts to look bedraggled during summer, you can cut the plants back completely—even mow them down—and they will sprout fresh new growth.

This invasive plant thrives on neglect. As such, it is an excellent choice for growing at a cottage or other infrequently used property where there isn't much time to maintain a lawn. Avoid planting this perennial near a lawn because it will quickly creep in. It is an attractive alternative to a lawn under large

A. podagraria 'Variegatum' (above & below)

shade trees where the lack of light and water will benefit rather than harm this plant.

Recommended

A. podagraria is rarely grown because it is unstoppably invasive. The cultivar **'Variegatum'** has attractive, white-margined foliage. It is reputed to be less invasive than the species, but it is still very prone to spreading if left unchecked.

Problems & Pests

May be afflicted by leaf blight. If this occurs, cut back the damaged foliage to renew the plants.

Hens and Chicks

Sempervivum

Height: 8–15 cm (3–6") **Spread:** 30–61 cm (12–24") to indefinite
Flower colour: red, yellow, white, purple; foliage **Blooms:** summer **Zones:** 2–8

IF YOU ARE LOOKING FOR A PERENNIAL THAT IS HAPPY IN SMALL
spaces and poor, dry soil, try hens and chicks. True to its botanical name,
which means 'always living,' it produces lots of baby plants that are easy to
propagate. A surefire sign that hens and chicks is happy is when flowers
emerge in summer. Although this plant doesn't flower often, when it does,
it has an other worldly kind of appeal that many gardeners find intriguing.
In recent years, there has been a renewed interest in succulents, and many
striking cultivars and hybrids of hens and chicks have become available.

This reliable, low-maintenance plant will add plenty of interest
to your garden for minimal effort. One of the most effective
ways I've seen hens and chicks used was in a living wreath.
Truly spectacular!

Planting

Seeding: Not recommended; remove and replant young rosettes to propagate

Planting out: Spring

Spacing: 30–61 cm (12–24") apart

Growing

Grow these plants in **full sun** or **partial shade**. The soil should be **poor to average** and **very well drained**. Add fine gravel or grit to the soil to provide adequate drainage. Once a plant blooms, it dies. When you deadhead the faded flower, pull up the soft parent plant as well. The whole plant may be left in place and the old rosettes removed periodically to provide space for the new daughter rosettes that sprout up, seemingly by magic. Divide by removing new rosettes and rooting them.

Tips

These plants make excellent additions to rock gardens and rock walls, where they will even grow right on the rocks. Hens and chicks can grow on almost any surface—in the past they were grown on tile roofs, and it was believed they would protect the house from lightning.

Recommended

S. arachnoideum (cobweb house-leek) is identical to *S. tectorum* except that the tips of the leaves are entwined with hairy fibres, giving the appearance of cobwebs. The species grows to 7.5 cm (3") tall and 30 cm (12") wide. **'Clairchen'** has

S. tectorum

pale green leaves covered in white webbing and **'Kappa'** leaves turn red later in the season.

S. tectorum forms a low-growing mat of fleshy leaved rosettes. Each rosette is about 15–25 cm (6–10") across, but they quickly produce small rosettes that grow and multiply to fill almost any space. Flowers may be produced in summer but are not as common in colder climates. The species grows to 15 cm (6") tall and 61 cm (24") wide. **'Atropurpureum'** has dark reddish purple leaves. **'Limelight'** has yellow-green, pink-tipped foliage. **'Pacific Hawk'** has dark red leaves that are edged with silvery hairs.

Problems & Pests

Hens and chicks is generally pest free. Failing to amend a poorly drained location may result in problems with rust and root rot.

S. tectorum 'Atropurpureum' and 'Limelight'

Hops
Humulus

Height: 3–6 m (10–20') **Spread:** 61 cm (24") dependent on width of support
Flower colour: green; foliage **Blooms:** summer **Zones:** 3–8

IF YOU NEED A VERY FAST-GROWING VINE, THEN HOPS IS FOR YOU.
It will cover a fence in a season or two and can be trained over a pergola or up
a trellis in half the time it takes for other vines to produce. If you are interested in growing hops for the fine art of brewing beer, it's important to
choose a named selection or cultivar that is a true female clone because only
a female plant produces usable fruit. The species is beautiful in its own right,
but certainly one of the most attractive hops is 'Aureus'. It produces an abundance of richly coloured, chartreuse leaves throughout the season. Many
newly introduced varieties are also available and are well worth searching for.

Planting

Seeding: Sow seed indoors at 15–18°C (59–64°F) in early spring. *H. japonicus* and its cultivars may be directly sown in late spring once the threat of frost has passed. *H. japonicus* 'Variegatus' rarely comes true to type when seeded.

Planting out: Spring, summer

Spacing: 61 cm (24")

Growing

Hops prefers **full to partial sun.** The soil should be **moist, moderately fertile, organically rich** and **well drained.** The lighter leaved cultivars require full sun to maintain the bright foliar colour. Divide in spring or fall, or propagate by stem cuttings in spring. Some type of support is necessary when trained as a climber; otherwise, it will creep along the ground as a groundcover.

Tips

Hops is most often trained as a climber on trellises, arbors, a variety of fencing, old trees, obelisks or along the sides of a buildings. It can be left to crawl along the ground around shrubs and trees as well.

Recommended

H. lupulus vigorously produces hairy vines, densely covered in coarse, deep green, toothed leaves. Fragrant green flowers emerge in early summer and change to tan with age. **'Aureus'** is strictly ornamental. It bears golden yellow foliage and reaches a mature height of 6 m (20'). If you make beer, try **'Magnum,'** a variety mostly grown for its fruit. It produces a very

H. lupulus 'Aureus'

Hops fruit is used to flavor beer; many varieties have been created and cultivated solely for that purpose.

high yield of hops that have a 'middle' flavour.

H. japonicus **'Variegatus'** is a twining perennial vine with hairy stems and sharply toothed, dark leaves that are mottled and streaked with white. Spikes of green flowers are borne in mid- to late summer. Its mature height is 3 m (10').

Problems & Pests

Hops may encounter problems with whitefly, powdery or downy mildew, anthracnose, ringspot virus and *Verticillum* wilt.

Hosta

Plantain Lily

Hosta

Height: 10–91 cm (4–36") **Spread:** 30 cm–1.2 m (12"–4')
Flower colour: white, purple; foliage **Blooms:** summer and fall **Zones:** 2–8

FEW WOULD DEBATE THAT HOSTA TAKES THE CAKE FOR BEING THE
most popular shade perennial ever. A few years ago, its popularity skyrock-
eted and with good reason. Hosta is a spectacular foliage plant that thrives
for years without needing to be divided. Variations in hosta colour, size and
variegation are almost as unlimited as the ways in which you can use this
plant. The only drawback is that you need to be a bit patient with hosta
when you first plant it because it takes a bit of time to really get going.
Once it does, you'll find yourself wanting more and more.

Planting

Seeding: Direct sow or start indoors in early spring. Young plants can take three or more years to reach flowering size.

Planting out: Spring

Spacing: 30 cm–1.2 m (12"–4') apart

Growing

Hosta prefers **light shade** or **partial shade** but tolerates full shade. Some will even tolerate full sun. Morning sun is preferable to afternoon sun. The soil should be **fertile**, **moist** and **well drained**, but most soils are tolerated. Hosta is fairly drought tolerant, especially when surrounded by mulch for moisture retention. Division is not required but can be done every few years in spring or summer to propagate attractive cultivars you want more of.

Tips

Hosta makes a wonderful woodland plant and looks great combined with ferns and other finely textured plants. Hosta is also good in a mixed border, particularly to hide the ugly, leggy lower stems and branches of some shrubs. Hosta's dense growth and thick, shade-providing leaves make it excellent for suppressing weeds. Hosta flowers are attractive and often fragrant.

Recommended

Hostas have been subjected to a great deal of crossbreeding and hybridizing. The result has been hundreds of cultivars, many of whose exact parentage is uncertain. The cultivars below have been

H. fortunei 'Albomarginata' (above)

grouped with the most generally accepted parent species.

H. '**Blue Angel**' grows 46–76 cm (18–30") tall and 91–1.2 m (3–4') wide and has wavy, blue-green, heart-shaped foliage and white flowers.

H. fortunei (fortune's hosta) is the parent of many hybrids and cultivars. It has broad, dark green foliage and bears lavender purple flowers in mid-summer. It quickly forms a dense clump of foliage, growing 30–61 cm (12–24") tall and spreading

H. 'Gold Standard'

61–91 cm (24–36"). **'Albomarginata'** has variable cream or white margins on the leaves. **'Aureomarginata'** has yellow-margined leaves and is more tolerant of sun than many cultivars.

H. **'Francee'** is often listed without a species. It has puckered, dark green leaves with a narrow white margin. It grows 38–53 cm (15–21") tall and 76–91 cm (30–36") wide. In early summer it bears lavender flowers on 76 cm (30") stems.

H. **'Frances Williams'** ('yellow edge') has rounded, puckered, blue-green leaves with yellow-green margins. The flowers are almost white. The variety grows to 61 cm (24") tall and 91 cm (39") wide.

H. **'Gold Standard'** forms into a clump of heart-shaped, chartreuse leaves with dark green edges that continually change in colour throughout the season. Lavender

blue flowers are borne on 1 m (36")
tall stems in mid-summer.

H. **'Great Expectations'** is another
specimen with pale yellow or cream
leaves that have wide, irregular,
blue-green margins. The flowers are
almost white. It grows to 51–61 cm
(20–24") tall and 76 cm (30") wide.

H. **'Honeybells'** has sweetly fragrant,
light purple flowers that grow to 91
cm (36") in height. The foliage is
heart shaped, pale green and shiny.
This hosta grows vigorously to 76 cm
(30") tall and 1.2 m (4') wide.

H. plantaginea (fragrant hosta) has
glossy, bright green leaves with distinctive veins. It grows 45–75 cm
(18–30") tall and spreads to about 91
cm (36") wide, bearing large, white,
fragrant flowers in late summer.
'Aphrodite' has white double flowers.

H. 'Royal Standard'

H. 'Royal Standard' is durable and low growing. It grows 10–20 cm (4–8") tall and spreads up to 91 cm (36"). The dark green leaves are deeply veined, and the flowers are light purple.

H. sieboldiana (Siebold's hosta) forms a large, impressive clump of blue-green foliage. It grows about 91 cm (36") tall and spreads up to 1.2 m (4'). Early-summer flowers are a light greyish purple that fades to white. **'Elegans'** (var. *elegans*) has deeply puckered, blue-grey foliage and light purple flowers. It was first introduced to gardens in 1915 and is still popular today.

H. sieboldii (Seersucker hosta) has undulating, narrow, green leaves with white margins. In late summer and early fall it bears light purple flowers with darker purple veins

H. 'Francee'

H. sieboldiana 'Elegans'

inside. It grows 30–75 cm (12–30")
tall and spreads about 50–61 cm
(20–24"). **'Alba'** has light green
leaves with undulating margins and
white flowers. **'Kabitan'** has narrow,
bright yellow foliage with undulating green margins. This compact
cultivar grows about 20 cm (8") tall
and spreads 30 cm (12").

H. **'Sum & Substance'** tolerates
sun and is pest resistant. It grows to
61–91 cm (24–36") tall and 1.5–1.8
m (5–6') wide with thick, smooth,
pale yellow to chartreuse foliage.
Pale lavender flowers bloom in mid-
summer on 76–91 cm (30–36") tall
stems.

Problems & Pests

Slugs, snails, leaf spot, crown rot
and chewing insects such as black
vine weevils are all possible problems for hostas.

*Hostas are considered by some
gardeners to be the ultimate in
shade plants. They are available
in a wide variety of leaf shapes,
colours and textures.*

Iris

Iris

Height: 10 cm–1.2 m (4"–4') **Spread:** 15 cm–1.2 m (6"–4') **Flower colour:** many shades of pink, red, purple, blue, white, brown, yellow; foliage **Blooms:** spring, summer **Zones:** 2–8

THIS GROUP OF PLANTS IS WONDERFULLY DIVERSE. THE COLOUR selections are endless, so you are sure to find something that suits your personal taste. Once you look past the stunning blooms, you'll find that the foliage is attractive in its own right. Grassy, sword-like leaves reach to the sky, spreading over the years into a clump of well-groomed foliage. Dwarf iris are the most charming, both in stature and form, but all irises deserve a place in your garden. Whether iris is planted along a serpentine pathway or in border groupings, the striking colour combinations will cause you to stop every time.

Planting

Seeding: Not recommended; germination is erratic and hybrids and cultivars may not come true to type

Planting out: Late summer or early fall

Spacing: 5 cm–1.2 m (2"–4') apart

Growing

Irises prefer to grow in **full sun** but tolerate very light or dappled shade. The soil should be **average** or **fertile** and **well drained**. Japanese iris and Siberian iris prefer a moist, well-drained soil. Divide in late summer or early fall.

Tips

Iris is a popular border plant, but Japanese iris and Siberian iris are also useful alongside a stream or pond, and dwarf cultivars make attractive additions to rock gardens.

Wash your hands after handling iris because it can cause severe internal irritation if ingested. Don't plant it near places where children play.

I. sibirica

Recommended

I. germanica (bearded iris) produces flowers in all colours. This iris has been used as the parent plant for many desirable cultivars. Cultivars may vary in height and width from 15 cm to 1.2 m (6"–4'), and are grouped as miniature dwarf, standard dwarf and intermediate. Flowering periods range from mid-spring to mid-summer, and some cultivars flower again in fall. (Zones 3–8)

I. sibirica cultivar

I. pallida (sweet iris) isn't as common as the cultivars, all of which have foliage that complements showy flowers. **'Aureo-variegata'** produces strap-like leaves with gold variegations and bicoloured flowers in purple and yellow. **'Variegata'** bears similar coloured flowers, but the foliage is a pale, grey-green with creamy white variegations. Species and cultivars of *I. pallida* generally mature to 61 cm (24") tall and 30 cm (12") wide. (Zones 3–8)

I. pumila (dwarf bearded iris, miniature beared iris) are true miniatures and probably the most familiar irises available. A wide variety of colours exist, including combinations, solids and patterns in a palette of shades. The foliage is grass-like, but broader than other iris species. On average they grow to heights of 10–20 cm (4–8").

I. germanica cultivar

I. pallida 'Variegata'

I. setosa is a beardless iris with medium green leaves that are tinted with shades of red at the base. Blue to purple flowers emerge in late spring to early summer. Depending on the cultivar, the mature size will vary from 15–91 cm (6–36") tall.

I. sibirica (Siberian iris) is more resistant to iris borers than other species. It grows 61 cm–1.2 m (24"–4') tall and 91 cm (36") wide. It flowers in early summer; cultivars are available in shades of mostly purple, blue and white. **'Ruffled Velvet'** bears mid- to late season blooms, growing 55 cm (22") tall. It bears reddish purple, ruffled flowers. **'Silver Edge'** produces large blue flowers, edged in silver.

I. germanica cultivars (above & below)

The iris is depicted on the wall of an Egyptian temple dating from 1500 BC, making it one of the oldest cultivated flowers.

Problems & Pests

Several problems are quite common to irises, but close observation will prevent them from becoming severe. Iris borers are a lethal problem. They burrow their way down the leaf until they reach the root, where they continue eating until there is no root left at all. The tunnels they make in the leaves are easy to spot, and if infected leaves are removed and destroyed, or if the borers are squished within the leaf, they will never reach the roots.

Leaf spot is another problem that can be controlled by removing and destroying infected leaves. Give the plants the correct growing conditions. Too much moisture for some species will allow rot diseases to settle in and kill the plants. Slugs, snails and aphids may also cause some trouble.

Jacob's Ladder

Polemonium

Height: 20–75 cm (8–30") **Spread:** 20–40 cm (8–16") **Flower colour:** purple, white, blue; foliage **Blooms:** late spring and summer **Zones:** 2–8

THE COMMON NAME JACOB'S LADDER REFERS to a dream of the Biblical patriarch Jacob. In this dream, Jacob saw angels ascending and descending a ladder into heaven. This name also refers to the physical characteristic of this plant's leaves, which are arranged along the stems like rungs on a ladder. Naming derivations aside, this perennial is really heavenly to grow. The species, *P. caeruleum*, does have a tendency to self-sow quite profusely. Not to worry though, because it is easily eradicated if you find you are a bit overwhelmed by the ladder-like stems.

Planting

Seeding: Start seed in spring or fall. If seeding indoors, keep soil temperature at about 21° C (70° F). Seed can take up to a month to germinate.

Planting out: Spring

Spacing: 20–40 cm (8–16") apart

In ancient Greece, P. caeruleum *was mixed with wine and used to treat dysentery, toothache and poisonous bites. Later in Europe it was used to treat rabies and syphilis.*

Growing

Jacob's ladder species grow equally well in **full sun** or **partial shade**. The soil should be **fertile, humus rich**, **moist** and **well drained**. Deadhead regularly to prolong blooming. These plants self-seed readily. Division is rarely required but should be done in late summer if desired.

Tips

Include Jacob's ladder in borders and woodland gardens. Use *P. reptans* in rock gardens and to edge paths. Use *P. caeruleum* as a tall focal point in planters.

Recommended

P. caeruleum (Jacob's ladder) forms a dense clump of basal foliage. Leafy, upright stems are topped with clusters of purple flowers. This plant grows 45–91 cm (18–30") tall and spreads about 30 cm (12"). The leaflets of the foliage are organized in a neat, dense, ladder-like formation. **'Album'** has white flowers. **'Apricot Delight'** produces many mauve flowers with apricot-pink centres. **'Brise d'Anjou'** has creamy white leaflet margins, but does not bear as many flowers as the species. **'Snow and Sapphires'** is a taller version of the former variegated cultivar with clear, crisp white variegations. The sky blue flowers are fragrant and much larger than the other variegated varieties. **'White Ghost'** produces twisted leaves infused with white and purple variegations.

P. reptans (creeping Jacob's ladder) is a mounding perennial, 20–40 cm (8–16") tall, with an equal spread.

P. caeruleum 'Brise d' Anjou'

It bears small blue or lilac flowers in late spring and early summer. (Zones 3–8)

Problems & Pests

Powdery mildew, leaf spot and rust are occasional problems.

P. caeruleum 'Album'

Japanese Painted Fern

Athyrium

Height: 30–61 cm (12–24") **Spread:** 30–61 cm (12–24") **Flower colour:**
no flowers; grown for foliage **Zones:** 4–8

REGIONS WITH HOT, DRY SUMMERS ARE OFTEN NOT THE
best places to grow ferns. However, the Japanese painted fern is an
exception. I was thrilled to discover that this little beauty does so
well in our dry prairie climate, in almost any soil type in most
locations. It is easy to grow and stands out among other
foliage plants. The only important thing to remember
is to shelter it from hot afternoon sun. When given
what it requires, Japanese painted fern will thrive
and flourish.

Planting

Seeding: Not recommended

Planting out: Spring

Spacing: 30 cm (12")

*Try to find out
whether a store-
bought plant was
propagated from
spores or division.
When this species is
grown from spores,
its foliage is more
colourful.*

A. nipponicum cultivar (above); 'Pictum' (below)

Growing

Japanese painted fern requires **partial shade** to maintain its colourful foliage. If it is planted in full shade, the colour may not develop, whereas full sun will cause the colour to fade or the leaves to scorch. The soil should be **moderately fertile**, **moist**, **neutral to acidic** and **humus rich**. Divide in spring when necessary.

It is important to apply a thick layer of mulch in fall to maintain a better moisture level around the roots and to protect the crown from exposure.

Tips

Japanese painted fern is very attractive when planted en masse, within mixed borders or shade gardens. The interesting foliage stands out beside other ferns in a woodland setting.

Recommended

A. nipponicum is a creeping, compact fern that grows 30–45 cm (12–18") tall and wide. It bears long, mid-green fronds with reddish purple midribs. The cultivars are far more readily available and attractive than the species, with new additions added yearly. This species has been known to hybridize freely with other *Athyrium* species. **'Pictum'** (formerly *Metallicum*) grows 30 cm (12") tall and wide. It produces fronds with purplish red stalks and metallic grey segments that are flushed with burgundy. **'Samurai Sword'** bears deep burgundy, arching fronds. **'Ursula's Red'** has broad, silver fronds, flushed and veined wine red. It grows 30–61 cm (12–24") tall and wide.

Problems & Pests

Problems are rare, though rust is possible.

Japanese Spurge

Pachysandra

Height: about 20 cm (8") **Spread:** 45–61 cm (18–24") **Flower colour:** white, inconspicuous; foliage plant **Blooms:** early spring **Zones:** 3–8

IN A GARDEN, GROUNDCOVERS ARE OFTEN THE PLANTS THAT really tie the entire landscape together, so it is important that they be attractive and of good form. Japanese spurge is a luxurious evergreen groundcover that will help to enhance your garden beyond your wildest imagination. It is rather slow to get established, but it's well worth the wait. This plant has the ability to grow right over tree roots, which other groundcovers often have difficulty doing. Because the foliage grows in whorls at the top of the stems, Japanese spurge always appears tidy, offering a lush mat of green well into the cool days of fall.

Planting

Seeding: Not recommended

Planting out: Spring or fall

Spacing: 45–61 cm (18–24") apart

Growing

Japanese spurge prefers **light to full shade** and tolerates any soil that is **moist**, **acidic**, **humus rich** and **well drained**. Division is not required but can be done in spring for propagation.

'Variegata' (above), P. terminalis (below)

Tips

Japanese spurge is a durable groundcover under trees, along north walls, in shady borders and in woodland gardens.

When snow coverage is poor or after a rough winter, Japanese spurge foliage can appear a little ragged come spring. Remove the damaged foliage, encouraging new growth to emerge in late spring to early summer, filling in the gaps.

Make sure to mulch heavily in the fall to protect the evergreen nature of this perennial. Remove the mulch in the spring when there is no longer a risk of frost.

Recommended

P. terminalis (Japanese spurge) forms a low mass of foliage rosettes. It grows about 20 cm (8") tall and can spread almost indefinitely, but it usually reaches 45–61 cm (18–24") in width in colder zones. **'Green Carpet'** remains more compact, producing finely detailed, smaller leaves. **'Green Sheen'** produces darker foliage with a glossy sheen. **'Variegata'** has white margins or silver-mottled foliage. It is not as vigorous as the species.

Problems & Pests

Problems with leaf blight, root rot, scale insects and slugs can occur.

Joe Pye Weed
Boneset
Eupatorium

Height: 91 cm–3 m (3–10') **Spread:** 75–91 cm (30–36") **Flower colour:** purple, white, pink **Blooms:** summer and fall **Zones:** 3–8

THIS VIGOROUSLY GROWING PERENNIAL CAN REACH HEIGHTS up to about 2 m (7') in one season once established, which is really quite extraordinary. Along with having great presence, it also has an artistic appeal. I like to see the cultivar 'Atropurpureum' placed beside plants that have purplish foliage within the landscape. This placement really capitalizes on the purplish tint of the leaves and stems, making an already stately plant even more attractive, especially when in bloom. However, any variety you choose to include in your garden is sure to give you great satisfaction, both in the garden and in your fresh cut arrangements.

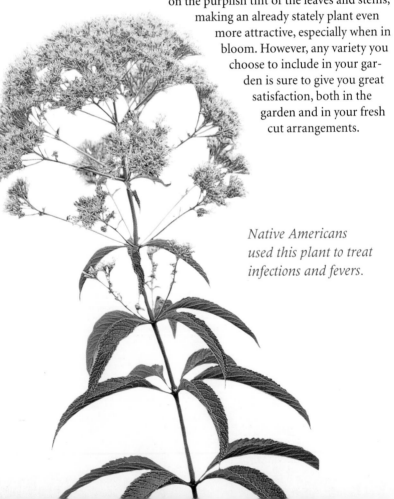

Native Americans used this plant to treat infections and fevers.

Planting

Seeding: Sow seed indoors or in a cold frame at 12–16°C (55–61°F)

Planting out: Spring, summer

Spacing: 91 cm (36")

Growing

Eupatorium prefers **full sun** and will tolerate partial shade. It responds well to just about any soil condition as long as it remains **consistently moist**. Propagate by division in spring, but only if necessary.

Tips

Joe Pye weed works well in mixed beds and borders, as a specimen or in a woodland setting.

Recommended

E. maculatum grows into an enormous, colourful clump. Large umbrella-like clusters of pinky purple flowers are borne in late summer and early fall. The flowers are held high above the bold green leaves by rigid, dark purple stems. It grows 2.1–3 m (7–10') tall and 91 cm (36") wide. **'Atropurpureum'** bears dark pinkish purple flowers on dark purple stems. **'Bartered Bride'** produces clusters of white flowers. **'Gateway'** is a little more striking in contrast to others. Deep magenta flowers are borne among large, deep green leaves and dark stems. Very compact compared to the species, this cultivar reaches heights of only 1.5–1.8 m (5–6') heights. (Zones 4–8)

E. rugosum (boneset, white snakeroot) is a mounding perennial that grows 91 cm–1.2 m (3–4') tall and 75 cm (30") wide. Pure white, fuzzy

E. rugosum

flowers are formed in clusters. This species is more tolerant of dry shade. **'Chocolate'** produces deep brown foliage that greens with age, and bright white clusters of flowers.

Problems & Pests

Rust, powdery mildew, leaf spot, slugs and snails can all become problems.

E. rugosum 'Chocolate'

Lady's Mantle
Alchemilla

Height: 8–61 cm (3–24") **Spread:** 30–61 cm (12–24") **Flower colour:**
yellow, green; foliage **Blooms:** early summer to early fall **Zones:** 2–8

I LIKE TO ENCOURAGE GARDENERS TO TRY DIFFERENT DESIGN
styles in their gardens. Quite often, gardeners will get stuck on ideas that
plants used for edging must be of low stature, which isn't always true. The
common lady's mantle is an average of 61 cm (24") high and will create a
wonderful edging for any moist, shady areas in the garden. It is attractive
throughout the year, but I like the appearance best in the late spring when
the plants are covered in beautiful chartreuse blooms. As a gardener, I can't
help myself and often stop and stroke the soft, velvety leaves. Perhaps this
plant's loveliest feature is its toothed leaf edges, which capture moisture and
result in beaded dewdrops hovering atop the
fine hairs on the leaf surface. This always
allows for budding photographers to capture special images after the morning dew.

Planting

Seeding: Sow fresh seed directly into the garden or into containers; transplant into the garden while seedlings are small

Planting out: Spring

Spacing: 50–61 cm (20–24")

Growing

Lady's mantle will grow best in **light shade** or **partial shade**, with protection from the afternoon sun. This plant dislikes hot locations. The soil should be **fertile, humus rich**, **moist** and **well drained**. Lady's mantle is drought resistant once it is established. Division is rarely required but can be done in spring before flowering starts or in fall once flowering is complete. If more plants are desired, move some of the self-seeded plants that are bound to show up to where you want them.

Tips

Lady's mantle is ideal for grouping under trees in woodland gardens and along border edges where it softens the bright colours of other plants. A wonderful location is alongside a pathway that winds through a lightly wooded area.

If your lady's mantle begins to look tired and heat-stressed during summer, rejuvenate it by trimming it back so new foliage can fill in.

Recommended

A. alpina (alpine lady's mantle) is a diminutive, low-growing plant that has soft white hairs on the backs of the leaves, giving the appearance of a silvery margin to each leaf. Tiny

A. mollis

A. alpina

clusters of yellow flowers are borne in summer. It grows 8–13 cm (3–5") tall and spreads up to 50 cm (20").

A. mollis (common lady's mantle) is the most frequently grown species. It forms a mound of soft, rounded foliage. Sprays of yellowish green flowers held above the foliage may be borne from early summer to early fall. It grows 20–61 cm (8–24") tall and spreads up to about 30–61 cm (12–24")

Problems & Pests

Lady's mantle rarely suffers from any problems, though fungus may be a problem during warm, wet summers.

Lamb's Ears

Stachys

Height: 15–61 cm (6–24") **Spread:** 45–61 cm (18–24") **Flower colour:** pink, purple; foliage **Blooms:** summer **Zones:** 2–8

YOUNG AND OLD, BEGINNER TO HORTICULTURIST—ALL IT TAKES is one glimpse of this adorable perennial to fall completely in love with it. It's no surprise that it's called lamb's ears—it's almost impossible to stop touching the soft, woolly leaves. For me it conjures up images of young lambs frolicking in the spring sunshine. Better yet, this plant is also quite attractive as edging along a perennial border. The delicate colour and texture of the leaves will soften the hardest edges along brick pathways and retaining walls. Lamb's ears is an ideal perennial to grow in our dry climate; it tends to fail in regions that experience extreme heat and humidity.

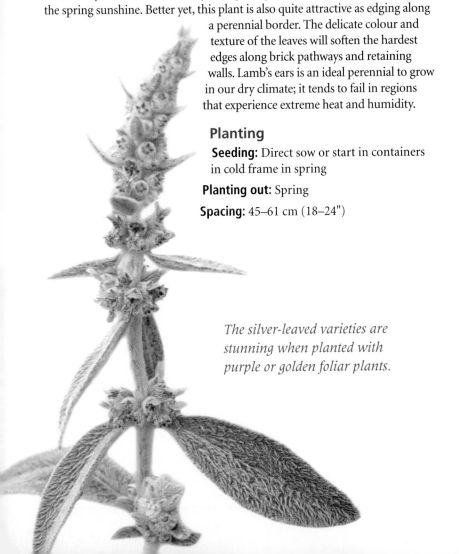

Planting

Seeding: Direct sow or start in containers in cold frame in spring

Planting out: Spring

Spacing: 45–61 cm (18–24")

The silver-leaved varieties are stunning when planted with purple or golden foliar plants.

Growing

Lamb's ears grows best in **full sun**. The soil should be of **poor** or **average fertility** and **well drained**. Remove spent flower spikes to keep plants looking neat. Select a flowerless cultivar if you don't want to deadhead. Divide in spring.

Tips

Lamb's ears makes a great groundcover in a new garden where the soil has not yet been amended. As long as good drainage is provided, lamb's ears will do well. It can be used to edge borders and pathways, providing a soft, silvery backdrop for more vibrant colours in the border.

This perennial is considered to be a very low-maintenance plant.

Recommended

S. byzantina (*S. lanata*) forms a mat of thick, woolly rosettes of leaves. It grows 15–45 cm (6–18") tall, with a spread of 45–61 cm (18–24"). Pinkish purple flowers are borne all summer. **'Big Ears'** has purple leaves that are twice as big as those of the species. **'Primrose Heron'** produces golden, fuzzy foliage, fading to a pale, soft yellow-green late in the season. The flowers are a bright purple-pink. **'Silver Carpet'** has silvery white, fuzzy foliage; it rarely, if ever, produces flowers. (Zones 3–8)

S. grandiflora **'Rosea'** is more upright in form, producing erect stems up to 61 cm (24") tall. The flower colour is similar to *S. byzantina*; however, the foliage is heart shaped, softly textured with pattern

S. grandiflora

and the occasional hair, and deep green rather than silver. **'Superba'** has deeper purple-pink flowers.

Problems & Pests

Fungal leaf problems, including rot, powdery mildew, rust and leaf spot, are rare but can occur in hot, humid weather. Diseased or damaged foliage can be cut back. New foliage will sprout when the weather cools down.

S. byzantina

Lamium
Dead Nettle
Lamium

Height: 15–30 cm (6–12") **Spread:** 30–61 cm (12–24") **Flower colour:** pink, purple, white, yellow; foliage **Blooms:** summer **Zones:** 2–8

LAMIUM IS A RELIABLE, HANDSOME GROUNDCOVER FOR SHADY areas, and that is sometimes a hard thing to come by. The foliage has such fantastic colour that it creates a powerful composition in the garden. *L. maculatum*, or spotted dead nettle, is one the most versatile and attractive species for prairie gardens. The cultivated varieties in this group offer myriad foliar colours in shades of chartreuse, silver and green with solid or combined variegations. Interesting flowers complement the attractive foliage for a show-stopping effect. Lamium can be a little on the invasive side, however, so be careful to choose the right location for this vigorous grower.

Though lamium is often confused with nettles because of its common name, it is actually a member of the mint family.

Planting

Seeding: Sow seed indoors or in a cold frame in early spring; cultivars will not come true to type

Planting out: Spring, summer

Spacing: 30–61 cm (12–24")

Growing

White- and purple-flowered lamium prefer **partial shade** whereas yellow-flowered varieties require **full shade**. Overall, whatever the flower colour, all are tolerant to partial sun at best. The soil should be **moist** and **well drained**. Although tolerant of most soil conditions, it grows less vigorously in poor soils. These plants are drought tolerant when grown in the shade, but they can develop bare patches if the soil is allowed to dry out for extended periods. Divide and replant in spring or fall if bare spots become unsightly. Some of the species will root where the stem touches the ground. Stem cuttings can be planted out in spring as well.

L. galeobdolon 'Florentium'

Lamium flowers closely resemble tiny snapdragons and are an important source of nectar for bees.

L. maculatum cultivar

L. maculatum 'Beacon Silver'
L. maculatum 'White Nancy'

Tips

Lamium is frequently used as a groundcover in shady beds, mixed borders or in group plantings. It also works well in a woodland setting.

Lamium will remain more compact if sheared back after flowering. Keep in mind that lamium can be quite invasive and is likely to overwhelm less vigorous plants. If your plants become invasive, pull some of them up, making sure to remove the fleshy roots.

Recommended

L. galeobdolon (yellow archangel, false lamium) forms a dense 20–30 cm (8–12") tall mat of silver-streaked foliage. Tall, wiry stems emerge from the mounds of leaves supporting small yellow clusters of flowers. **'Florentium'** (*Variegatum*) isn't as upright, but is more of a creeper. Silver-centred leaves are edged in green. **'Herman's Pride'** bears coarser foliage that is speckled with white. **'Silver Angel'** has more of a prostrate form and silvery foliage. (Zones 3–8)

L. maculatum (spotted dead nettle) grows 15–30 cm (6–12") tall and 30–61 cm (12–24") wide. This species has been used in just about every possible way, from a groundcover to a hanging basket trailer, but it's considered a little too vigorous for rock or alpine gardens. Small, silvery green leaves grow among pink, white and purple clusters of flowers. **'Anne Greenaway'** has three bands of colour on each leaf. A central streak of silver is surrounded by green and edged with yellow.

Lavender flowers then emerge in late spring atop the colourful foliage. **'Aureum'** produces variegated chartreuse foliage and pink flowers. It's considered less vigorous and requires part to full shade. **'Beacon Silver'** bears purplish flowers and silvery variegated leaves with darker edging and pink flowers. It's known to self-seed. **'Orchid Frost'** bears silver-accented foliage edged in blue-green and topped with deep pink blooms. **'White Nancy'** has silvery white foliage and pure white flowers.

Problems & Pests

Lamium may experience problems with downy or powdery mildew, leaf spot, slugs and snails.

L. galeobdolon 'Florentium'

Lamium was used in folk medicine in the past for its astringent properties. It was also grown in Europe as a pot herb.

L. maculatum 'Anne Greenaway'

Liatris
Blazing Star
Spike Gayfeather, Gayfeather
Liatris

Height: 45–91 cm (18–36") **Spread:** 45–61 cm (18–24") **Flower colour:** purple, white; foliage **Blooms:** summer **Zones:** 2–8

LIATRIS IS NOT JUST A LONG-LASTING CUT FLOWER FOR FLORISTS, but also a wonderful addition to your garden. Planting liatris in clumps gives the tall, spiky blooms further landscape appeal and a bigger impact overall. The species, a North American native wildflower, is a beautiful complement to any natural planting area, but the cultivated varieties are nothing short of spectacular. Aside from its appeal to humans, liatris is also very attractive to the butterfly and bee population. In fact, many pollinating insects are known to make their way to the tall, colourful flower spikes to collect whatever pollen might be available. I like to plant this perennial beside my bog garden because there it receives adequate moisture without being at risk of getting root rot.

Planting

Seeding: Direct sow in fall; plants may take two to four years to bloom from seed

Planting out: Spring

Spacing: 45–61 cm (18–24") apart

Growing

Liatris prefers **full sun**. The soil should be of **average fertility, sandy** and **humus rich**. Water well during the growing season, but don't allow the plants to stand in water during cool weather. Mulch during summer to prevent moisture loss.

Trim off the spent flower spikes to promote a longer blooming period and to keep the plants looking tidy. Divide every three or four years in fall. The clump will appear crowded when it is time to divide.

Tips

Use these plants in bog gardens, borders and meadow plantings. Liatris doesn't like to sit in water during cool weather and may develop root rot during winter. Plant in a location that has good drainage.

Liatris does well when grown in planters.

Recommended

L. spicata is an erect, clump-forming plant. It grows 45–91 cm (18–36") tall and spreads 45–61 cm (18–24"). The flowers are pinkish purple or white. **'Floristan Violet'** has purple flowers. **'Floristan White'** has white flowers. **'Kobold'** has deep purple flowers.

'Floristan White'

Problems & Pests

Slugs, stem rot, root rot, rust and leaf spot are possible problems.

'Kobold'

Lily
Lillium

Height: 30 cm–1.8 m (12"–6') **Spread:** 30–61 cm (12–24") **Flower colour:** cream, pink, yellow, orange, white, red, purple, solids and bicolours, patterns in every shade **Blooms:** summer **Zones:** 2–8

THIS GROUP OF PLANTS IS MADE UP OF A VAST NUMBER OF SPECIES, hybrids and cultivars. There is sure to be a lily that will work in your garden, regardless of light or soil conditions. But, as with daylilies, roses, tulips and petunias, where does one begin to choose from the many and varied colour combinations, forms, heights and groups of the lily family? My best advice would be to start with one, but make sure to plant at least three to five plants together for greater impact. Pick a variety bearing blossoms in your favourite colour or one with extra long stems for cutting. Don't let it overwhelm you, and just have fun. Lilies have often been included in the many fresh flower arrangements I've put together over the years, and will continue to be in the future.

Planting

Seeding: Sow ripe seed in a cold frame in early spring, or indoors under lights at 18–21°C (65–70°F)

Planting out: Spring, summer

Spacing: 30–61 cm (12–24")

Growing

Most lilies prefer **full sun** while others prefer **partial shade**. Overall, a minimum of six hours of sunlight a day should suffice for any lily, or a full day's sun for the top part of the plant and shade for the crown or base. The soil should be **well drained**, **light** and **organically rich**. Lily bulbs are very prone to damage and bruising and should be handled very carefully. Once harvested, the bulbs should never be allowed to dry out or they'll die. Lily roots prefer to remain cool. Apply a thick layer of mulch around the crown, or plant a groundcover near the base to help the ground to remain cool. It's recommended to deadhead; however,

Asiatic lily

the foliage should be allowed to die back on its own. This will enable the bulb to be well fed for the following year. When the clump begins to thin out in the centre over time, lift and divide immediately after flowering.

Tips

Lilies are beautiful in just about any setting, but they are most effective in mixed beds and borders, woodland or wild settings, cottage gardens or en masse.

Recommended

Asiatic Hybrids are considered the most reliable lilies for prairie conditions. They come in white, yellow, orange, pink, red and lavender. Patterns of stripes or dots and stars can also occur from one hybrid to another, and the flowers can face up, out or down. Blooming periods can differ, too. Bright morning sun is best, with some shade during the

hottest part of the day. Mature sizes range from 61 cm–1.2 m (24"–4') tall and 30 cm (12") wide.

Aurelian Hybrids (trumpet lilies) have fragrant, trouble-free, trumpet-shaped flowers in a variety of bright colours, including pink, apricot, orange, white and yellow. These lilies are a little more tender, and they require winter mulch for protection. Mature sizes range from 1.2–1.8 m (4–6') tall and 45 cm (18") wide. Hybrids from this group may require staking because of their height; otherwise, they are care free. (Zones 4–8)

Martagon Lilies (common turkscap lily) vigorously produce stately stems 1.2–1.8 m (4–6') tall, topped with down-facing blooms. It's not uncommon to see 40–50 flowers per stem, perched high above clumps of dark, shiny foliage borne in low

Martagon Lily

L. lancifolium (below)

mounds. Martagons are increasing in popularity, and for good reason. They are long-lived, hardy, fragrant and available in a wide variety of colours. Martagons are usually a little more expensive than others, but consider them an investment. This group requires seven years to bloom when grown from seed, but the wait is well worth it. They will clump over time, and should only be disturbed once dormant. They can be left for many years before division is even necessary. Martagons prefer lighter soils but grow quite successfully in heavy clay soils in full to partial sun. (Zones 4–8)

Oriental Hybrids bloom a little later than most, and bear fragrant, large, starry flowers in shades of white, pink and red that are sometimes banded or spotted. Relatively short-lived and considered a little fussy, these hybrids require a light, loamy, organically rich soil that is slightly acidic. Winter mulch is recommended for protection on the prairies. Mature sizes range from 91 cm–1.8 m (3–6') tall and 45 cm (18") wide. (Zones 4–8)

L. cernuum (nodding lily) grows 30–50 cm (12–20") tall in full to partial sun. It bears soft purple-pink flowers accented with spots. (Zones 3–8)

L. lancifolium grows to 1.2 m (4') tall, producing flowers in shades of white, cream, yellow, pink and red, all speckled with brown spots. The most recognizable and traditional colour available is orange, which is best known as the tiger lily.

L. michiganese grows 61 cm–1.5 m (24"–5') tall in an upright form. It bears oval-shaped leaves on dark stems that support nodding, oranged-red flowers with burgundy spots at base of each petal. (Zones 4–8)

L. regale (regal lily) is an easy-to-grow species that matures to 1.8 m (6') tall. It bears up to 25 super fragrant white flowers with purple outer stripes at one time. (Zones 4–8)

L. rubellum bears funnel-shaped, pink flowers with burgundy spots at the base. The fragrant flowers are borne atop 30–80 cm (12–32") tall stems. It prefers partial shade and acidic, moist soil. (Zones 3–7)

Problems & Pests

Grey mould, viruses, aphids, slugs, red lily beetles, snails, wildlife (deer, birds, voles, rabbits, groundhogs) can all cause damage. Don't get discouraged by the lengthy list of critters. For the most part, when planted in the right location, lilies are trouble free.

Lily bulbs have no real period of dormancy. The fleshy roots have no outer protective layer. The bulbs should be replanted immediately after being dug up or after being purchased. Make sure to keep moist packing material around each bulb until it is planted.

Lily-of-the-Valley

Convallaria

Height: 15–30 cm (6–12") **Spread:** indefinite **Flower colour:** white, pink; foliage **Blooms:** spring **Zones:** 1–8

I OFTEN HAVE MORE SUITABLE SPOTS FOR LILY-OF-THE-VALLEY than any other invasive groundcover. It spreads by rhizomes and will quickly and easily colonize a large area in a season or two. I once had a small strip of soil on the north side of my farmhouse that seemed unable to support the growth of anything. As a last resort, I planted patches of lily-of-the-valley. Lo and behold, in no time at all, the patches began to weave into a thriving bed of green. Even though the soil conditions were poor, the vigorous growth habit prevailed. I was thrilled and frequently cut the flowers for fresh arrangements and bouquets. They have a delicate elegance and a pleasant, though intense, fragrance that is second to none.

Planting

Seeding: Not recommended; very easy to propagate by division

Planting out: Spring or fall

Spacing: About 30 cm (12"); quickly spreads to fill an area

Growing

Lily-of-the-valley grows well in **full sun to full shade**. The soil should be of **average fertility**, **humus rich**, and **moist**, but almost any soil conditions are tolerated. This plant is drought resistant. Division is rarely required but can be done whenever you need more plants. Pairs of leaves grow from small pips, or eyes, that form along the root. Divide a length of root into pieces, leaving at least one pip on each piece.

Tips

Plant this versatile groundcover in a woodland garden, bordering a pathway or beneath shade trees where little else will grow. Its dense growth and shallow roots keep weeds down but won't interfere with shrubs.

Lily-of-the-valley can be quite invasive. Don't grow it with plants that are less vigorous and likely to be overwhelmed, such as alpine plants in a rock garden.

Lily-of-the-valley flowers are known for their delightful scent. In fall, dig up a few roots and plant them into pots. Overwinter the pots in a sheltered location, such a window well, cold frame or unheated porch. In early spring, bring the pots indoors to enjoy the flowers and their scent.

'Rosea'

Lily-of-the-valley is currently being researched for its potential medicinal qualities.

Recommended

C. majalis forms a mat of foliage. It grows 15–25 cm (6–10") tall and spreads indefinitely. Small arching stems lined with fragrant, white, bell-shaped flowers are produced in spring. **'Albostriata'** and **'Aureovariegata'** have white- or yellow-striped leaves, respectively. **'Flore Pleno'** has white double flowers and tends not to be quite as invasive as the species. **'Fortin's Giant'** has larger leaves and flowers than the species and can grow up to 30 cm (12") tall. **'Rosea'** (var. rosea) has light pink or pink-veined flowers.

Problems & Pests

Occasional problems with mould and stem rot can occur.

Lupine
Lupinus

Height: 46–91 cm (18–36") **Spread:** 30–46 cm (12–18") **Flower colour:**
white, cream, yellow, pink, red, orange, purple, blue; some bicoloured; foliage
Blooms: early to mid-summer **Zones:** 3–8

LUPINES IN BLOOM ARE SIMPLY UNFORGETTABLE. THEIR NODDING
blossoms, which resemble tiny bonnets, are perfectly balanced on tall, slender stems and move up and down gracefully in a breeze. The plant's blue-
tinted, lacy foliage lends a dainty quality to its appearance, and gives it an
old-fashioned appeal. One summer a number of years ago, I had the good
fortune to spend some time on the east coast of
Canada. The roadsides everywhere were filled with a
rainbow of colour. On closer inspection, and to my
delight, the rainbow turned out to be none other
than lupines in glorious bloom. I came away from
that trip with a new appreciation for this prairie
classic. It's something I'll never forget.

Planting

Seeding: Soak seeds in warm water for 24 hours, then plant directly outdoors in mid-fall or mid-spring. If you start seeds indoors, you may need to place planted seeds in the refrigerator for four to six weeks after soaking them.

Planting out: Spring or fall

Spacing: About 30–46 cm (12–18") apart

Growing

Lupine grows best in **light shade** or **partial shade**. The soil should be of **average to high fertility**, **sandy**, **well drained** and **slightly acidic**. Protect lupine plants from drying winds. Deadheading is recommended to encourage more flowering as the season progresses, but lupine may self-seed if the spent spikes are left in place. One solution is to leave just a couple of spikes in place once flowering is finished to allow some seedlings to fill in as the older plants die out.

Lupines are in the same plant family as beans and peas. However, the pods and seeds of lupines will cause stomach upset if ingested.

This perennial can be short-lived. Carefully removing the small offsets that develop at the base of the plant and replanting them will provide you with more plants. Division is not required. Lupine dislikes having its roots disturbed.

Tips

Lupines are wonderful when massed together in borders or in cottage and natural gardens.

Recommended

There are many species of lupines, but they are rarely grown in favour of the many popular hybrids. Most lupines form a dense basal mound of foliage from which tall spikes emerge, bearing many colourful, pea-like flowers.

Gallery Hybrids are dwarf hybrids. They grow about 46–61 cm (18–24")

tall and spread about 30–46 cm
(12–18"). They are available with
flowers in blue, red, pink, yellow or
white.

Russell Hybrids were among the
first groups of hybrids developed.
They grow about 61–91 cm
(24–36") tall, spread 30–46 cm
(12–18") and bear flowers in a wide
range of solid colours and
bicolours.

Problems & Pests

Aphids are the biggest problem for
lupines. Slugs, snails, leaf spot,
downy mildew, powdery mildew,
rust, stem rot and damping off (in
seedlings) can cause occasional
trouble.

*The fuzzy, peapod-like capsules that
form along the spike once the flowers
fade can be removed, or left to ripen
so that seeds can be collected.*

Lysimachia
Loosestrife
Lysimachia

Height: 5 cm–1.2 m (2"–4') **Spread:** 46–91 cm (18–36") **Flower colour:** yellow, white; foliage **Blooms:** spring, summer **Zones:** 2–8

THE COMMON NAME LOOSESTRIFE MAY CONJURE UP IMAGES OF wetlands completely overtaken by a truly beautiful but noxious weed called purple loosestrife. Unfortunately, common names can be rather confusing as they may also refer to another plant entirely. Loosestrife, more commonly known as lysimachia in Saskatchewan and Manitoba, is a lovely perennial to grow with a wide array of positive attributes. Gooseneck loosestrife is one of most unique varieties, and is aptly named for the graceful bend in the flower stalk that resembles the neck of a goose. Each and every lysimachia has its own exceptional qualities that work well with a great many other perennials, including coral bells, goat's beard and bergenia.

Tall, upright varieties are frequently used in fresh floral arranging.

Planting

Seeding: Sow seed indoors or directly outside in early spring

Planting out: Spring, summer

Spacing: 46–91 cm (18–36")

Growing

Loosestrife prefers **full to partial sun**. The soil should be **rich**, **fertile**, **moist** and **well drained**. It is best not to allow the soil to dry out during hot summers. Divide in spring or fall.

Tips

Loosestrife works well in a herbaceous border or bog garden or along a pond border. The low-growing species are best suited for groundcover.

Recommended

L. ciliata (fringed loosestrife) is an erect, vigorously growing form 1.2 m (4') tall and 61 cm (24") wide. It bears single or double, star-shaped, yellow flowers with reddish brown centres. Hairy, mid-green leaves are vigorously produced on slender stems. **'Firecracker'** bears reddish bronze foliage in a loose, upright clump. Nodding yellow flowers are borne on the stalk tips, most often in pairs. This cultivar is also slightly smaller at maturity. (Zones 3–8)

L. clethroides (gooseneck or Japanese loosestrife) grows 61–91 cm (24–36") tall and 91 cm (36") wide. Tall, dense, white flower spikes stand on thick, purple stems that are slightly bent like a goose's neck. Deep green, bushy foliage turns a brilliant bronzy red in autumn.

L. punctata 'Alexander'

L. punctata

This species prefers a moist location and is best suited to bog or waterside plantings. It also tolerates partial shade and is very effective in masses, though it can be mildly invasive.

L. nummularia (creeping Jenny, moneywort) is unique among other loosestrife species. Its round leaves grow flatly on opposite sides of creeping stems. Yellow flowers are borne throughout the season. It has a tendency to become invasive, but it is easily maintained by gently cultivating the runners out. It is not afraid of shade and is ideal for rock walls, containers or as a shady groundcover. The species grows 5–10 cm (2–4") tall and 46–61 cm (18–24") wide. **'Aurea'** produces golden foliage with yellow flowers. This cultivar may require some midday shade to prevent or reduce leaf scorch.

L. ciliata 'Firecracker'
L. nummularia

L. punctata (yellow, golden or garden loosestrife) is an upright, bushy, spreading clump of 46–91 cm (18–36") tall leafy spikes. Bright yellow, cupped flowers with orange centres are borne along the spike to the tip, amongst the foliage. **'Alexander'** has a similar overall appearance but with white and green variegated foliage. It grows slightly smaller than the species.

Problems & Pests

Rust and leaf spot are the only problems lysimachia may encounter.

Lysimachia is often confused with purple loosestrife (Lythrum salicaria), a plant that is considered a noxious weed on the prairies.

'Alexander'

L. clethroides

Mallow

Malva

Height: 20 cm–2 m (8"–6.5') **Spread:** 30–61 cm (12–24") **Flower colour:** purple, pink, white, blue; foliage **Blooms:** summer, fall **Zones:** 3–8

MALLOW IS AN ATTRACTIVE PERENNIAL ON ITS own, but it is far more impressive when planted in larger groupings. Mallow is immediately recognizable as a relative of hollyhock. Both plants share similar characteristics, including saucer-shaped blossoms born on tall, rigid spikes. Like the hollyhock, mallow is considered a short-lived perennial that will self-sow throughout the garden. Bare, well-weeded spaces are often the best locations for self-seeding mallow, as the seeds that fall to the ground must have good contact with the soil in order to successfully germinate and grow. Little else is needed in order to enjoy this perennial for years to come.

Planting

Seeding: Direct sow in spring or early summer, or start indoors in late winter to early spring

Planting out: Spring or summer

Spacing: 30–61 cm (12–24")

Growing

Mallow grows well in **full sun** or **partial shade**. The soil should be of **average fertility**, **moist** and **well drained**. Mallow is drought tolerant. In very rich soils, it may require staking. Mallow can be propagated by basal cuttings taken in spring.

Mallow self-seeds. Cutting plants back by about half in late May will encourage more compact, bushy growth, but will delay flowering by a couple of weeks. Transplant or thin out seedlings if they are too crowded. Mallow does not need dividing.

Tips

Use mallow in a mixed border or a wild or cottage garden. Deadhead the flowers to keep your plants blooming until the snow flies.

Mallows also make good cut flowers.

M. sylvestris 'Primley Blue' (photos this page)

Recommended

M. alcea (hollyhock mallow) is a loose, upright, branching plant. It grows 61 cm–1.2 m (24"–4') tall and spreads 46–61 cm (18–24"). This plant bears pink flowers with notched petals all summer. **'Fastigiata'** is tall, narrow and upright as well, growing 80 cm (32") tall, and bearing medium pink flowers.

M. moschata (musk mallow) is a bushy, upright plant with musk-scented leaves. It grows about 91 cm (36") tall and spreads about 61 cm (24"), bearing pale pink or white flowers all summer long. **'Pink Perfection'** bears soft pink flowers, and **'White Perfection'** produces pure white flowers with pink centres.

M. sylvestris (cheeses, tall mallow, high mallow) may be upright or spreading in habit. It can grow from 20 cm–1.2 m (8"–4') tall and spreads

M. sylvestris 'Primley Blue'
M. alcea 'Fastigiata'

to 30–61 cm (12–24"). The pink flowers have darker veining and are produced all summer. There are many cultivars of this species available. **'Bibor Felho'** has rose purple flowers with darker purple veins that reach 1.5–2 m (4–6') heights. **'Braveheart'** grows 91 cm (36") tall, with darkly veined, light purple-pink flowers. **'Mystic Mix'** bears flowers in dark purple, mauve and blue. This mix can reach heights of 2 m (6.5'). **'Primley Blue'** has light purple-blue flowers. This is a prostrate cultivar that grows only about 20 cm (8") tall. **'Zebrina'** has pale pink or white flowers with purple on 1–1.5 m (3–4') tall stalks. (Zones 4–8)

M. sylvestris 'Bibor Felho'

Problems & Pests

Problems with rust, leaf spot and spider mites can occur occasionally.

Mallow is reputed to have a calming effect when ingested and was used in the Middle Ages as an antidote for aphrodisiacs and love potions.

M. sylvetris 'Zebrinus'

Maltese Cross
Rose Campion
Lychnis

Height: 61 cm–1.2 m (24"–4') **Spread:** 30–46 cm (12–18") **Flower colour:** magenta, pink, salmon, white, scarlet, red **Blooms:** summer **Zones:** 2–8

MALTESE CROSS WAS NAMED BECAUSE EACH INDIVIDUAL FLOWER is shaped in the image of the cross. It is thought that originally maltese cross was brought back to Europe from Turkey in the saddlebags of the Knights of Malta during the Crusades. A romantic tale for a reliable, prairie standard. Who knew it had such exotic beginnings? Tales aside, this vigorous perennial is highly sought after by those with a preference for bright, glowing colour palettes. Butterflies are also fond of this prolific bloomer and will return in fall after the plant has received a hard prune in late spring to encourage new, lush foliage and an additional blooming cycle.

Maltese cross species make beautiful, carefree additions to a border, cottage garden or naturalized garden.

The genus name, Lychnis, is Greek for 'lamp,' a reference to the brilliant glow of the flowers.

Planting

Seeding: Start seeds in late spring; best germination will occur if you keep the soil between 20–21° C (68–70° F) if seeding indoors

Planting out: Spring

Spacing: 30–46 cm (12–18")

Growing

Maltese cross will grow equally well in **full sun** or **partial shade**. The soil should be of **average fertility** and **well drained**. These plants can be short-lived, but they tend to self-seed and repopulate the garden with new plants as old ones die out. They reseed easily in gravel pathways, and young plants can easily be transplanted from there. Basal cuttings can also be taken to propagate the plants. Division can be done in spring though these short-lived plants may not need it.

Tips

These tall plants may need some support, particularly in a windy location. Peony supports or twiggy branches pushed into the soil before the plants get too tall are best and are less noticeable than tying the plants to stakes.

Recommended

L. chalcedonica (Maltese cross) is a stiff, upright plant. It grows 91 cm–1.2 m (3–4') tall and spreads 30–46 cm (12–18"). The scarlet flowers are borne in clusters in early and mid-summer. Some support may be required to keep this plant standing upright. **'Alba'** has white flowers. **'Dusky Salmon'** is a newer

L. coronaria

cultivar, bearing soft salmon, finely cut flowers.

L. coronaria (rose campion) forms an upright mass of silvery grey leaves and branching stems. It grows 61–91 cm (24–36") tall and about 46 cm (18") wide. The plant is dotted in late summer with magenta pink flowers, which are very striking against the silvery foliage. **'Alba'** has white flowers with silvery grey foliage. **'Angel's Blush'** has white flowers with reddish pink centres. **'Atrosanguinea'** has red flowers. (Zones 3–8)

Marsh Marigold

Caltha

Height: 46 cm (18") **Spread:** 46 cm (18") **Flower colour:** yellow, white;
foliage **Blooms:** summer **Zones:** 2–8

WHILE ON A SCHOOL FIELD TRIP MANY YEARS AGO, I HAD THE
pleasure of seeing the most magnificent marsh marigold specimen to date.
A large, established grouping of marsh marigolds was blooming like the dick-
ens along a meandering stream. One of the clumps had obviously been there
for many years because of its sheer size. Since that day, I have been striving to
transform my marsh marigold into the mammoth specimen I saw that day,
but to no avail. Must have been something in the water.

Planting

Seeding: Sow ripe seed in a partly shaded cold frame, or indoors in early spring or fall

Planting out: Spring

Spacing: 46 cm (18")

Growing

Marsh marigold grows well in **full sun** or **partial shade**. The soil should be **humus rich**, **wet to boggy**, without drainage being a concern. When division is necessary, it should be done in either early spring or fall.

Tips

Marsh marigold is frequently used as a marginal water plant, providing a blast of colour during the summer months. It works well in just about any water feature environment, as long as it receives a minimum of six hours of sunlight. It is ideal for a damp space where nothing else grows.

For those who don't have a water feature, but who want to add a marsh marigold to their landscape, this is how to do it. Punch holes into a large, plastic pail or tub filled with peat moss, leaving enough space to plant in. Dig a hole large enough to incorporate the tub, and place it into the hole. Once the peat moss is saturated, and as long is it's kept consistently moist, it should replicate the conditions of a bog garden. Once the plant begins to look spent, usually in late summer, allow it to dry out while it goes dormant.

Marsh marigold is poisonous if eaten in large quantities.

'Alba'

Recommended

C. palustris grows to a height and spread of 46 cm (18") and is a perennial native to wetlands in Saskatchewan and Manitoba. Rounded, shiny, thick green leaves form into a clump, followed by bright yellow, buttercup-like flowers. **'Alba'** is also very compact, but pure white flowers emerge in early spring. **'Flore Pleno'** (*Plena*) bears vivid yellow, double flowers. The latter cultivar requires full sun and boggy conditions to thrive.

Problems & Pests

Rust fungus, leaf gall and powdery mildew can all become problematic.

C. palustris

Masterwort

Astrantia

Height: 30–75 cm (12–30") **Spread:** 46 cm (18") **Flower colour:** greenish white, pink, maroon; foliage **Blooms:** summer to fall **Zones:** 4–8

MASTERWORT IS A VERSATILE PERENNIAL THAT LOOKS GREAT planted in a border and is adored by florists for fresh use in cut bouquets, everlasting arrangements and crafts. Perennials like this keep giving long past the growing season. When in bloom, the flowers resemble tiny, exploding fireworks displays. The flowers will last much longer than a quick flash in the sky, however. Papery bracts surround the true flowers, giving this perennial its flamboyant appeal. After an afternoon of planting masterwort in your garden, you too can have a daily fireworks display, all summer long.

Planting

Seeding: Sow seed indoors or in a cold frame in early spring

Planting out: Spring to fall

Spacing: 46 cm (18")

Growing

Masterwort prefers **full sun to partial shade**. The soil should be **moist**, **fertile** and **humus rich**. *A. major* tolerates drier conditions and requires full sun. 'Sunningdale Variegated' requires full sun to maintain its vivid foliar colour. Divide in spring. As long as the roots are kept moist, masterwort tolerates hot summer sun.

Tips

This plant is suited to moist and fertile woodland conditions or near the edges of water features, including streams, ponds or bogs.

Cover the crown with a thick layer of mulch in fall for protection from winter exposure.

Recommended

A. carniolica **'Rubra'** (dwarf red masterwort) is a compact selection, bearing deep purply red flowers surrounded by reddish green bracts. Dense, lacy foliage builds into clumps. It grows 30–40 cm (12–18") tall and 46 cm (18") wide.

A. major (great masterwort) bears distinctive flowers atop showy bracts in pale pink to white. This self-seeder produces loose clumps of dark, deeply cut foliage and blooms for a long time. Its grows to 75 cm (30") tall and 46 cm (18") wide. **'Hadspen Blood'** has deep red

A. major 'Rubra'

bracts and flowers. **'Lars'** bears dark red flowers for an especially long period of time. **'Rosea'** is a slightly taller cultivar that bears rich pink blooms. **'Rubra'** bears flowers and bracts in red to pink colours. **'Sunningdale Variegated'** is primarily grown for its variegated, creamy white and green foliage. Tall, wiry stems stand above luxurious foliage tipped with pink-flushed white blooms.

A. maxima (large masterwort) grows 46–61 cm (18–24") tall and 46 cm (18") wide. It bears large pink or white flowers atop sharp, greenish pink bracts. A vigorous producer, this plant spreads quickly underground without being invasive.

Problems & Pests

Grey mould, mildew, slugs and aphids can all be possible problems.

Meadow Rue

Thalictrum

Height: 61 cm–1.5 m (24"–5') **Spread**: 61–91 cm (24–36") **Flower colour**: pink, purple, yellow, white; foliage **Blooms**: spring or summer **Zones**: 3–8

MEADOW RUE IS PERFECT ANYWHERE IN THE BORDER, BUT I FEEL it adds a special element when placed front and centre. Like the columbine, meadow rue's lacy foliage is well behaved and attractive, so it's best displayed on the edge of a border so that it doesn't get lost among other plants. The light and airy sprays of starry flowers reach to the sky without totally obscuring the view behind. Meadow rue is easy to please and requires little in the way of care or concern. The flowers are wonderful in fresh arrangements, as an accent to bolder, brighter blossoms, from spring well into late summer.

Meadow rue's unique flowers are generally petal-less. They consist of showy sepals and stamens.

Planting

Seeding: Direct sow in fall or indoors in early spring. Keep the soil temperature at about 21° C (70° F).

Planting out: Spring

Spacing: About 61–91 cm (24–36") apart

Growing

Meadow rue prefers **light** or **partial shade** but tolerates full sun if the soil remains moist. The soil should be **humus rich**, **moist** and **well drained**. These plants rarely need to be divided. If necessary for propagation, divide in spring as the foliage begins to develop. They may take a while to re-establish themselves once they have been divided or have had their roots disturbed.

Tips

In the middle or at the back of a border, meadow rue makes a soft backdrop for bolder plants and flowers and is beautiful when naturalized in an open woodland or meadow garden.

These plants often do not emerge until quite late in spring. Mark the location where they are planted so that you do not inadvertently disturb the roots if you are cultivating the soil around them before they begin to grow.

Do not plant individual plants too close together because their stems can become tangled.

Recommended

T. aquilegifolium (columbine meadow rue) forms an upright

T. aquilegifolium

mound 61–91 cm (24–36") tall, with an equal spread. Pink or white plumes of flowers are borne in early summer. The leaves are similar in appearance to those of columbines. **'Thundercloud'** ('Purple Cloud') has dark purple flowers. **'White Cloud'** has white flowers.

T. delvayi (Yunnan meadow rue) forms a clump of narrow stems that usually needs staking. It grows 1.2–1.5 m (4–5') tall and spreads about 61 cm (24"). It bears fluffy purple or white flowers from midsummer to fall. **'Album'** has white flowers. **'Hewitt's Double'** is a popular cultivar that produces numerous tiny, purple, pompom-like flowers.

Problems & Pests

Infrequent problems with powdery mildew, rust, smut and leaf spot can occur.

Meadowsweet

Filipendula

Height: 61 cm–2.4 m (24"–8') **Spread:** 46 cm–1.2 m (18"–4') **Flower colour:** white, cream, pink; foliage **Blooms:** late spring, summer **Zones:** 2–8

THIS PRETTY PLANT IS FOUND IN MANY AREAS OF THE WORLD. Lucky for us that many of the varieties grow and thrive in our climate. I once had a very large area planted with *F. rubra* (queen of the prairie) next to a sitting area in my garden. It had a unique fragrance that drew people in. Senses other than sight are often neglected in many garden designs, but all the senses should be taken into consideration when designing and planting a garden. In order of importance, our sense of smell is second only to our visual appreciation, and meadowsweet is a perfect perennial to appeal to our noses. This is especially true in our garden 'rooms,' where we like to linger, relax and enjoy a cup of tea at the end of the day.

Planting

Seeding: Germination can be erratic. Start seed in cold frame in fall, keeping soil evenly moist.

Planting out: Spring

Spacing: 46–1.2 m (18"–4')

Growing

Meadowsweet plants prefer **partial** or **light shade** but tolerate full sun if the soil remains sufficiently moist. The soil should be **fertile**, **deep**, **humus rich** and **moist**. Meadowsweet tends to self-seed, so you may want to deadheaded, but the faded seedheads are quite attractive when left in place. Divide in spring or fall. You may need a sharp knife to divide meadowsweet because it grows thick, tough roots. Alternatively, transplanting the seedlings may be an easier way to get new plants.

Tips

Most meadowsweet species are excellent plants for bog gardens or wet sites. Grow them alongside streams or in moist meadows. Meadowsweet may also be grown in the back of a border, if kept well watered. *F. vulgaris* prefers dry soil and is a good choice for a dry area. If you want to have this plant in your garden but do not have room for the larger ones, nor the moisture, then try 'Rosea' or 'Flore Pleno,' both of which prefer average to dry soils.

F. ulmaria was used in past times to flavour mead and ale. Today it is gaining popularity for flavouring vinegars and jams. It may also be made into a pleasant wine similar to dandelion wine.

F. rubra

Recommended

F. palmata 'Rubra' vigorously produces upright plumes of deep pink flowers. Large leaves are jaggedly cut and palm shaped. It can reach 2–2.25 m (6–8') in height. (Zones 3–8)

F. purpurea (Japanese meadowsweet) forms a clump of stems and large, deeply lobed foliage. It grows up to 1.2 m (4') tall and spreads about 61 cm (24"). It bears pinkish red flowers that fade to pink in late summer. **'Elegans'** has fragrant white flowers. The spent flowerheads develop a red tint, so it is not essential to deadhead. (Zones 4–8)

F. palmata 'Rubra'

F. ulmaria 'Variegata'

F. rubra (queen-of-the-prairie) forms a large, spreading clump. It grows to be 1.8–2.4 m (6–8') tall and 1.2 m (4') wide. It bears clusters of fragrant, pink flowers from early to mid-summer. **'Venusta'** bears very showy pink flowers that fade to light pink in fall. (Zones 3–8)

F. ulmaria (meadowsweet, queen-of-the-meadow) bears creamy white flowers in large clusters. It grows to 61–91 cm (24–36") tall and 61 cm (24") wide. **'Aurea'** has yellow foliage that matures to light green as summer progresses. **'Flore Pleno'** has double flowers. **'Variegata'** foliage features creamy white and pale yellow, patchy variegations. (Zones 3–8)

F. vulgaris (dropwort, meadowsweet) is a low-growing species. It grows up to 61 cm (24") tall and 46 cm (18") wide. **'Flore Pleno'** has

white, double flowers and **'Rosea'**
has pink flowers.

Problems & Pests

Powdery mildew, rust and leaf spot
can be troublesome.

*It is thought that the name
meadowsweet is derived from the
Anglo-Saxon word medesweete
because it was often used to
flavour mead.*

*In the 16th century, it was
customary to strew floors with
rushes and herbs to warm the floor
underfoot, to freshen the air and to
combat infections; meadowsweet
was the herb Queen Elizabeth I
preferred for this purpose.*

F. ulmaria 'Variegata'

F. ulmaria

Monkshood

Aconitum

Height: 61 cm–1.8 m (24"–6') **Spread:** 30–46 cm (12–18") **Flower colour:** purple, blue, white; foliage **Blooms:** late summer **Zones:** 2–8

THE UNIQUE BLOSSOM SHAPE OF THIS PLANT GAVE rise to its common name along with a variety of other names alluding to the helmet-like shape of the flowers. Just a few examples include Turk's cap, friar's cowl, soldier's cap, helmet flower, cukoo's cap and Thor's hat. In Japan, a native species of similar appearance is called *hana-tori kabuto*, meaning literally 'flower-bird samurai helmet.' All species are attractive, but I find myself drawn to azure monkshood, *A. charmichaelii*, more often than not. It displays a dazzling combination of deeply cut foliage combined with bright blue flowers. Better yet, the flowers are on show for a lengthy period of time, allowing us to enjoy them almost all summer long.

The upper petals of monkshood flowers are fused to make an enclosure that looks like the cowl worn by medieval monks.

Planting

Seeding: Germination may be irregular. Seeds planted in garden in spring may bloom the following summer; seeds planted later will not likely bloom until next year.

Planting out: Spring; bare-rooted tubers may be planted in fall

Spacing: 30–46 cm (12–18") apart

Growing

Monkshood prefers to grow in **slightly shaded** areas but tolerates sun if the climate is cool. These plants will grow in any moist soil but prefer to be in a **rich soil** with lots of **organic matter** worked in. Monkshood prefers conditions to be on the cool side. It does poorly when the weather gets hot, particularly if conditions do not cool down at night. Mulch the roots to keep them cool. These plants require a period of dormancy in winter. Divide about every

three years in late fall or early spring. It will take some time for plants to re-establish themselves.

Tips

Monkshood plants are perfect for cool, boggy locations along streams or next to ponds. They make tall, elegant additions to a woodland garden in combination with lower-growing plants. Monkshood often

A. x *cammarum* 'Bicolour' (below)

requires staking to prevent the tall flower spikes from falling over.

When dividing or transplanting monkshoods, the crown of the plant should never be planted at a depth lower than where it was previously growing. Burying the crown any deeper will only cause it to rot and the plant to die.

Do not plant monkshoods near tree roots because these plants cannot compete with trees.

Recommended

A. x *cammarum* is a group of hybrids that contains several of the more popular cultivars. **'Bicolor'** bears blue and white flowers. The flower spikes are often branched. **'Bressingham Spire'** bears dark purple-blue flowers on strong spikes. It grows up to 91 cm (36") tall but needs no staking.

A x *cammarum* 'Bicolor' (above & below)

A. charmichaelii (azure monkshood) forms a low mound of foliage
from which the flower spikes
emerge. The foliage generally grows
to about 61 cm (24") in height, but
the plant can grow up to 1.8 m (6')
tall when in flower. Purple or blue
flowers are borne from mid- to late
summer, a little later than those of
other species. **'Arendsii'** bears dark
blue flowers on strong spikes that
need no staking.

A. napellus (common monkshood)
is an erect plant that forms a basal
mound of finely divided foliage. It
grows 91 cm–1.5 m (36–5') tall and
spreads 30–46 cm (12–18"). This
plant bears dark purple-blue flowers
from mid- to late summer.

Problems & Pests

Delphinium leaf tier moth larvae,
aphids, powdery mildew, downy
mildew, rust and different forms of
rot may become problematic.

A. napellus (above & below)

Mullein

Verbascum

Height: 91 cm –1.8 m (3–6') **Spread:** 46–61 cm (18–24") **Flower colour:** pink, purple, maroon, yellow, white, orange; foliage **Blooms:** summer
Zones: 3–8

YELLOW-FLOWERED MULLEIN IS DRAMATIC IN STATURE alone, but it is far more striking when planted beside any purple-leaved plant. Certainly the trend of late has been to co-ordinate foliage and blooms in contrasting colours to emphasize their vividness. Purple or burgundy and bright lemon yellow play off one another, tricking the eye into thinking that the yellow is brighter and that the deep purple and burgundy are far richer. This combination also creates a stage to showcase the silver-white, felted foliage of *V. bombyciferum.* Any of the coral bells, the purple-leaved *Prunus* trees or shrubs or the tried and true Thunderchild ornamental crabapple tree (*Malus* 'Thunderchild') would be stellar accompaniments for this statuesque beauty.

V. nigrum *was used as an herbal remedy for a number of ailments, including colic and coughs. Witches from the Middle Ages were said to use it in their love potions, hence the common name of hag taper.*

Planting

Seeding: Start seeds in containers in cold frame in late spring or early summer; may not flower until third season

Planting out: Spring

Spacing: 46 cm (18") apart

Growing

Grow this plant in **full sun**. The soil should be **poor, alkaline and well drained**. When planted in soil that is too rich, the plants become floppy and fall over. Mullein will rot if planted in a location with moist soil or where water from run-off or overflowing gutters hits the foliage.

This plant is short-lived, but self-seeding will keep it growing in your garden. Removing the spent flower spikes may encourage new blooms. Mullein may be divided in spring, though this is rarely necessary.

M. bombyciferum (1st year below & 2nd year above)

V. bombyciferum (above & below)

Tips

Use in the middle or at the back of a sunny border. Mullein also looks good in natural gardens.

Recommended

V. bombyciferum (giant silver mullein) produces silvery white, felted leaves that form into a rosette initially, later sending out tall flower spikes covered in bright yellow blossoms. The species can grow 1.5–1.8 m (5–6') tall and 46–61 cm (18–24") wide. **'Banana Custard'** produces green foliage with a silvery cast and tall, pastel yellow flower spikes.

V. nigrum (black mullein, hag taper) is a clump-forming perennial that reaches 91 cm (36") in height. Tall spikes displaying yellow flowers with purple centres emerge from the central rosette of foliage. The deep green leaves taper at the tips and carry a dense layer of black hairs. (Zones 4–8)

V. phoeniceum (purple mullein) produces a large clump of broad leaves in a rosette form. A tall flower spike emerges from the centre bearing flowers in shades of white, pink, pale lavender, maroon and deep violet. The species grows 61 cm–1.2 m (2–4') tall and 30–46 cm (12–18") wide. The seed of *V. phoeniceum* is often sold as a 'mixed hybrid,' but it isn't a hybrid at all; it's just a mix of different colours of this particularly variable species. (Zones 4–8)

Problems & Pests

Powdery mildew, fungal leaf spot and caterpillars may cause problems.

Common mullein (Verbascum thapus) *was brought to North America by European settlers, who used it as a remedy for coughs and diarrhea. It was smoked by American Indians to treat asthma, bronchitis and other lung problems. An insecticide for mosquito larvae is also made from the methanol extracted from this plant.*

Obedient Plant
False Dragonhead
Physostegia

Height: 46 cm–1.2 m (18"–4') **Spread:** 61 cm (24") **Flower colour:** pink, purple, white **Blooms:** mid-summer to fall **Zones:** 2–8

MY FAMILY MADE AN INTERESTING DISCOVERY IN OUR GARDEN recently. They were enchanted by the notion that each individual flower along the stalk of this plant can be positioned in different directions and will stay put where it is placed. Although obedient plant isn't currently on the top ten favourites list of gardeners in Saskatchewan and Manitoba, it continues to have a bright future. All the more reason to stock up on more of them in the upcoming season. Obedient plant is very well suited to a number of settings, including children's gardens for the obvious appeal, and butterfly and cutting gardens. Once cut, the flowers maintain their colour and strength in fresh arrangements, offering a soft touch to summery bouquet.

Planting

Seeding: Sow in early fall or in spring. Soil temperature should be about 21–24° C (70–75° F). Protect fall-started seedlings from winter cold.

Planting out: Spring or fall

Spacing: 61 cm (24") apart

Growing

Obedient plant prefers **full sun** and tolerates partial or light shade. The soil should be of **average to high fertility** and **moist**. In a fertile soil, this plant will be more vigorous and will possibly need staking. Choose a compact cultivar to avoid the need for staking. Plants can become invasive. Divide in early to mid-spring, once ground can be worked, every two years or so to curtail invasiveness.

Tips

Use in borders, cottage gardens and informal and natural gardens. Obedient plant can be cut for use in fresh arrangements.

Recommended

P. virginiana has a spreading root system from which upright stems sprout. It grows 61 cm–1.2 m (24"–4') tall and spreads 61 cm (24"), or more. **'Miss Manners'** grows tall and sturdy, producing pure white blooms atop dark green foliage. This cultivar doesn't require staking and was developed for its non-invasive habit. **'Summer Snow'** is a compact, less invasive plant with white flowers. **'Variegata'** is a desirable variegated specimen with cream-margined leaves and bright

P. virginiana

pink flowers. **'Vivid'** grows 46–61 cm (18–24") tall and bears medium purple-pink flowers on a compact form. Obedient plant blooms late in the season, averaging two to four weeks in mid-summer to fall.

Problems & Pests

Rare problems with rust and slugs are possible.

'Variegata'

Ostrich Fern
Fiddlehead Fern
Matteuccia

Height: 91 cm–1.2 m (3–4') **Spread:** 61–91 cm (24–36") **Flower colour:** green-brown to black fronds **Blooms:** fertile fronds appear in spring and remain until fall **Zones:** 2–8

I HAVE OFTEN HEARD THAT THIS FERN CAN BECOME A PROBLEM because of its spreading, invasive nature. I have to admit that I have never experienced this; in fact, I feel quite the opposite. I usually respond with a smile and let people know that more emerging fronds only allows for more steamed fiddleheads on their dinner plates. My first experience with ferns was in my grandmother's garden. Even as a child, I knew the way she combined ferns and daylilies was something special. The possibile garden uses for this plant are endless because ostrich ferns blend beautifully with just about anything. Plant them en masse for impact, together with bold-flowered plants as an accent or in a woodland setting to showcase their native heritage.

*Most ferns pre-date
the dinosaurs.*

Planting

Seeding: Sow ripe spores indoors in early spring at 15°C (59°F)

Planting out: Spring to fall

Spacing: 61–91 cm (24–36")

Growing

Ostrich fern prefers **partial to full shade**. The soil should be **organically rich, moist, neutral to acidic** and **well drained**. Established clumps can be divided in early spring. Make sure to plant the crown slightly above soil level to prevent crown rot.

Tips

Ferns are native to shady, woodland settings under canopies of large trees. Areas that simulate these conditions are best. They also work well in mixed borders, en masse and in foliage gardens for texture.

Recommended

M. struthiopteris is easy to grow and bears long, broad, feather-like fronds from the centre or crown. It has a light, airy appearance. Dark brown to black, fertile fronds emerge from the centre in late summer.

Problems & Pests

Ostrich ferns are carefree; however, crown rot can occur when the crown has been planted too deeply. This can also occur in locations with poor drainage.

Penstemon

Penstemon

Height: 46 cm–1.5 m (18"–5') **Spread:** 30–61 cm (12–24") **Flower colour:** white, yellow, pink, purple, red **Blooms:** spring, summer, fall **Zones:** 3–8

AN EYE-CATCHING GROUPING OF 'HUSKER RED' WAS RESPONSIBLE for my personal 'penstemania.' Gardeners have created entire websites devoted to this easy-to-keep, drought-tolerant perennial. 'Husker Red' was selected as the Perennial Plant of the Year in 1996 and since that time has become a garden classic. I have to warn you, however, that planting one will leave you wanting more. Who can help themselves, with the huge selection of penstemons available in such a great range of colours? Penstemon is a dream to grow and requires little for its success, but well-drained soil is imperative because this plant cannot tolerate wet feet.

Planting

Seeding: Start indoors in late summer or early spring, keeping soil temperature at 13–18° C (55–64° F)

Planting out: Spring or fall

Spacing: 30–61 cm (12–24")

Growing

Penstemon prefers **full sun** but tolerates partial shade. The soil should be of **average to rich fertility** and **well drained**. These plants are drought tolerant and can rot in wet soil. Mulch in winter to protect from cold. Pinch plants when they are approximately 30 cm (12") tall to encourage bushy growth. Divide every two to three years in spring.

Tips

Ideal for use in a mixed or herbaceous border, cottage or rock garden.

Twiggy branches pushed into the ground around young penstemon plants will provide them with support as they grow.

P. digitalis 'Husker Red'

Recommended

P. barbatus (beard-lip penstemon) is an upright, rounded perennial. It grows 46–91 cm (18–36") tall and spreads 30–46 cm (12–18"). Red or pink flowers are borne from early summer to early fall. **'Alba'** has white flowers. **'Elfin Pink'** bears compact spikes of clear pink. **'Hyacinth Mix'** is a mix of pink, lilac, blue and scarlet. **'Praecox Nanus'** ('Nanus Rondo') is a compact, dwarf plant that grows about half the size of the species. It bears pink, purple or red flowers. **'Prairie Dusk'** has tall spikes of tubular, rose purple flowers and **'White Bedder'** bears white flowers that are tinged in pink.

P. digitalis (foxglove penstemon) is a very hardy, upright, semi-evergreen perennial. It grows 61cm–1.5 m (24"–5') tall and spreads 46–61 cm (18–24"). It bears white flowers,

P. digitalis 'Husker Red' (below)

often veined with purple, all summer. **'Husker Red'** has red stems with red-purple new foliage and is good for mass planting. The flowers are white and veined with red. (Zones 4–8)

P. fruticosus **'Purple Haze'** is slightly different than other penstemons. It has evergreen foliage and is considered a subshrub. Typically a mounding plant, when placed near a wall edge or overhang, it will trail over the side for a showy display of abundant purple flowers in late spring. Great for rock gardens or tiered beds as edging. It may require some winter protection. (Zones 4–8)

Problems & Pests

Powdery mildew, rust and leaf spot can occur, but serious problems are rare.

Over 200 species of Penstemon *are native to varied habitats, from mountains to open plains, throughout North and South America.*

Peony

Paeonia

Height: 30 cm–1.2 m (12"–4') **Spread:** 15–80 cm (6–32") **Flower colour:** white, cream white, yellow, pink, red, purple; foliage **Blooms:** spring, early summer **Zones:** 2–8

IT'S NOT UNCOMMON TO SEE MATURE PEONY PLANTS STILL standing tall and blooming profusely in old, abandoned farmyards. The buildings may have fallen down over the years and be in a serious state of disrepair, but certain perennials continue to flourish despite the tall grasses and weeds that seem set to overtake them. Peonies just never fail to amaze me with their resilience, strength and unequalled beauty. I have only one problem with them, however. I never seem to install peony hoops around their bases until it's too late. I have been found in the garden long after they're tall and filled out, carefully pulling the foliage through the rings. I think it's time to try the new compact hybrids that do not require staking, for their sake and mine.

Planting

Seeding: Not recommended. Seeds may take two to three years to germinate and many more years to grow to flowering size.

Planting out: Spring or fall

Spacing: 30–80 cm (12–32")

Growing

Peony prefers **full sun**, but it tolerates partial shade. The planting site should be well prepared before the plants are introduced. Peonies like **fertile**, **humus-rich**, **moist** and **well-drained** soil, to which lots of compost (but not composted manure) has been added. Division is not required, but it is usually the best way to propagate new plants, and should be done in fall.

P. lactiflora cultivar

Tips

These are wonderful plants that look great in a border when combined with other early-flowering plants.

In the past, peonies were used to cure a variety of ailments. They are named after Paion, who was the physician to the Greek gods.

P. tenuifolia

Despite their exotic appearance, peonies are tough and hardy perennials that can survive winter temperatures of up to -40° C (-40° F).

They may be underplanted with bulbs and other plants that will die down by mid-summer, when the emerging foliage of peonies will hide the dying foliage of spring plants.

Planting depth is a very important factor in determining whether or not a peony will flower. Tubers planted too shallowly or too deeply will not flower. The buds or eyes on the tuber should be 2.5–5 cm (1–2") below the soil surface.

Cut back the flowers after blooming and remove any blackened leaves to prevent the spread of grey mould. Red peonies are more susceptible to disease.

Use wire tomato cages or peony hoops to support the stems and top-heavy flowers in early spring, shortly after the stems begin to emerge.

Recommended

Peonies may be listed as cultivars of a certain species or as interspecies hybrids. There are hundreds available.

P. lactiflora (common garden peony, Chinese peony) forms a clump of red-tinged stems and dark green foliage. It grows up to 75 cm (30") tall, with an equal spread, and bears single, fragrant white or pink flowers with yellow stamens. Some popular hybrid cultivars are '**Dawn Pink,**' with single, rose pink flowers; '**Duchesse de Nemours,**' which has fragrant, double, white flowers tinged yellow at the base of each interior petal; and '**Prince of Darkness,**' with double, velvety, dark red flowers in mid-season. These cultivars are often sold as hybrids and not as cultivars of this species.

'Sarah Bernhardt' displays large, double, fragrant pink flowers.

P. officinalis (common peony) forms a clump of slightly hairy stems and deeply lobed foliage. It bears single red or pink flowers with yellow stamens. It grows 61–80 cm (24–32") tall, with an equal spread. Two of the cultivars are **'Alba Plena'** with white, double flowers and **'Rubra Plena'** with red, double flowers. (Zones 3–8)

P. suffruticosa (tree peony) is a shrubby plant that develops woody stems. A vast number of hardy and tender cultivars are available in different colours and sizes. Tree peonies are often grafted onto garden peony roots to improve their cold hardiness. The following are considered to be hardy and can grow quite tall, reaching heights of 1. 2 m (4') or more. They produce bold foliage and very showy flowers. **'Deep Dark Purple'** bears intensely fragrant, fully double, dark magenta flowers approximately 15–20 cm (6–8") wide. **'Godaishu'** has very large, upfacing, semi-double, white blossoms. **'High Noon'** bears bright yellow flowers showcasing a central cluster of orange stamens. (Zones 3–8)

P. tenuifolia (fernleaf peony) looks slightly different than the aforementioned species. It exhibits delicate, finely cut foliage and single, deep red flowers that emerge earlier than those of garden peonies. It grows 30–46 cm (12–18") tall and wide. (Zones 3–8)

Problems & Pests

Peonies may have trouble with *Verticillium* wilt, ringspot virus, tip blight, stem rot, grey mould, leaf blotch, nematodes, tarnished plant bug or Japanese beetles.

Phlox

Phlox

Height: 5 cm–1.2 m (2"–4') **Spread:** 30–91 cm (12–36") **Flower colour:** white, blue, purple, pink, red **Blooms:** late spring, fall **Zones:** 2–8

SO MANY PHLOX, SO LITTLE TIME. THEY ALL HAVE A NUMBER of great qualities, but I love the scented varieties the most. They produce a heady, sweet scent that conjures up all sorts of romantic pictures in my mind when I smell them. The taller varieties are ideal for cutting because they last quite a long time, carrying the fragrance wherever they go. For those with a butterfly or hummingbird garden, phlox effectively attracts both, though the richly coloured types are far more attractive to hummingbirds and can substitute for the bright red feeders you might hang from your soffits.

Planting

Seeding: Not recommended

Planting out: Spring

Spacing: 30–91 cm (12–36") apart

Growing

Moss phlox prefers to grow in **partial shade**. Garden phlox and wild sweet William prefer to grow in **full to partial sun**. All three species like **fertile, humus-rich, moist, well-drained** soil. Divide in fall or spring. Creeping phlox spreads out horizontally as it grows. The stems grow roots where they touch the ground. These plants are easily propagated by detaching the rooted stems in spring or early fall. Do not prune creeping phlox in fall—it is an evergreen and will have next spring's flowers already forming.

Tips

Low-growing species are useful in a rock garden or at the front of a border. Taller species may be used in the middle of a border where they

P. subulata (above)

are particularly effective if planted in groups.

Garden phlox requires good air circulation to prevent mildew. Wild sweet William is more resistant to powdery mildew than garden phlox.

Recommended

P. **'Chatahoochee'** is a low, bushy plant. It grows 15–30 cm (6–12") tall and spreads about 30 cm (12"). It

P. paniculata

P. paniculata 'David'

P. paniculata 'Eva Cullum' (above)
P. subulata 'Candy Stripe' (below)

produces lavender blue flowers with darker purple centres for most of the summer and early fall. This hybrid enjoys a lightly shaded spot in the garden. (Zones 4–8)

P. maculata (wild sweet William, early phlox) forms an upright clump of hairy stems and narrow leaves that are sometimes spotted with red. It grows 61–91 cm (24–36") tall and spreads 46–61 cm (18–24"). Pink, purple or white flowers are borne in conical clusters in the first half of summer. This species resists powdery mildew. **'Miss Lingard'** bears large clusters of fragrant, white flowers early in the season. **'Omega'** bears white flowers with light pink centres. **'Rosalinde'** bears dark pink flowers. 'Miss Lingard' and 'Rosalinde' are taller than the species, usually 75 cm (30") or taller. (Zones 3–8)

P. paniculata (garden phlox) has many cultivars. They vary greatly in size from 50 cm–1.2 m (20"–4') tall with a spread of 61–91 cm (24–36"). There are many colours available, often with contrasting centres. Garden phlox blooms in summer and fall. **'David'** bears white flowers and is resistant to powdery mildew. **'Eva Cullum'** is a compact phlox, bearing pink flowers with a dark red eye. **'Norah Leigh'** grows to 75 cm (30") tall with creamy white variegated leaves. The flowers are bright white with a dark pink eye. **'Starfire'** bears crimson red flowers. **'Windsor'** has deep pink flowers. (Zones 3–8)

P. stolonifera (creeping phlox) is a low, spreading plant. It grows 10–15 cm (4–6") tall, spreads about 30 cm (12") and bears flowers in shades of

purple in spring. This species tolerates heavy shade. **'Ariane'** produces
white flowers and pale green foliage.
'Blue Ridge' bears soft blue blooms
and **'Sherwood Purple'** has purplish blue flowers.

P. subulata (creeping phlox, moss
phlox, moss pinks) is very low
growing, only 5–15 cm (2–6") tall,
with a spread of 50 cm (20"). It also
has cultivars with flowers that
bloom in various colours from late
spring to early summer. **'Candy
Stripe'** bears bicoloured pink and
white flowers. **'G.F. Wilson'** vigorously produces a mat of lavender
blue flowers among tightly packed,
tiny leaves. **'Rosette'** is a very compact, mounding perennial that bears
pale pink flowers in mid-spring.

Problems & Pests

Occasional problems with powdery
mildew, stem canker, rust, leaf spot,
leaf miners and caterpillars are
possible.

P. maculata

*Phlox comes in many forms, from
low-growing creepers to tall,
clump-forming uprights. The
many species can be found in
varied climates from dry, exposed
mountainsides to moist, sheltered
woodlands.*

P. subulata

Pincushion Flower

Scabiosa

Height: 30–61 cm (12–24") **Spread:** 61 cm (24") **Flower colour:** purple, blue, white, pink **Blooms:** summer **Zones:** 2–8

THE NAME 'SCABIOSA' IS DERIVED FROM THE WORD 'SCABIES,' which is the Latin word for mange. Not the most complimentary name for such a pretty plant, but it was believed to give relief to those infected with mange when the infected area was rubbed with the leaves. Never having the misfortune of getting mange, I grow pincushion flower for its power to attract a vast array of butterflies to my garden. Little is needed for this perennial to flourish throughout the summer, but for maximum bloom, it is helpful to remove the flowers once they begin to look spent.

The rounded, densely petalled blooms serve as a perfect landing pad for butterflies.

Planting

Seeding: Direct sow in spring or summer

Planting out: Spring

Spacing: 61 cm (24") apart

Growing

Pincushion flower prefers **full sun** but tolerates partial shade. The soil should be **light, moderately fertile, neutral** or **alkaline** and **well drained.** Divide in early spring whenever the clumps become over-grown.

S. caucasica cultivar

Tips

These plants look best when they are planted in groups in a bed or border. They are also used as cut flowers.

Remove the flowers as they fade to promote a longer flowering period. Cutting flowers at their peak every few days for indoor use will make this maintenance chore more enjoyable.

Recommended

S. caucasica forms a basal rosette of narrow leaves. Blue or lavender flowers are borne on long stems that grow up to 61 cm (24") tall, with an equal spread. **'Fama'** bears sky blue flowers with silvery white centres. **'House's Hybrids'** (Isaac House Hybrids) is a group of slightly smaller plants with large, shaggy, blue flowers. **'Miss Wilmont'** bears white flowers.

Several hybrids have been developed from crosses between *S. caucasica* and ***S. columbaria***, a smaller species. These hybrids may be listed as cultivars of either species.

S. Butterfly Blue'

'Butterfly Blue' bears lavender blue flowers from early summer until frost. **'Pink Mist'** grows about 30 cm (12") tall and bears many pink blooms all season. (Zones 3–8)

Problems & Pests

Pincushion flower or other kinds of *Scabiosa* rarely have any problems. Sometimes aphids can be trouble-some.

Pinks

Dianthus

Height: 5–46 cm (2–18") **Spread:** 20–61 cm (8–24") **Flower colour:** pink, red, white, lilac purple **Blooms:** spring, summer **Zones:** 2–8

THE COMMON NAME PINKS DOES NOT REFER TO THE COLOUR of the flowers but to the fringed edges of the petals. More specifically, the fringing resembles an edge trimmed with pinking shears. Seamstresses will certainly recognize the reference. If you're not familiar with the name pinks, you may recognize the other common name for this genus: carnation. If maiden pinks are more up your alley, then this tells me you prefer a low-maintenance perennial with a long blooming season. As with most perennials, when the clump begins to die out in the centre, simply dig it up, divide it into sections and dispose of the centre portion; then replant the rest. Now there's enough to share, and it really is that simple.

Planting

Seeding: Not recommended; cultivars do not come true to type from seed

Planting out: Spring

Spacing: 20–61 cm (8–24") apart

Growing

Pinks prefer **full sun** but tolerate light shade. A **well-drained, neutral** or **alkaline soil** is required. The most important factor in the successful cultivation of pinks is drainage—they hate to stand in water. Mix sand or gravel into their area of the flowerbed to encourage good drainage.

Pinks may be difficult to propagate by division. It is often easier to take cuttings in summer, once flowering has finished. Cuttings should be 2.5–8 cm (1–3") long. Strip the lower leaves from the cuttings and keep them humid, but be sure to give them some ventilation so that fungal problems do not set in. Division each year or two will keep plants vigorous. Divide pinks in early spring.

Tips

Pinks are excellent plants for rock gardens and rock walls, and for edging flower borders and walkways.

Deadhead as the flowers fade to prolong blooming. Leave a few flowers in place to go to seed. The plants will self-seed quite easily. Seedlings may differ from the parent plants, often with new and interesting results.

The tiny, delicate petals of pinks can be used to decorate cakes. Be sure to remove the white part at the base of the petals before using them or they will be bitter.

D. plumarius cultivar

D. plumarius cultivar

The Cheddar pink is a rare and protected species in Britain. It was discovered in the 18th century by British botanist Samuel Brewer, and it became as locally famous as Cheddar cheese.

D. gratianopolitanus

Recommended

D. x *allwoodii* (Allwood pinks) forms a compact mound and bears flowers in a wide range of colours. Cultivars generally grow 20–46 cm (8–18") tall, with an equal spread. **'Beatrix'** bears double, pink, fragrant clusters of flowers with narrow, grassy foliage. **'Doris'** bears semi-double, salmon pink flowers with dark pink centres. It is popular as a cut flower. **'Laced Romeo'** bears spice-scented, red flowers with cream-margined petals. **'Sweet Wivelsfield'** bears fragrant, two-toned flowers in a variety of colours.

D. *deltoides* (maiden pinks) grows 15–30 cm (6–12") tall and about 30 cm (12") wide. The plant forms a mat of foliage and flowers in spring. This is a popular species in rock gardens. **'Brilliant'** ('Brilliancy,' 'Brilliance') bears dark red flowers.

D. gratianopolitanus (Cheddar pink) usually grows about 15 cm (6") tall but can grow up to 30 cm (12") tall and 46–61 cm (18–24") wide. This plant is long-lived and forms a very dense mat of evergreen, silver-grey foliage with sweetly scented blooms in summer. **'Blue Hills'** bears deep-pink flowers and silvery blue foliage to a height of 15 cm (6"). **'Mountain Mist'** can tolerate heat better than other *Dianthus* cultivars. It bears soft pink flowers that poke through mounds of blue foliage. **'Petite'** is an even smaller plant, growing 5–10 cm (2–4") tall, with pink flowers.

D. plumarius (cottage pink) is noteworthy for its role in the development of the many popular cultivars known as garden pinks. It is generally 30–46 cm (12–18") tall and 61 cm (24") wide, although smaller cultivars are available. They all flower in spring and into summer if deadheaded regularly.

D. plumarius

The flowers can be single, semidouble or fully double and come in many colours. **'Spring Beauty'** bears double flowers in many colours with more strongly frilled edges than the species. (Zones 3–8)

Problems & Pests

Providing good drainage and air circulation will keep most fungal problems away. Occasional problems with slugs, blister beetles, sow bugs and grasshoppers are possible.

D. deltoides

Poppy
Papaver

Height: 30 cm –1.2 m (12"–4') **Spread:** 30–91 cm (12–36") **Flower colour:** yellow, red, orange, pink, white; foliage **Blooms:** spring, early summer **Zones:** 2–8

NEVER BEFORE HAD I SEEN POPPIES LIKE THE ONES IN THE Cotswolds in England. I was staying in a little town called Stow-on-the-Wold, and decided to go for a walk to watch the sunset. I hiked down to the bottom of a very large hill to an old Roman well which is the town's main water supply. Behind the well was a narrow winding pathway that led up a wooded hillside. On impulse I decided to explore the rather steep pathway. At the top, the trees disappeared, and I was suddenly looking at an entire field completely filled with poppies. In the background was the most beautiful sunset, perfectly echoing the pinks, reds and scarlets of the poppies. I'll never look at poppies the same way again.

Planting

Seeding: Direct sow in spring or fall

Planting out: Spring

Spacing: 30–91 cm (12–36") apart

Growing

Grow these plants in a location that receives **full sun**. The soil should be **average to fertile** and must be **well drained**. Plants will die back after flowering and send up fresh new growth in late summer, which should be left in place for winter insulation. Division is rarely required but may be done in fall once the new rosettes begin to form.

Tips

Small groups of poppies look attractive in an early summer border.

Because poppies go completely dormant by mid-summer, they may leave a bare spot in a border. Baby's breath and catmint plants make good companions and will fill in any blank spots left in the border later in summer.

P. nudicaule (above & below)

Use of poppy seeds in cooking and baking can be traced as far back as the ancient Egyptians.

Recommended

P. nudicaule (Iceland poppy) grows to 30–46 cm (12–18") tall and wide. Iceland poppies freely self-seed and are usually biennial. The colours range from yellow, white and orange to pastel shades of salmon and pink. Light-green, hairy stems support the delicate, single, cup-shaped flowers that emerge from mounds of lacy blue-green leaves.

P. orientale (Oriental poppy) forms an upright, oval clump. It grows 46 cm–1.2 m (18"–4') tall and spreads 61–91 cm (24–36"). Red, scarlet, pink or white flowers with prominent black stamens are borne in late spring and early summer. **'Allegro'** has bright scarlet-red flowers. **'Brilliant'** matures to a similar size and produces vibrant red flowers in late spring. The hairy foliage dies down by mid-summer. **'Carneum'** grows

P. orientale cultivars (above & below)

75–91 cm (30–36") tall and 46–61 cm (18–24") wide. In late spring, enormous, satiny, soft salmon flowers emerge from large clumps of coarse, hairy foliage. **'Pizzicato'** is a dwarf cultivar, with flowers in a wide range of colours. It forms a mound 46–61 cm (18–24") tall, with an equal spread.

Problems & Pests

Problems with powdery mildew, leaf smut, grey mould, root rot and damping off may occur.

The use of poppies to pay homage to the armed forces began after WWI, when the British legion sold poppies to commemorate soldiers who died in that war. Poppies were chosen because they grew in vast numbers on the battlefields of Flanders, Belgium.

P. orientale cultivars (above & below)

Potentilla
Cinquefoil
Potentilla

Height: 8–46 cm (3–18") **Spread:** 15–61 cm (6–24") **Flower colour:** yellow, red, orange, pink, white; foliage **Blooms:** summer **Zones:** 2–8

POTENTILLA INSTANTLY BRINGS TO MIND THE WOODY ORNAMENTALS or shrubs so commonly found in landscape designs. Most people don't even realize that there is a lesser known herbaceous ornamental called potentilla or cinquefoil. Deservedly, it is gaining in popularity and offers a low-growing alternative to more familiar perennials such as tickseed or asters. Potentilla is similar to the shrubby types when you compare the flowers, however. The perennial bears blossoms reminiscent of tiny, single roses in striking, bright colours and warm hues atop hairy, green foliage. Although this plant has cultural preferences similar to its shrubby relatives, it is unique unto itself and ideal for most garden settings.

Planting

Seeding: Start in containers in early spring; if seeding indoors, keep soil moist and temperature at about 21° C (70° F)

Planting out: Spring or fall

Spacing: 15–61 cm (6–24") apart

Growing

Potentilla grows equally well in **full sun** or **partial shade**. These plants are very drought tolerant but should be protected from hot afternoon sun. The soil should be of **poor to average fertility** and **well drained**. Divide in spring or fall, whenever the centre of the plant begins to thin or die out.

Tips

Potentilla plants make attractive additions to borders, rock gardens and rock walls. Group taller types close together to support each other. Cut back the cultivar 'Miss Willmott' to keep it neat and compact.

Recommended

P. nepalensis (Nepal cinquefoil) forms a loose clump of trailing stems. It grows 30–46 cm (12–18") tall and spreads up to 61 cm (24"), bearing rose pink flowers from late spring to early summer. **'Miss Willmott'** bears scarlet flowers with darker, contrasting centres.

P. neumanniana is mat forming, growing about 10 cm (4") tall and spreading 30 cm (12"). It bears bright yellow flowers from spring through summer. **'Nana'** is even more compact, growing 8 cm (3")

P. neumanniana 'Nana'

tall and spreading 15 cm (6"). The flowers are yellow. (Zones 3–8)

P. tridentata (three-toothed cinquefoil, shrubby fivefingers) is a low-growing species that produces a mat of shiny everygreen foliage. Tiny, rounded, white flowers balance out the leaves, which change to bronze in the fall. It grows 10–25 cm (4–10") tall and 25–30 cm (10–12") wide.

Problems & Pests

Occasional problems with mildew, leaf blister, rust and fungal leaf spot can usually be prevented with good drainage.

P. nepalensis 'Miss Willmott'

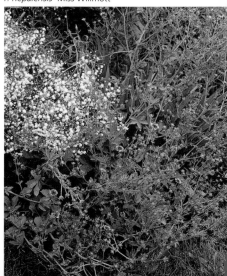

Prairie Mallow

Sidalcea

Height: 61 cm–1.2 m (24"–4') **Spread:** 30 cm (12") **Flower colour:** pink
Blooms: summer **Zones:** 4–8

PRAIRIE MALLOW REMINDS ME OF A BABY HOLLYHOCK—ALL OF
the splendor of a hollyhock but in a more manageable size. This perennial is
ideal for gardeners who adore hollyhocks but who don't have a hope of ever
growing them because of a lack of suitable space. This is one perennial that
will look great in any garden regardless of your design style. I remember seeing
a similar variety growing wild in the
Wenatchee Mountains in Washington
State. I was so impressed with the
wave after wave of colour that
graced the area for most of the
summer that I had to come home
and plant some mallow in my
garden. Only a small area of my
garden is reserved for this
beauty, but it will always
remind me of the fields of
prairie mallow that I had the
opportunity to enjoy many
years ago.

Planting

Seeding: Sow seed indoors or in a cold frame in spring or fall

Planting out: Spring

Spacing: 30 cm (12")

Growing

Prairie mallow prefers **full sun** but tolerates partial sun. The soil should be of **average fertility**, **organically rich**, **moist**, **light**, **sandy**, **neutral to slightly acidic** and **well drained**. Division should be done in spring. Winter mulch may be necessary for protection, with or without reliable snow coverage. Cut back after blooming to encourage a second flush of flowers. Prairie mallow generally dislikes lime soils.

Tips

Prairie mallow has an old world appearance, traditional enough for mixed beds or borders and cottage gardens. It is stunning when planted in masses, allowing for bunch upon bunch of fresh cut flowers.

Recommended

S. malviflora (checkerbloom) grows into an upright, narrow clump of rounded, kidney-shaped leaves. Tall spikes of pink flowers are borne in summer. **'Brilliant'** grows 61–75 cm (24–30") tall and 30 cm (12") wide and bears deep pink flowers. **'Elsie Heugh'** has large, soft pink-fringed flowers. It grows 91 cm–1.2 m (3–4') tall. **'Party Girl'** is a mix that produces different shades of pink. Its mature size is 61–91 cm (24–36") tall. All of the flowers display a cluster of prominent stamens.

S. malviflora cultivar (above); *S. malviflora* (below)

Problems & Pests

Slugs and rust are the only potential problems.

Prickly Pear Cactus

Opuntia

Height: 15–30 (6–12") **Spread:** 20–30 cm (8–12") **Flower colour:** yellow; foliage **Blooms:** summer **Zones:** 3–8

WHILE I WAS GROWING UP, MY FAMILY WOULD SPEND TIME IN wild areas of Saskatchewan that have a large population of cacti. Soon after arriving, in fact, before the car door had even closed, one or more of us would kneel, sit or lay on a prickly pear cactus while playing. Upon hearing the inevitable screams, my mom would quickly come to the rescue, patiently removing the spines from our little behinds, knees and fingers. Needless to say, if you grow cactus, take a cue from my mom, and always have tweezers ready.

The edible fruits (tunas) are reddish green and egg shaped with ruby red pulp that tastes a little like watermelon.

Planting

Seeding: Sow presoaked seed indoors in winter or early spring at 21°C (70°F)

Planting out: Spring, summer

Spacing: 20–30 cm (8–12")

Growing

Prickly pear cactus prefers **full to partial sun**. The soil should be of **average fertility**, **sharply drained**, **gritty** and **organically rich**. Propagate root stem segments when available.

Always use a piece of folded newspaper to handle this plant. Make sure to dispose of the newspaper afterwards to avoid getting pricked by thorns that may have embedded themselves in the paper.

Tips

Prickly pear cactus is perfect for alpine or rock gardens, trough or desert gardens, xeriscaping or a well-drained, mixed border.

Contact with the bristles can cause an intense irritation to the skin. It is very important to wear protective gloves because the bristles are very difficult to remove from the skin.

Recommended

O. humifusa will slowly mature to a 15–30 cm (6–12") height and a 20–30 cm (8–12") spread. Round to oval, flat, thick pads are covered with bristles and the occasional prickle. The fleshy pads grow on top of one another, appearing to balance edge to edge. Large, bright yellow, papery flowers with prominent stamens emerge on the pad edges.

O. humifusa (photos this page)

The flowers last only for a couple of days, after which the fruit begins to develop.

Problems & Pests

Black and leaf spot, mealy bugs, scale, viruses and bacterial soft rot.

Primrose

Primula

Height: 10–91 cm (4–36") **Spread:** 15–61 cm (6–24") **Flower colour:** red, orange, pink, purple, blue, white, cream, yellow; foliage **Blooms:** spring, early summer **Zones:** 2–8

DESPITE THE MISCONCEPTION THAT IT'S DIFFICULT, IF NOT impossible, to grow primroses on the prairies, there are a tremendous number of primrose varieties to choose from. I'm here to tell you that it is possible, and in fact incredibly easy to grow them in Saskatchewan and Manitoba. The vast majority of primrose varieties bloom in spring, early spring at that, a seeming confirmation that the cold winter months are fading away and that warm spring days are on the horizon. Primroses require little in the way of care. Moist, organically rich soil and lots of sunshine go a long way. Once established, you'll reap the rewards of endless waves of colourful, sunny spring blossoms for many years to come.

Planting

Seeding: Sow ripe seeds directly in the garden at any time of year; start them indoors in early spring or in cold frame in fall or late winter

Planting out: Spring

Spacing: 15–61 cm (6–24") apart

Growing

Choose a location for these plants with **full sun** or **partial shade**. The soil should be **moderately fertile, humus rich**, **moist**, **well drained** and **neutral** or **slightly acidic**. Pull off yellowing or dried leaves in fall for fresh new growth in spring. Overgrown clumps should be divided after flowering or in early fall.

Tips

Primroses may be incorporated into many areas of the garden. Moisture-lovers may be included in a bog garden or a moist spot. Woodland primroses grow well in a naturalistic garden or under the shade of taller shrubs and perennials in a border or rock garden.

P. florindae (above)

Species with flowers on tall stems look excellent when planted in masses; species with solitary flowers peeking out from the foliage are interesting when dotted throughout the garden in odd spots.

Recommended

P. auricula (auricula primrose) forms a rosette of smooth, waxy foliage. Large flowers are clustered at the tops of stout stems. The plant grows up to 20 cm (8") tall and spreads 25 cm (10"). The flowers are

usually yellow or cream, but there are many cultivars with flowers in many colours.

P. denticulata (drumstick primrose) grows 30 cm (12") tall and 25 cm (10") wide. The flowers form ball-shaped clusters in shades of white, pink, purple and blue. This species is considered very hardy in locations with reliable snow coverage.

P. florindae (Himalayan cowslip) will grow to a height of 61–91 cm (24–36") and a spread of 30–61 cm (12–24"). Large, drooping clusters of yellow or orange blooms are produced in summer, later than other *Primula* species. Large, toothed leaves cluster tightly on the ground, supporting the tall flower stems. (Zones 3–8)

P. x polyanthus (polyantha primrose, polyantha hybrids) usually grows 20–30 cm (8–12") tall, with an equal spread. The flowers are clustered at

P. x polyanthus hybrid (below)

the tops of stems of varying heights. It is available in a wide range of solid colours or bicolours. (Zones 3–8)

P. saxatilis requires some afternoon shade and resents being too dry for any length of time. Over time it reaches 10–15 cm (4–6") heights and 22 cm (9") widths. Soft green, deeply cut, rosette-shaped leaf clusters emerge in early spring. Fuzzy stalks appear later in summer, tipped with delicate clusters of slender-petalled, pink flowers. (Zones 3–8)

P. vialii forms a rosette of deeply veined leaves. The flowers are borne in small spikes that bloom from the bottom up. The blooms have a two-toned appearance as the red buds open to reveal light violet flowers. It grows 30–61 cm (12–24") tall and spreads about 30 cm (12"). (Zones 3–8)

P. vulgaris (English primrose, common primrose) grows 15–20 cm (6–8") tall and 20 cm (8") wide. The flowers are solitary and borne at the ends of short stems that are slightly longer than the leaves. (Zones 4–8)

Problems & Pests
Slugs, strawberry root weevils, aphids, rust and leaf spot are possible problems for primrose plants.

Primrose flowers can be made into wine or candied as edible decoration.

P. x polyanthus (below); P. vialli (above)

Purple Coneflower
Echinacea

Height: 61 cm–1.5 m (2–5') **Spread:** 46 cm (18") **Flower colour:** purple, pink, white; with rusty orange centres **Blooms:** summer **Zones:** 3–8

PURPLE CONEFLOWER HAS RISEN TO HEIGHTS LIKE FEW OTHER perennials have, based on its medicinal claims to fame and beauty. Aside from its many ornamental qualities, this sassy perennial has been proven to boost immunity, thereby aiding in the prevention of the common cold. New and old varieties are superb for mixed border plantings, naturalized areas or planted en masse. They attract a wide variety of pollinating insects, butterflies and bees throughout the summer months. If you leave your border clean up until the following spring, you will also have the pleasure of viewing many of our feathered friends munching away on the leftover seedheads on cold winter days.

E. purpura (photos this page)

Planting

Seeding: Direct sow in spring

Planting out: Spring

Spacing: 46 cm (18") apart

Growing

Purple coneflower grows well in **full sun** or **very light shade**. It tolerates any **well-drained** soil, though it prefers **average** or **rich soil**. The thick taproot makes this plant drought resistant, but it prefers to have regular water. Deadheading early in the season is recommended as it prolongs the flowering season. Later in the season you may wish to leave the flowerheads in place.

The plants may self-seed, providing more plants. If you don't want them to self-seed, then remove all the flowerheads as they fade. Pinch plants back in early summer to encourage bushy growth that is less prone to mildew. Divide every four years or so in spring or fall.

Tips

Use purple coneflower in meadow gardens and informal borders, in large groups or as single plants.

The dry flowerheads make an interesting feature in fall and winter gardens.

Echinacea was discovered by native peoples and was one of their most important medicines. It is a popular immunity booster in herbal medicine today.

'White Lustre' (above); 'Magnus' (below)

Recommended

E. purpurea is an upright plant with prickly hairs all over. It grows up to 1.5 m cm (5') tall and spreads 46 cm (18"). The cultivars are generally about half this height. It bears purple flowers with orangy centres from mid-summer to fall. **'Kim's Knee High'** is a dwarf, compact form, growing to 61 cm (24") tall. The pink petals are reflexed back rather than straight out from the flowers' centres. Its companion is **'Kim's Mop Head,'** which reaches a similar height; however, it displays white flowers on a compact form. **'Magnus'** bears large purple flowers, up to 18 cm (7") across, with orange centres. **'White Lustre'** produces white flowers surrounding orange centres. **'White Swan'** is a compact plant with white flowers. **'Ruby Giant'** produces fragrant, large, 13–18 cm

(5–7") wide, bright pink flowers on tall, erect 91 cm (36") stems. The petals extend out flat, with upcurved tips surrounding bright yellow centres.

Problems & Pests

Powdery mildew is the biggest problem. Other possible problems are leaf miner, aster yellows, stem rot, damping off, *Fusariam* crown and root rot, *Botrytis* blight, bacterial spot and grey mould. Vine weevils may attack the roots. Although this may be a daunting list, when purple coneflower is planted in the right location, it will thrive.

Purple coneflower seed is an important food source for goldfinches and chickadees.

'Magnus' (below)   'Magnus' & 'White Swan' (above)

Rudbeckia
Black-Eyed Susan
Rudbeckia

Height: 46 cm–3m (18"–10') **Spread:** 30–91 cm (12–36") **Flower colour:** yellow or orange, with brown or green centres **Blooms:** mid-summer to fall **Zones:** 2–9

THIS IS ONE PERENNIAL THAT HAS RACED TO THE TOP OF THE popularity list. It is simply spectacular when planted en masse. Just give it full sun, and sit back and enjoy the show. Rudbeckia is great for late-season colour, and we often neglect to include enough late-blooming perennials in our borders. In addition to its many other attributes, rudbeckia can withstand the light fall frosts that are so typical of the prairies. It does not fully give up until the temperatures drop to about -7° C (19° F). My favourite is the cultivar 'Indian Summer' because of its bright and sunny disposition. If I had to pick a fault of this cultivar, it would be that it needs to be treated as an annual in areas colder than zone 3.

Planting

Seeding: Indoors in early spring or outdoors in a cold frame; soil temperature 16–18° C (61–64° F)

Planting out: Spring

Spacing: 30–91 cm (12–36")

Growing

Rudbeckia grows well in **full sun** or **partial shade**. The soil should be of **average fertility** and **well drained**. Fairly heavy clay soils are tolerated. Regular watering is best, but established plants are drought tolerant.

Divide in spring or fall every three to five years. Pinch plants in June to encourage shorter, bushier growth.

Tips

Use rudbeckia in wildflower or naturalistic gardens, in borders and in cottage-style gardens. It is best planted in masses and drifts.

Though deadheading early in the flowering season keeps the plants

R. hirta

Rudbeckia cut flowers are long lasting in arrangements.

R. hirta cultivar

R. lanciniata (above), *R. fulgida* (below)

flowering vigorously, seedheads are often left in place later in the season for winter interest and as food for birds in fall and winter.

Recommended

R. fulgida is an upright, spreading plant. It grows 18–36" tall and spreads 12–24". The orange-yellow flowers have brown centres. **Var.** *sullivantii* **'Goldsturm'** bears large, bright golden yellow flowers. **'Pot of Gold'** is almost identical to 'Goldsturm' but more compact in form.

R. hirta (gloriosa daisy) produces large flowers from midsummer to fall. A great many varieties are part of this group of hybrids, including **'Indian Summer,'** which bears golden orange flowers on tall stems. This variety is bushy enough to support the statuesque flowers. **'Prairie Sun'** produces single, golden flowers with yellow tips. The centre of each

flower is quite prominent and green. These are two of the taller varieties, reaching 91 cm–1.2 m (3–4') heights. **'Sonora'** is a smaller variety that bears yellow flowers with a brown band surrounding the prominent rustic centre. The **'Toto'** series is a bushy, compact group of plants with single blossoms. **'Toto Gold'** has bright golden orange flowers and **'Toto Rustic'** bears rich mahogany red to brown petals tipped in yellow.

R. laciniata (cutleaf coneflower) forms a large, open clump. It grows 4–10' tall and spreads 24–36". The yellow flowers have green centres. **'Goldquelle'** is a compact form bearing large, double yellow flowers.

Problems & Pests

Rare problems with slugs, aphids, rust, smut and leaf spot are possible.

R. hirta cultivar (above); *R. fulgida* (below)

Russian Sage

Perovskia

Height: 91 cm–1.2 m (3–4') **Spread:** 91 cm–1.2 m (3–4') **Flower colour:** blue, purple; foliage **Blooms:** mid-summer to fall **Zones:** 4–8

IT IS WORTH FINDING SPACE FOR THE RECIPIENT OF THE 1995 Perennial Plant of the Year award. Members of the Perennial Plant Association vote annually on which plant to give this prestigious award to. The criteria necessary to become a winner include versatility in a wide range of climates, low-maintenance qualities and multi-season interest. Rest assured that any perennial that receives this prestigious award will be a surefire winner in your garden. Of all the flowering sage varieties, Russian sage offers the most impressive haze of lavender blue flowers available today.

The airy habit of this plant creats a mist of silver and purple in the garden.

Russian sage is rarely troubled by pests or diseases.

Planting

Seeding: Not recommended; germination can be very erratic

Planting out: Spring

Spacing: 91 cm–1.2 m (3–4') apart

Growing

Russian sage prefers **full sun**. The soil should be **poor to moderately fertile** and **well drained**. Russian sage does not need dividing.

Tips

The silvery foliage and blue flowers combine well with other plants in the back of a mixed border and soften the appearance of daylilies. Russian sage may also be used in a natural garden or on a dry bank.

Cut the plant back to 30 cm (12") in fall or early spring to encourage vigorous, bushy growth.

Recommended

P. atriplicifolia is a loose, upright plant with silvery white, finely divided foliage. It grows 91 cm–1.2 m (3–4') tall, with an equal spread. The small, lavender blue flowers, borne in late summer and fall, are loosely held on silvery, branched stems. **'Blue Spire'** is an upright plant with deep

'Longin'

blue flowers and feathery leaves. The airy habit of this plant creates a mist of silver-purple in the garden. **'Filigran'** has delicate foliage and an upright habit. **'Longin'** is narrow and erect and has more smoothly edged leaves than other cultivars.

P. atriplicifolia

Sandwort

Arenaria

Height: 2.5–30 cm (1–12") **Spread:** 15–30 cm (6–12") **Flower colour:** white flowers with yellow eyes **Blooms:** late spring, early summer **Zones:** 2–8

ALTHOUGH SANDWORT IS STILL RELATIVELY UNKNOWN ON THE prairies, it is definitely worth adding it to your landscape. I don't know why sandwort isn't a bestseller, but I am sure that in the future, growers everywhere will stock it. My first sandwort was the small but classy *A. montana* that bloomed floriferously in my rock garden. In late spring, the large flowers almost completely covered the low-growing mat of foliage. Another prime place for this lovely little groundcover is along pathways, as it will quite happily creep along the edges, just enough to soften the hardscape but not overstep its bounds.

Sandwort forms an attractive mat of foliage that is inviting to bare feet.

Planting

Seeding: Direct sow in fall

Planting out: Spring or fall

Spacing: 15–30 cm (6–12") apart

Growing

Sandwort likes to grow in **full sun** or **light shade**. The soil should be **poor** or **average**, **sandy** and **well drained**. Divide in spring or fall when the centre of the plant begins to thin out.

Tips

Sandwort does well in a rock garden, on a stone wall or between the paving stones of a path.

This plant likes to be watered regularly but doesn't like standing in water. To avoid spending all summer watering it, plant sandwort beneath taller shrubs and apply a mulch to the soil surface. Sandwort has shallow roots and will not compete with the larger shrubs. Both the mulch and the sandwort plant will protect the roots of the bigger shrub.

Recommended

A. capillaris (threadleaf sandwort, mountain sandwort) is a loosely mat-forming perennial. It grows 30 cm (12") tall. The thread-like foliage blends with the tall, narrow stems, which support white, star-shaped flowers in bloom from late spring to early summer.

A. ciliata (fringed sandwort) has a prostrate form with densely packed foliage and non-flowering shoots. It reaches 7 cm (3") tall. It's considered very hardy and suitable for alpine trough gardens and rock gardens.

A. montana

A. montana (mountain sandwort) forms a low mat of foliage. It grows 2.5–20 cm (1–8") tall and spreads about 30 cm (12"). It bears white flowers in late spring. This species has a reputation for being one of the easiest alpine plants to grow.

A. purpurascens (alpine sandwort, pink sandwort) grows 8 cm (3.5") tall and 15 cm (6") wide. Trailing, star-shaped, pink flowers are borne in summer on a mat of tiny, glossy, dark leaves. This species may require a little winter protection and is a little shy to flower, but well worth the wait. (Zones 3–8)

Problems & Pests

Occasional problems with rust or anther smut are possible.

Saxifrage
Rockfoil
Saxifraga

Height: 10–61 cm (4–24") **Spread:** 15–30 cm (6–12") **Flower colour:** red, pink, white **Blooms:** spring, summer **Zones:** 3–8

I HAVE SUCH GREAT AWE FOR THIS GROUP OF PLANTS. THEY continue to astound me time and again with their tenacity and toughness, thriving in the unlikeliest places. Although I've lost a number of these little darlings over the years, there is rarely a shortage of varieties to be grown. There isn't enough space or time in the day to grow them all, based on the great number of saxifrages I'd still like to grow. Many of the saxifrage that I have experimented with were considered marginal or not fully hardy in my zone. This never discouraged me, however. Their petite size makes them easy to protect in the cold winter months, so why not test the hardiness limits? Sometimes discoveries are made from pushing the boundaries.

Planting

Seeding: Sow seed into an open frame in fall

Planting out: Spring, summer

Spacing: 15–30 cm (6–12")

Growing

Saxifrage requires **deep to partial shade**. The soil should be **humus rich**, **moist** and **very well drained**. A gravelly surface is best to allow the foliage to be slightly above the soil and reduce the potential for rot. Spring is the best time for division. Propagate individual rosettes in late spring or early summer.

S. x urbium

Tips

Saxifrage is generally a tiny perennial that loves a location with excellent drainage. Alpine, trough and rock gardens offer the cultural requirements that it demands. It also works well as edging along the front of mixed beds and borders.

Saxifraga is an enormous group of plants that all require slightly different care and conditions. Explore what's available, but be aware of their cultural requirements.

S. x arendsii cultivar

When planted in masses, it acts as groundcover, but it's just as effective when placed in between pavers or stepping stones along a pathway.

Recommended

S.* x *arendsii (mossy saxifrage) produces ground-hugging mats of bright green foliage, reaching 10–20 cm (4–8") heights and 30 cm (12") widths. Cup-shaped, red, pink or white flowers emerge on short stems through tightly packed leaves. This species resents drought, preferring a cool and moist location. **'Cloth of Gold'** produces a mat of golden yellow, lacy foliage and white flowers. (Zones 4–8)

S. cotyledon (pyramidal saxifrage) has larger, greyish leaves in a rosette clump approximately 20 cm (8") wide. Dense panicles of white flowers emerge in summer, reaching a height of 46–61 cm (18–24").

S. paniculata (encrusted saxifrage) bears tightly mounded clusters of 30 cm (12") wide grey-green foliage

S. cotyledon cultivar (above); *S. paniculata* (below)

rosettes with lime-encrusted margins. Starry white flowers emerge on short 25 cm (10") stems. This species is considered one of the easiest *Saxifraga* to grow. **'Foster's Red'** has deep red flowers. This cultivar prefers a lime soil and remains smaller than the species. **'Minutifolia'** bears red-tinted flower stems and rosettes.

S. x *urbium* (London pink) vigorously spreads its large, spoon-shaped rosettes 15–30 cm (6–12") wide. Soft pink, airy blooms emerge in late spring. **'Aureopunctata'** (golden London pride) produces 20–30 cm (8–12") tall, spotted, gold foliage. **'Primuloides'** remains very tiny, bearing little rosettes; it is suitable for shady rock gardens. It grows 10 cm (4") tall. (Zones 4–8)

Problems & Pests

Aphids, slugs, vine weevil grubs and spider mites are all possible.

S. x *urbium* (above); *S.* x *urbium* cultivar (below)

S. x *urbium* 'Aureopunctata'

Sea Holly

Eryngium

Height: 70–91 cm (28–36") **Spread:** 46–70 cm (18–28") **Flower colour:** blue, white; foliage **Blooms:** summer **Zones:** 2–8

AT MY FIRST DRIED FLOWER ARRANGEMENT WORKSHOP, MY students were thrilled with the colour retentive quality and unique form of sea holly blossoms. One student in particular fell head over heels in love with sea holly and created an exquisite arrangement that hangs in her front hall to this day. Later she noted her inability to grow sea holly in her own garden because of a lack of sunlight. After our discussion, we agreed to share what sea holly I had in my garden to renew her everlasting arrangements. Every summer, she has come to harvest a few stems, as there is always more than I can ever use. Some of the best perennials are meant to be shared, and sea holly is no exception, because there simply is no end to its uses, fresh or dried.

Planting

Seeding: Sow ripe seed indoors or in a cold frame in early spring

Planting out: Spring, summer

Spacing: 46–70 cm (18–28")

Growing

Some sea holly varieties require slightly different cultural conditions than others. Overall the minimum requirements are **full sun** in **dry, well-drained, moderately fertile to poor soil**. It is drought tolerant owing to its long taproot, which can make transplanting and division difficult or unsuccessful. Although it is slow to re-establish, you may need to divide it every couple of years.

E. alpinum (above); *E. amethystinum* (below)

Tips

Sea holly is frequently used in xeriscaping, mixed borders, everlasting or cutting beds. It has also been known to stand on its own as a specimen. Smaller varieties are well suited to alpine and rock gardens.

Recommended

E. alpinum (alpine sea holly) grows 70 cm (28") tall and 46 cm (18") wide. Finely cut, spiny-toothed, silvery grey foliage is produced on upright, stiff, grey stems. Spiny, but delicate, feathery collars sit under the prominent, silvery lavender flowerheads. This species is tolerant of a little shade and prefers the moisture level in the soil to hinge on dry. (Zones 3–8)

E. amethystinum (amethyst sea holly) is a clump-forming perennial that grows 70 cm (28") tall and wide. Spiny, mid-green leaves are finely cut and jagged. Silvery blue stems emerge, supporting steely, purplish blue spiky flowers, balanced on silvery green bracts.

E. planum (flat sea holly, blue sea holly) grows into a 91 cm (36") tall

and 46 cm (18") wide clump of dark, toothed leaves with heart-shaped bases. The silvery grey foliage and stems are tinted blue and are leathery looking. Spherical, spiny, light blue flowers sit above spiky bracts. This plant is considered one of the hardiest and longest lived species.

Problems & Pests

Powdery mildew, root rot, slugs and snails can be a problem from time to time.

Sea Lavender
Perennial Statice
Limonium

Height: 61–75 cm (24–30") **Spread:** 61–75 cm (24–30") **Flower colour:**
lavender blue, white; foliage **Blooms:** summer **Zones:** 2–8

IT'S NO SURPRISE THAT SEA LAVENDER WAS NAMED FOR ITS
preference for the salt meadows and marshes in its native habitat. It grows
naturally along the Atlantic coast from Labrador to Florida, and westward
along the gulf to Texas. The common name also refers to the flower plumes'
resemblance to blue-grey sea spray blown over the meadows and prairies
from seas beyond. Anything that evokes visions of the sea has instant appeal
for me. Sea lavender never failed to please when I began to grow and sell it as
an everlasting on the commercial
market years ago. The blooms
are as beautiful when left to
sway to and fro in the garden
as they are fresh in a vase or
dried for crafts, to be enjoyed well
beyond our gardening season.

Planting

Seeding: Sow seed directly in early spring

Planting out: Early spring to late fall

Spacing: 61–75 cm (24–30")

Growing

Sea lavender prefers **full sun**. The soil should be **sandy** and **well drained**. Division can be done in the spring but only if necessary. Owing to its long taproot, sea lavender is highly drought tolerant and a little resentful of being moved. You'll have to have patience while waiting for it to re-establish.

L. latifolium

Tips

Sea lavender is well suited for xeriscaping, mixed beds and borders or an everlasting or cutting garden.

Recommended

L. latifolium grows 61–75 cm (24–30") tall and wide. Wide, rounded leaves form in large clumps of leathery, dark rosettes. Tall, wiry stems emerge in summer, supporting large, airy panicles of tiny purple flowers. Up to a dozen stems are in full bloom consistently throughout the summer. **'Violetta'** bears darker blossoms and **'Blue Cloud'** produces bluish purple flowers.

Problems & Pests

Rust, leaf spot, flower spot, grey mould and crown rot can all cause damage.

L. latifolium cultivar

Sedum
Stonecrop
Sedum

Height: 5–61 cm (2–24") **Spread:** 46 cm (18"–indefinite) **Flower colour:** yellow, white, red, pink; foliage **Blooms:** summer, fall **Zones:** 2–8

ADMIRERS OF SUCCULENT PLANTS ARE ALWAYS KEEN TO PICK UP the newest sedum introductions every year while the rest of us try our best to keep up. These easy-keepers are available in every form, size, texture and colour, bearing succulent leaves in the most foreign shapes imaginable. They resemble cacti without the thorns. Gardeners new to this plant are always amazed at the diversity of sedums available. As it is autumn while I am writing this, it seems fitting to be able to look out my office window and enjoy the sight of one of the hottest sedums on the market. The aptly named *S.* 'Autumn Joy' is more spectacular in autumn than at any other time of the year. It bears large, showy clusters of flowers until the snow begins to fly.

S. spectabile 'Brilliant'

Planting

Seeding: Indoors in early spring. Seed sold is often a mix of different species; you might not get what you hope for or expect, but you can just as easily be pleasantly surprised.

Planting out: Spring

Spacing: 46–61 cm (18–24") apart

Growing

Sedum prefers **full sun** but tolerates partial shade. The soil should be of **average fertility**, **very well drained** and **neutral to alkaline**. Divide in spring, when needed. Prune back 'Autumn Joy' in May by one-half and insert pruned parts into soft soil. Cuttings will root quickly. Early summer pruning of upright species and hybrids will give compact, bushy plants.

Tips

Low growing sedums make excellent groundcovers. They are frequently used in rock gardens or cascading over rock walls. They also edge beds and borders wonderfully. The taller types give a beautiful late-season display in a bed or border.

S. spurium cultivar

Recommended

S. acre (gold moss stonecrop) grows 5 cm (2") high and spreads indefinitely. The small, yellow-green flowers are borne atop mid-green foliage in summer. **'Aureum'** produces succulent, yellow foliage.

S. 'Autumn Joy' (autumn joy sedum) is a popular upright hybrid.

S. acre (above); S. spurium (below)

The flowers open pink or red and later fade to deep bronze over a long period in late summer and fall. The plant forms a clump 61 cm (24") tall, with an equal spread.

S. 'Mohrchen' forms an upright clump of stems. It grows about 61 cm (24") tall, with an equal spread. Bronze-red summer foliage brightens to ruby red in the fall. Clusters of pink flowers are borne in late summer and fall.

S. spectabile (showy stonecrop) is an upright species with pink flowers borne in late summer. It forms a clump 46 cm (18") tall and wide. **'Brilliant'** bears bright pink flowers. **'Neon'** bears vibrant, pinkish purple flowers in late summer. Both cultivars mature to a similar size to the species.

S. spurium (two-row stonecrop)
forms a mat about 10 cm (4") tall
and 61 cm (24") wide. The flowers
are deep pink or white. **'Fuldaglut'**
bears reddy bronze foliage with
deep pink flowers. **'Tricolour'** bears
unique foliage in red, white and
green. Pink flowers are borne on
5–8 cm (2–3") tall plants.

S. telephium **'Sunset Cloud'** grows
to 30 cm (12") tall and 61 cm (24")
wide. It produces toonie-sized,
round, purple leaves on arching
stems. Russet-coloured flowers
emerge in mid-summer, clustered
atop colourful stems. (Zones 4–8)

S. **'Vera Jameson'** is a low, mounding
plant with purple-tinged stems and
pinkish purple foliage. It grows up to
30 cm (12") tall and spreads 46 cm
(18"). Bunches of dark pink flowers
are borne in late summer and fall.

Problems & Pests

Slugs, snails and scale insects may
cause trouble for these plants.

S. spectabile cultivar (above); *S.* 'Autumn Joy' (below)

*Low-growing sedums make an
excellent groundcover under
trees. Their shallow roots survive
well in the competition for space
and moisture.*

Siberian Bugloss
Brunnera

Height: 30–46 cm (12–18") **Spread:** 46 cm (18") **Flower colour:** purple, blue; foliage **Blooms:** spring to early summer **Zones:** 2–8

I AM A FOOL FOR FORGET-ME-NOT FLOWER TYPES, AND THIS relative of *Mysotis* is no exception. This is a terrific perennial to grow solely for the blooms, but when mixed with delicate-looking plants, its bold foliage is hard to beat. Siberian bugloss specimens are effective on their own but pack more punch in small groupings, especially 'Jack Frost,' which bears silvery, variegated foliage topped with sky blue flower sprays. Purple or chartreuse flowers and foliage are the ideal companions for this perennial because contrasting colours emphasize the best attributes of this stunning perennial even further, resulting in an inspiring colour combination.

Planting
Seeding: Sow seed indoors or in a cold frame in early spring to extend the season

Planting out: Spring

Spacing: 46 cm (18")

Growing

Siberian bugloss is most successful in **partial to full shade**. The soil should be **humus rich**, **moist** and **well drained**, but it tolerates dry, poor soils. Siberian bugloss self-seeds readily and spreads underground by rhizomes. Division is only necessary when the centre begins to die out. This form of propagation should be done in spring.

Tips

Siberian bugloss is eye catching when planted in masses or left as a large specimen. It works well in woodland and shade gardens, alongside streams or ponds, under tall trees as a groundcover, or within a naturalized setting.

Recommended

B. macrophylla is a clump-forming perennial that grows 30–46 cm (12–18") tall and 46 cm (18") wide. Upright stems support blue flowers. **'Dawson's White'** (Variegata) bears blotchy foliage with irregular creamy white variegations and soft blue flowers. This cultivar is more insistent about a location in full shade; otherwise, leaf scorch may be a problem. **'Hadspen Cream'** bears pale green foliage, lightly edged in creamy white. The variegations are narrower and more irregular. Pale blue flowers emerge in mid- to late spring.

Problems & Pests

No serious insect or disease problems affect Siberian bugloss. Slugs and snails may cause a little damage but will only show up from time to time.

B. macrophylla

Bugloss *comes from the Greek meaning 'ox tongue,' probably in reference to the roughness and shape of the leaves.*

'Dawson's White'

Snow-in-Summer

Cerastium

Height: 5–30 cm (2–12") **Spread:** 30–91 cm (12–36") **Flower colour:** white; foliage **Blooms:** late spring, early summer **Zones:** 2–8

GARDENERS NEVER FAIL TO BE IMPRESSED BY SNOW-IN-SUMMER. I once taught a landscape design workshop in a very remote area in south-west Saskatchewan. I happened to include an image of snow in summer nestled beneath some very mature Colorado spruce trees in my presentation, and this showy but drought-tolerant plant was the star event of the entire day. At the time, I wasn't aware that this stellar performer was a relative unknown in that part of the province. Needless to say, the next time I was there, I found it thriving in gardens everywhere. Once gardeners had discovered this plant's preference for drier regions, it took off like a shot and remains popular to this day.

Planting

Seeding: Start seeds early indoors or sow directly in garden for flowers in first year

Planting out: Spring

Spacing: 30–61 cm (12–24") apart

Growing

Grow snow-in-summer in **full sun** or **partial shade**. This plant will grow in any type of **well-drained** soil but may develop root rot in wet soil. The richer the soil, the more invasive this plant becomes, but it will do well in poor soil. Snow-in-summer tends to die out in the middle as it grows, so dividing it every two years will ensure that it maintains even coverage.

Tips

Snow-in-summer is well suited to sunny, hot locations. It may be used under taller plants as a groundcover, along border edges and to prevent erosion on sloping banks. It is attractive on a rock wall but might overwhelm less vigorous plants.

Cutting the plant back after it has finished flowering and again later in summer will help keep growth in check and prevent the plant from thinning out excessively in the centre. It can spread up to 91 cm (36") in a single year.

C. tomentosum (photos this page)

Recommended

C. tomentosum forms a low mat of silvery grey foliage. It grows 15–30 cm (6–12") tall and spreads 61 cm (24") or more. This plant bears white flowers in late spring. **'Silberteppich'** ('Silver Carpet') is a more compact cultivar. **Var. *compactae*** is a shrubbier variety that spreads less and **'Yo Yo'** is a low-growing variety with silvery grey leaves. It grows to 15 cm (5") tall.

Soapwort
Saponaria

Height: 10–61 cm (4–24") **Spread:** 46 cm (18") **Flower colour:** pink, white, red **Blooms:** spring, summer, fall **Zones:** 2–8

SOAPWORT IS APTLY NAMED BECAUSE IT CONTAINS SAPONIN IN ITS roots. Saponin is a compound that will form a soapy solution when mixed with water. This extract is still used in detergents and commercial foaming agents. Aside from its commercial applications, soapwort is an attractive and versatile plant to include in a prairie landscape. *S. ocymoides* or rock soapwort is a darling variety bearing little downy leaves smothered in bright pink flowers. The cultivar 'Rubra Compacta' is especially stunning, producing deep crimson flowers. I say all of this with an note of caution, however. Early in my gardening years, I tangled with *S. offinalis*, or bouncing bet. Although attractive, this variety can be rather persistent, and I still find it cropping up in my garden occasionally like a bad cold that never really goes away.

Planting
Seeding: Start seeds in the early spring. Keep the planted seeds in a cool dark place, about 15–18° C (61–65° F), until they germinate. Move into a lighted room as soon as germination begins.

Planting out: Spring

Spacing: 46 cm (18") apart

Growing

Soapwort grows best in **full sun**. The soil should be of **average fertility**, **neutral to alkaline** and **well drained**. Poor soils are tolerated. Divide in spring every few years to maintain vigour and control spread.

Tips

Use soapworts in borders, rock gardens and on rock walls. Soapworts can overwhelm less vigorous plants. Cut rock soapwort back after flowering to keep it neat and compact.

Recommended

S. ocymoides (rock soapwort) forms a low, spreading mound. It grows 10–15 cm (4–6") tall and spreads about 46 cm (18"). The plant is completely covered in bright pink flowers in late spring and continues to flower sporadically all summer. '**Alba**' has white flowers. '**Rubra Compacta**' is very low growing, with dark pink flowers.

S. officinalis (soapwort, bouncing bet) is an upright plant. It grows up to 61 cm (24") tall and spreads about 46 cm (18"). This plant is aggressive and can quickly spread even farther with good growing conditions. Pink, white or red flowers are borne from summer to fall. Cultivars are not as invasive as the species. '**Rosea Plena**' bears fragrant, pink, double flowers in early summer.

Problems & Pests

Infrequent, but slugs and snails can be problematic in moist locations.

S. officinalis (above)

S. ocymoides & *S. ocymoides* 'Alba' (centre)

S. officinalis 'Rosea Plena' (below)

Solomon's Seal

Polygonatum

Height: 46 cm–1.2 m (18"–4') **Spread:** 61–91 cm (24–36") **Flower colour:** white; foliage **Blooms:** spring, summer **Zones:** 2–8

IT CAN BE FUN TO LEARN ABOUT THE HISTORICAL SIGNIFICANCE of plant names, and Solomon's seal is no exception. The common name is said to be derived from the scar left on the creeping rhizomes after the flowering stems die off in the fall. This scar is said to resemble the seal of King Solomon, the king of Israel from 961–931 BC. The seal became synonymous with Solomon, who allegedly used the symbol to repel demons and to call upon angels. Conversely, poet Geoffrey Grigson (1915–85) claimed that it was called Solomon's seal because the flowers resembled the seal on a letter. Regardless, this plant has claimed its own place in history, and that's only the beginning.

Planting

Seeding: Sow seed indoors or in a cold frame in early spring

Planting out: Spring

Spacing: 61–91 cm (24–36")

Growing

Solomon's seal prefers **partial to full shade**. The soil should be **fertile, humus rich**, **moist** and **well drained**. Propagate by division in spring once the rhizomes have begun to grow. Make sure not to damage the young shoots. Division can also be done in the fall.

Tips

Solomon's seal seems to brighten up the dullest shade garden. The flowers emerge in such a unique way that they attract attention wherever they're planted. It is also useful in mixed beds and borders. It looks most at home in woodland settings or naturalized areas. It is suitable as a groundcover when planted in groups.

The berries are highly poisonous. Be cautious planting in areas that are easily accessible to children or pets.

When division of the rhizomes is necessary, be sure that each division has at least one bud eye.

Recommended

P. commutatum (small Solomon seal) is a spreading, arching plant that grows into a 91 cm–1.2 m (3–4') tall and 61–91 cm (24–36") wide clump. White, solitary, tubular flowers are borne dangling from the leaf axils, followed by little black berries. (Zones 3–8)

P. falcatum '**Variegatum**' arching stems grow 46–61 cm (18–24") tall. The glossy leaves are edged creamy white on red-tinted stems.

P. multiflorum (many-flowered Solomon's seal) is a prolific bloomer, bearing clusters of pendent white

P. multiflorum (photos this page)

bells along the stems. This species will get 61–70 cm (24–30") tall and wide.

P. odoratum '**Variegatum**' (fragrant Solomon's seal) bears variegated foliage and fragrant, white flowers with green tips in spring. Black, round berries follow after the waxy flowers. Slow to establish, this popular perennial will grow 61 cm (24") tall and wide.

Problems & Pests

Slugs and sawfly larvae are possible.

Speedwell
Veronica
Veronica

Height: 1.2–61 cm (½–24") **Spread:** 20–46 cm (8–18") **Flower colour:** white, pink, purple, blue **Blooms:** summer **Zones:** 2–8

SPEEDWELL IS A SPLENDID PERENNIAL BECAUSE IT IS WELL behaved, beautiful and available in a wide variety of forms. Speedwell varieties offer lengthy blooming cycles throughout the growing season, depending on the type. *Veronica whitleyi*, a newcomer to the prairie landscape, produces grey-green foliage with the loveliest bright, sky blue flowers that smother the foliage in May and June; taller species, including *V. spicata*, will continue to bloom well into the month of August.

When planted among other flowering perennials and shrubs, you can expect some level of bloom throughout the growing season right up to a hard frost in the cool days of autumn.

Speedwell often attracts hummingbirds, butterflies and bees to the garden.

Planting

Seeding: Not recommended.
Seedlings do not always come true
to type. Seeds germinate quickly if
started indoors in early spring.

Planting out: Spring

Spacing: 46 cm (18") apart

Growing

Speedwells prefer **full sun**, but they
will tolerate partial shade. The soil
should be of **average fertility**, **moist**
and **well drained**. Divide in fall or
spring every three to five years.

Tips

Plant spike speedwell in masses in a
bed or border. Prostrate speedwell is
useful in a rock garden or at the
front of a border. Deadhead to
encourage longer blooming. For
tidier plants, shear back tall types to
15 cm (6") in June.

S. spicata cultivar (above)

V. x 'Sunny Border Blue' (below)

S. *spicata* 'Red Fox' (above)

V. *spicata* subsp. *incana* (below)

Recommended

V. austriaca (Hungarian speedwell) bears spikes of vibrant blue flowers in early summer. This clump-forming perennial matures to 20–30 cm (8–12") tall and wide. **'Crater Lake Blue'** produces intense blue, gentian-like flowers. **'Trehane'** is more compact than the species, with golden foliage.

V. gentianoides (broad-leaved speedwell) grows 30–40 cm (12–16") tall and wide. Tall spikes of pale blue flowers emerge from the low mounds of tightly packed leaves. **'Variegata'** produces creamy white variegations throughout the foliage with flowers similar in appearance to the species.

V. prostrata (creeping speedwell) is a mat-forming species with olive green foliage and short, sky blue flower spikes. It's well suited to rock gardens and grows 10–15 cm (4–6") tall and 30–46 cm (12–18") wide. (Zones 4–8)

V. repens (creeping speedwell) remains very low to the ground, maturing to only 1 cm (½") tall, but up to 30 cm (12") wide. It produces a densely packed carpet of tiny leaves speckled with little white flowers in late spring.

V. spicata (spike speedwell) is a low, mounding plant with stems that flop over when they get too tall. It grows 30–61 cm (12–24") tall and spreads 46 cm (18"). It bears spikes of blue flowers in summer. Many cultivars of different colours are available. **'Blue Carpet'** bears deep blue flowers on a very compact form. **'Icicle'** is a late bloomer, producing tall, white-spiked flowers. **Subsp. incana** has soft, hairy, silvery green leaves and deep purple-blue flowers. **'Red Fox'** has dark, red-pink flowers.

V. x **'Sunny Border Blue'** grows to a height of 30–46 cm (18–24") and a spread of 30 cm (12"). Considered more resistant to mildew than others, this hybrid has a dense, compact form. It bears short spikes of purple-blue flowers in summer. (Zones 3–8)

V. whitleyi (Whitley's speedwell) produces a low-spreading mat of tiny, grey-green, lacy leaves and small, blue flowers. It grows 5–10 cm (2–4") tall and 30–61 cm (12–24") wide.

V. spicata subsp. *incana* (above)

Problems & Pests

Problems with scale insects are possible, as are fungal problems such as downy mildew, powdery mildew, rust, leaf smut and root rot.

V. x 'Sunny Border Blue' (below)

Spiderwort
Trinity Flower
Tradescantia

Height: 30–61 cm (12–24") **Spread:** 46–61 cm (18–24") **Flower colour:** blue, purple, pink, white **Blooms:** late summer **Zones:** 3–8

SPIDERWORT ISN'T A PROLIFIC BLOOMER, BUT IT WILL CONTINUE to flower all summer if the nights are cool. It is important to deadhead regularly to encourage further blooming. The triangular flowers are borne in showy colours and are distinctly shaped. *T.* x *andersoniana* hybrids, old and new, offer an array of colours, sizes and forms to choose from. 'Snowcap' is especially striking, bearing extra large, pure white flowers. A more recent introduction, 'Blue and Gold,' produces glowing chartruese yellow, blade-like foliage and contrasting dark purple-blue flowers with bright yellow stamens. There's a spiderwort for everyone and every prairie garden setting.

John Tradescant, Tradescantia's *namesake, sailed on Sir Robert Maxwell's 1620 voyage to fight Barbary pirates. After retiring from the high seas, he established a garden in Lambeth, England and later became gardener to King Charles I.*

Planting

Seeding: Sow seed indoors in early spring at 21°C (70°F)

Planting out: Spring to fall

Spacing: 46–61 cm (18–24")

Growing

Spiderwort prefers **full sun to partial shade**. The soil should be **moist, fertile** and **well drained**. It tolerates poorly drained, lean soil, but the blooming will be greatly diminished. Division is possible in fall or spring. If allowed to dry out in full sun, it becomes vulnerable to scorch.

Tips

Spiderwort is perfect for waterside plantings or locations where it is moist for long periods. It also works well in shady borders and mixed beds or as a groundcover.

Contact with the foliage may irritate sensitive skin.

Recommended

T. x *andersoniana* produces upright clumps reaching 30–61 cm (12–24") in height and 46–61 cm (18–24") in width. Clusters of triangular flowers bloom in mid-summer until fall, on each stem's tip. **'Charlotte'** bears pink flowers and **'Concorde Grape'** bears frosted, blue-green foliage with deep purple flowers. **'Hawaiian Punch'** has magenta pink flowers, and **'Isis'** has white flowers with a touch of purple in the centre. **'Little Doll'** produces light blue blossoms atop a compact form with narrow foliage. **'Purple Dome'** has deep purple flowers and is probably the most common. **'Red Cloud'** produces cherry red blooms, and **'Snowcap'** bears extra large, pure white flowers.

Problems & Pests

Viruses, aphids and spidermites can all be problematic.

'Concorde Grape'

Sweet Woodruff

Galium

Height: 10–20 cm (4–8") **Spread:** 30–46 cm (12–18") **Flower colour:** white; foliage **Blooms:** late spring to mid-summer **Zones:** 3–8

IF YOU LOOK CLOSELY, AND USE YOUR IMAGINATION, YOU'LL SEE that the rounded clusters of leaves surrounding the stems of this plant resemble tiny umbrellas, as if they were sheltering little creatures below. The scented foliage and flowers are pleasing when dried, reminiscent of freshly mowed hay, and are often used in potpourri. Fresh leaves were used in medieval times to stuff mattresses. It has been used since the 13th century to flavour wine and was used medicinally for a variety of ailments. Today, sweet woodruff is mostly used as a lush, low-growing, shade-loving groundcover. Slow to establish but well worth the wait, it is ideal in a mixed border or spring bulb bed. As new foliage grows taller and thicker, it disguises the spent bulb foliage below, a win-win situation.

Planting

Seeding: Not recommended

Planting out: Spring or fall

Spacing: 30–46 cm (12–18") apart

Growing

This plant prefers **partial shade**. Sweet woodruff will grow well in full shade but with greatly diminished flowering. The leaves are prone to sun scorch in full sun. The soil should be **humus rich** and **evenly moist**. Divide plants in spring or fall.

Tips

Sweet woodruff is a perfect woodland groundcover. It forms a beautiful green carpet and loves the same conditions in which azaleas and rhododendrons thrive. Shear back after blooming to encourage plants to fill in with foliage and crowd out weeds.

Recommended

G. odoratum is a low, spreading groundcover with emerald green, lance-shaped leaves that have tiny, marginal prickles. Clusters of star-shaped, white flowers emerge in late spring. The tiny flowers contrast beautifully with the lush foliage to create a bright carpet suitable for any shady border.

Problems & Pests

Sweet woodruff may have problems with mildew, rust and fungal leaf spot.

The dried leaves were once used to scent doorways and refresh stale rooms.

G. odoratum (photos this page)

The wiry, creeping habit of sweet woodruff makes it an excellent groundcover, particularly under trees. The white flowers seem to glow at dusk.

Thrift
Sea Pink
Armeria

Height: 20–61 cm (8–24") **Spread:** 30–61 cm (12–24") **Flower colour:** pink, white **Blooms:** late spring, early summer **Zones:** 2–8

THRIFT IS NOT ONLY ATTRACTIVE TO US, BUT TO A HOST OF BEES and butterflies as well. There is something very charming about the little pompom-shaped flowers clustered overtop of a grassy mound of foliage. They remind me of a child's drawing of fluffy clouds overtop low, mounded hills. This evergreen perennial is easy to incorporate into your garden, especially in tiny pockets where little else will grow. When I daydream about my future retirement, I often picture myself planting sea thrift in between the spaces of a flagstone walk leading up from the seashore, so I can watch the pompoms wave in the coastal winds.

Planting

Seeding: Start seeds in spring or fall; soak for a few hours before planting

Planting out: Spring

Spacing: 30–61 cm (12–24") apart

Growing

Thrift requires **full sun**. The soil should be of **poor** or **average fertility** and **well drained**. Thrift is very drought tolerant. Divide in spring or fall.

Tips

This is a useful plant in rock gardens or at the front of a border.

If your thrift plant seems to be dying out in the middle of the clump, try cutting it back hard. New shoots should fill in quickly.

Recommended

A. **'Bees'** is a group of larger hybrids that grow 46–61 cm (18–24") tall, with an equal spread. The large white, pink or red flowers are borne in late spring and summer.

A. ***maritima*** forms a clump of grassy foliage. Ball-like clusters of white, pink or purple flowers are borne at the ends of long stems in late spring and early summer. The plant grows up to 20 cm (8") tall and spreads about 30 cm (12"). **'Alba'** has white flowers. **'Dusseldorf Pride'** bears deep pinkish red, round, clustered flowers.

Problems & Pests

Problems are rare with this durable plant. It may occasionally get rust or be attacked by aphids.

A. maritima 'Alba' (above); *A. maritima* (below)

Attract bees and butterflies to your garden with clumps of thrift.

Thyme
Thymus

Height: 2.5–46 cm (1–18") **Spread:** 10–40 cm (4–16") **Flower colour:** purple, pink, white **Blooms:** late spring, early summer **Zones:** 2–8

PARSLEY, SAGE, ROSEMARY AND THYME MAY BRING TO MIND AN Elizabethan folksong popularized by Simon and Garfunkel in the 1960s, but these herbs also lend an important element to the garden and kitchen. *T. praecox* subsp. *arcticus* is one of the many creeping varieties ideal for planting between paving stones, where it is sure to be trod upon and release its aroma. The fabulous scent conjures up images of great food and fellowship for me because I often use thyme when I cook for my friends and family. Thyme has historical, medicinal, culinary and horticultural significance and endless uses both inside and outside the home.

Planting

Seeding: Many popular hybrids, particularly the ones with variegated leaves, cannot be grown from seed. Common thyme and mother-of-thyme are good choices for starting from seed. Start indoors in early spring.

Planting out: Spring

Spacing: 10–40 cm (4–16")

Growing

Thyme prefers **full sun**. The soil should be **average** or **poor** and **very well drained**; it helps to have leaf mould worked into it. It is easy to propagate the cultivars that cannot be started from seed. As the plant grows outwards, the branches touch the ground and send out new roots. These rooted stems may be removed and grown in pots to be planted out the following spring. Unrooted stem cuttings may be taken in early spring, before flowering. Divide plants in spring.

T. x citriodorus 'Golden King' (above)

This large genus has species throughout the world that have been used in various ways in several cultures. Ancient Egyptians used it in embalming; the Greeks added it to baths and the Romans purified their rooms with it.

T. praecox subsp. *arcticus* (below)

T. *praecox* subsp. *arcticus* (above)

T. x *citriodorus* 'Argenteus' (below)

Tips

Thyme is useful in the front of borders, between or beside paving stones and on rock gardens and rock walls.

Once the plants have finished flowering, it is a good idea to shear them back by about half. This encourages new growth and prevents the plants from becoming too woody.

Recommended

T. x *citriodorus* (lemon-scented thyme) forms a mound 30 cm (12") tall and 25 cm (10") wide. The foliage does smell of lemon, and the flowers are pale pink. The cultivars are more ornamental. **'Argenteus'** has silver-edged leaves and **'Aureus'** has yellow-gold variegated leaves.

'**Golden King**' has leaves with yellow margins. (Zones 4–8)

T. praecox subsp. *arcticus* (*T serphyllum,* creeping thyme, mother-of-thyme) remains very low to the ground, maturing to a height of only 2–5 cm (1–2") and a spread of 30 cm (12"). This groundcover is frequently used for its practicality, fragrance and colour. Tiny flowers emerge from the tightly packed, hairy foliage in mid-summer. '**Albus**' (white creeping thyme) bears white flowers, and '**Elfin**' forms tiny, dense mounds of foliage that grow up to 5–7.6 cm (2–3") tall and 10 cm (4") wide. It rarely flowers. '**Highland Cream**' has lemon-scented, white-edged leaves and pale, pinky white flowers. '**Languinosis**' (woolly thyme) is a mat-forming plant up to 7.6 cm (3") high and 20–25 cm (8–10") wide, with fuzzy, grey-green leaves. It bears pink or purplish flowers in summer. '**Minimus**' grows 5 cm (2") high and 10 cm (4") wide. '**Purple Carpet**' bears pale purple flowers while '**Snowdrift**' has white flowers.

T. vulgaris (common thyme) forms a bushy mound of dark green leaves. The flowers may be purple, pink or white. It usually grows about 30–46 cm (12–18") tall and spreads about 40 cm (16"). '**Silver Posie**' is a good cultivar with pale pink flowers and silver-edged leaves. (Zones 3–8)

Problems & Pests
Rare. Seedlings may suffer from damping off and plants may get grey mould or root rot. Good circulation and drainage are the best ways to avoid these problems.

T. vulgaris (above)

In the Middle Ages, it was believed that drinking a thyme infusion would enable one to see fairies.

T. praecox subsp. *articus* 'Purple Carpet' (below)

Tiarella
Foam flower
Tiarella

Height: 10–30 cm (4–12") **Spread:** 15–61 cm (6–24") **Flower colour:** white, pink; foliage **Blooms:** spring, sometimes to early summer **Zones:** 3–8

I HAVE GREAT RESPECT FOR ANY PLANT THAT IS PART OF THE saxifrage family. You'll find saxifrage plants clinging to rocky cliffs beside the ocean, and they'll be some of the last plants you'll see when climbing up above the tree zone. Tiarella is native to woody areas of North America and Eastern Asia. It is a close relative of coral bells (*Heuchera*) and shares a great many similarities with that plant, including mounds of colourful foliage graced with airy sprays of flowers. Breeders have been steadily creating new cultivated varieties, so don't be surprised if you are inundated by wonderful new cultivars every spring.

Planting

Seeding: Start in cold frame in spring

Planting out: Spring

Spacing: 15–61 cm (6–24") apart

Growing

Foam flower prefers **partial**, **light** or **full shade,** avoiding afternoon sun. The soil should be **humus rich**, **moist** and **slightly acidic**. These plants adapt to most soils. Deadheading will encourage reblooming. Divide in spring.

Tips

Foam flower is an excellent groundcover for shaded and woodland gardens. It can be included in shaded borders and left to naturalize in wild gardens.

If foliage fades or rusts in summer, cut it partway to the ground and fresh new growth will emerge.

Foam flower spreads by underground stolons, which are easily pulled up to stop the plant from spreading too far.

Recommended

T. cordifolia grows 15–30 cm (6–12") tall and spreads 30 cm (12") wide. Fuzzy, divided leaves form into clumps, supporting white flower spikes in summer. The foliage turns a bronzy colour in the fall before dying back. **'Dark Eyes'** foliage is darker with a burgundy-black blotch in the centre. **'Filigree Lace'** bears white flowers with deeply divided, delicate foliage. **'Inkblot'** produces soft pink flowers with large, ink-blotched leaves. **'Skeleton Key'** has lacy, bronze leaves.

T. wherryi is similar to *T. cordifolia*, but it forms a clump and is more prolific. The species grows to 20 cm (8") tall and 15 cm (6") wide.

T. cordifolia (above & below)

'Heronswood Mist' produces mottled, creamy white, pink and green foliage and pale pink stems and flowers. **'Oakleaf'** forms a dense clump of dark foliage with pink flowers. (Zones 4–8)

Problems & Pests

Rust, powdery mildew and slugs are possible problems.

Trollius
Globe Flower
Trollius

Height: 20–91 cm (8–36") **Spread:** 41–61 cm (16–24") **Flower colour:** yellow, orange; foliage **Blooms:** spring to early summer **Zones:** 3–7

YELLOW FLOWERS BRING SUCH JOY AND COLOUR TO THE GARDEN. Trollius is a very handsome plant that resembles a tall but robust buttercup. When my family lived on a farm and my children were young, I used to spend a great deal of time in my kitchen cooking and canning. This allowed me to enjoy the garden view from my kitchen window. I have always thought it necessary to have a beautiful view out of any window you spend an inordinate amount of time in front of. I remember the bright yellow blossoms standing out in that garden view, drawing my eye in.
To this day, trollius reminds me of smiling, chubby-cheeked, blond little girls and our days on the farm.

Planting
Seeding: Sow fresh ripe seed in cold frame in fall or spring; seeds may take up to two years to germinate

Planting out: Spring or fall

Spacing: 46–61 cm (18–24")

Growing

Globe flower prefers **partial shade** but tolerates full sun if enough moisture is provided. These plants prefer cool, moist conditions and do not tolerate drought. The soil should be **fertile** and **heavy** and not be allowed to dry out. Globe flowers can be planted in well-drained soil as long as the soil remains moist. Prune out any yellowing leaves in summer. Division is rarely required but can be done in early spring or late fall.

Tips

Globe flower is the perfect plant for the side of a pond or stream. It will naturalize very well in a damp meadow garden or bog garden and can be used in the border as long as the soil remains moist. Globe flowers are long lasting as cut flowers.

Recommended

T. chinensis (Chinese globe flower) grows 61–91 cm (24–36") tall and 46 cm (18") wide. It produces yellow or orange, bowl-shaped flowers with pronounced stamens. **'Golden Queen'** grows to 61 cm (24") tall and has orange flowers. (Zones 3–7)

T. x *cultorum* (hybrid globe flower) forms perfectly globe-shaped flowers. Plants grow 61–91 cm (24–36") tall and 41–46 cm (16–18") wide. **'Cheddar'** bears semi-double flowers in pastel yellow shades. **'Earliest of All'** grows 46–51 cm (18–20") tall and produces pale yellow-orange flowers earlier than the other globe

T. chinensis (above & below)

flowers. **'Lemon Queen'** is a more compact variety that produces lemon yellow, double flowers. **'Orange Princess'** has large, deep orange flowers on plants 30–61 cm (12–24") tall.

T. pumilus (dwarf globe flower) is a low-growing rock garden or edging variety that grows 20–30 cm (8–12") tall and 25–30 cm (10–12") wide. Single, bright yellow flowers are small in comparison to other species and are borne atop a low mound of shiny foliage.

Problems & Pests

Powdery mildew may cause occasional problems.

Viola

Viola

Height: 10–15 cm (4–6") **Spread:** 10–30 cm (4–12") **Flower colour:** purple, blue, white, yellow, red **Blooms:** spring to fall **Zones:** 2–8

FEW OTHER PERENNIALS ARE AS CHARMING AS THE VIOLA. *V. tricolour*, or Johnny jump up, is the most popular perennial viola grown on the prairies. Its reputation as a self-sowing perennial is reliable, as you'll find it growing here, there and everywhere, and without becoming a nuisance. My youngest daughter, who loves to pick flowers but is not always allowed such freedom at her grandmother's, is always allowed to pick as many as she likes. When visiting, she can be sure that she will go home with at least one handful of these great little flowers, because there are always more than enough to go around.

Planting

Seeding: Sow ripe seed indoors, cold frame or directly outdoors in early to mid-spring; seed can also be sown directly outdoors in late fall

Planting out: Spring, summer

Spacing: 10–30 cm (4–12") apart

Growing

Violets will grow equally well in **partial shade** or **full sun**. The soil should be **fertile**, **humus rich**, **moist** and **well drained**. Violets self-seed freely and you may find them cropping up here and there in unlikely places in the garden. Cultivars may not set seed. Divide in spring or fall. Most species are short-lived, so make sure to propagate them in some manner yearly.

Tips

Violets are good for rock gardens, walls and the front of a border, but keep in mind that they can be invasive. They also work well in woodland and cottage garden settings, mixed beds or left to their own devices for naturalizing.

Recommended

V. obliqua (marsh blue violet) grows 15 cm (6") tall and 15–30 cm (6–12") wide. Large, lightly fragrant flowers emerge from mounds of heart-shaped leaves in late spring, sometimes white with blue eyes and veins. **'Royal Robe'** bears bright, purplish blue flowers. **'White Czar'** produces white blooms with yellow centres. All three of these violas are prolific self-seeders. (Zones 3–8)

V. sororia (woolly blue violet) forms a small clump of scalloped foliage with fuzzy undersides. It grows 15 cm (6") tall and spreads 15–30 cm (6–12"). Its flowers are purple or white with purple dots and streaks, borne in spring and summer. **'Freckles'** has white flowers that are speckled with light purple dots. **'Rubra'** bears burgundy red flowers, which is a very unusual colour for perennial violas. (Zones 3–8)

V. tricolor (Johnny jump up) grows 10–15 cm (4–6") tall and wide. This species is sometimes used as an annual, or left to re-establish itself naturally by self-seeding. Early spring, tiny purple and yellow bicolour flowers emerge from tiny clumps of leaves. Plant Johnny jump up in an area where it will be free to roam. **'Blue Elf'** produces vibrant, bluish purple flowers. **'Helen Mount'**

V. sororia 'Freckles'

is the traditional standard, with violet and yellow flowers on rounded foliage. This cultivar's flowers look similar to, but are much larger than, the species.

Problems & Pests

Mosaic viruses, downy and powdery mildew, crown and root rot, grey mould, spot anthracnose, fungal leaf spots, slugs, snails, aphids and violet leaf midge are all potential problems.

V. tricolor

Windflower

Anemone

Height: 15–61 cm (6–24") **Spread:** 15–61 cm (6–24") **Flower colour:** white, yellow, pink, blue; foliage **Blooms:** spring, summer or fall **Zones:** 2–8

WINDFLOWER IS BOTH DELICATE AND TOUGH. OVER THE COURSE OF history, the genus anemone has had a great many uses. Said to have sprung from the blood of Adonis, this plant is reputedly valuable in preventing fever, and has been used to treat bruised and freckled skin. The common name was derived from the belief that anemone blossoms were opened by the wind, which isn't entirely the case, but it's not far off. Prairie dwellers often grow snowdrop anemone, *A. sylvestris,* for its sheer simplicity, beauty and hardiness. I have many fond memories of the graceful white flowers waving in the wind early in spring, as sure sign of better things to come.

Planting
Seeding: Not recommended

Planting out: Spring

Spacing: 15–61 cm (6–24") apart

Growing

Anemone prefers **partial** or **light shade** and tolerates full sun. The soil should be of **average to high fertility**, **humus rich** and **moist**. *A. blanda* prefers a light, sandy soil. While dormant, anemone prefers dry soil. Divide in spring or fall. Grecian windflower prefers to be divided in summer.

Tips

Anemone makes a beautiful addition to lightly shaded borders, woodland gardens and rock gardens.

Recommended

A. altaica creeps very low to the ground. It grows only to 15–20 cm (6–8") tall and 30 cm (12") wide. It bears violet flowers that bloom in the spring above a mat of finely cut, dark green leaves with purplish stems.

A. blanda (Grecian windflower) is a low, spreading, tuberous perennial that bears blue flowers in spring. It grows 15–20 cm (6–8") tall, with an equal spread. **'Atrocaerulea'** bears deep blue flowers. **'Pink Star'** has pink flowers with yellow centres. **'White Splendor'** is a vigorous plant with white flowers. The short-lived blooms are hard to ignore. (Zones 4–7)

A. canadensis (meadow anemone) is a spreading perennial with slightly invasive tendencies. It grows 30–61 cm (12–24") tall, with an equal spread. The yellow-centred, white flowers are borne in late spring and early summer. This species needs regular watering when first planted to become established. (Zones 3–7)

A. blanda ' White Splendor'

A. sylvestris (snowdrop anemone, snowdrop windflower) produces scented, white, nodding flowers in spring. The ornate, dark green foliage spreads over 30 cm (12") wide and grows half as tall. This species is a self-seeder, suitable for naturalizing around trees and shrubs.

Problems & Pests

Rare but possible problems include leaf gall, downy mildew, smut, fungal leaf spot, powdery mildew, rust, nematodes, caterpillars and slugs.

A. sylvestris

Other Plants to Consider

Catmint
Nepeta 'Dropmore Blue'

Catmint grows well in **full sun** or **partial shade**, in **well-drained soil** of **average fertility**. Rich soil can lead to floppy growth. Pinch tips in June to delay flowering and make plants more compact. After blooming, cut plant back by one-third to one-half to encourage new growth and more blooms. This Canadian-bred hybrid was introduced in 1932, created by Dr. Frank Skinner in Manitoba. It produces dense, fragrant greyish green foliage, topped with clusters of bright blue flowers all summer, and grows 25–30 cm (10–12") tall and 30–46 cm (12–18") wide. (Zones 2–8)

Cornflower
Centaurea montana

Cornflower is attractive in borders, informal or natural gardens and large rock gardens. It grows well in **full sun** and **light shade**, in **moist, well-drained soil** of **poor** or **average fertility**. It may become straggly, floppy or invasive in rich soil. *C. montana* is a mounding or sprawling plant with cobalt blue flowers from late spring to mid-summer. White and pink cultivars are also available. It may self-seed. Cut plants back once blooming stops for more flowers in late summer. The species can grow 30–61 cm (12–24") tall and spread 46–61 cm (18–24"). Problems with downy or powdery mildew, rust or mould occur rarely. (Zones 3–7)

Fescue
Festuca glauca

Fescue is valued for its low-growing tufts of foliage and is frequently used in xeriscape settings, contemporary gardens and naturalized areas. It also works well in rock and alpine gardens. It prefers **full sun** and thrives in **poor to moderately fertile soil** that is **well drained** and somewhat **dry**. *F. glauca* produces steely blue tufts of fine, needle-like blades of grass. Most varieties produce tan-coloured spikes from mounds of blue grass, revealing small, tan flower plumes. Many cultivars and hybrids are available. To maintain its foliar colour, divide fescue every two or three years, or when it begins to die out in the centre. (Zones 3–8)

Foerster's Feather Reed Grass
Calamagrostis arundinacea
'Karl Foerster'

This hardy ornamental grass thrives in **full to partial sun**. Though it tolerates the poorest soils, it prefers **moist, humus rich** and **well-drained** soil. It is perfect for mixed borders and xeriscaped spaces. The long, elegant inflorescences add beauty to a winter landscape and last well into spring. This cultivar is a slow-growing, forming a clump of arching, narrow, green blades of grass. Tall, wiry stems emerge from the clump, bearing silvery bronze to pale purple-brown panicles of flowers. It can grow up to 1.5 m (5') tall when in flower in mid- to late summer. (Zones 3–8)

Gas Plant
Dictamnus albus

Gas plant makes an attractive addition to a border. This large, clump-forming plant grows 46–91 cm (18–36") tall and spreads 30–91 cm (12–36"), bearing spikes of pink-veined, white or pink flowers. Both the flowers and leaves have a lemon scent. Gas plant prefers **full sun** but tolerates partial shade. The soil should be **average to fertile, dry** and **well drained**. This plant can take several years to become established and flower. Don't divide gas plant; it resents being disturbed. Avoid touching the leaves; if oils in the leaves get on the skin and are exposed to sunlight, they can cause rashes, itching and burning. (Zones 2–8)

Goldenrod
Solidago hybrids

These hybrids have more attractive flowers than the common wild goldenrod species. They form clumps of strong stems 61–91 cm (24–36") tall and about 18" wide, with narrow leaves. Plumes of bright yellow flowers appear mid-summer to fall. 'Crown of Rays' has horizontally oriented flower sprays; 'Golden Shower' has more pendent flower sprays. Goldenrod prefers **full sun** but tolerates some shade. **Poor to average, light, well-drained soil** is best. Rich soil encourages green growth but not flowers. Useful for late-season colour in large borders, cottage gardens and wildflower gardens. It may overwhelm other plants. (Zones 3–7)

Height Legend: Low: < 30 cm (12") • Medium: 30–61 cm (12–24") • Tall: > 91 cm (36")

SPECIES by Common Name	COLOUR								BLOOMING			HEIGHT		
	White	Pink	Red	Orange	Yellow	Blue	Purple	Foliage	Spring	Summer	Fall	Low	Medium	Tall
Arabis	•	•						•	•	•		•		
Artemisia	•				•			•		•		•	•	•
Astilbe	•	•	•				•	•		•			•	•
Baptisia				•	•	•	•	•		•				•
Bellflower	•	•				•	•		•	•		•	•	
Bergamot	•	•	•				•			•			•	•
Bergenia	•	•	•				•	•	•				•	
Bishop's Hat	•	•	•		•			•	•			•	•	
Bitterroot	•	•		•	•			•	•	•		•		
Bleeding Heart	•	•	•				•	•	•	•			•	•
Buttercup	•				•					•	•	•	•	•
Chrysanthemum	•	•	•	•	•		•			•	•		•	
Cimicifuga	•							•		•	•			•
Clematis	•	•	•		•	•	•		•	•				•
Columbine	•	•	•	•	•	•	•		•	•		•	•	
Coral Bells	•	•	•		•		•	•	•	•			•	•
Corydalis	•				•	•	•	•	•	•		•	•	
Cranesbill	•	•	•				•	•		•		•	•	•
Crocus	•		•		•	•	•		•	•		•		
Cupid's Dart	•					•	•			•	•		•	•
Daylily		•	•	•	•		•	•	•	•				•
Delphinium	•	•			•	•	•	•	•	•		•	•	•
Elephant Ears				•	•			•		•	•		•	•
Euphorbia					•			•	•	•			•	•
Evening Primrose	•	•			•				•	•		•	•	•
False Solomon's Seal	•							•	•				•	•
Flax						•			•	•	•			
Fleece-Flower	•	•	•					•		•		•	•	•
Forget-Me-Not	•	•				•			•	•		•		
Foxglove	•	•	•		•		•			•			•	•
Gaillardia			•	•	•					•	•		•	•

Hardy	Semi-hardy	Tender	Sun	Part Shade	Light Shade	Full Shade	Moist	Well Drained	Dry	Fertile	Average	Poor	Page Number	SPECIES by Common Name
•			•					•			•	•	70	Arabis
•			•					•		•	•		72	Artemisia
•				•	•	•	•	•		•			76	Astilbe
•			•	•				•					80	Baptisia
•			•	•	•			•		•	•		82	Bellflower
•			•	•	•	•	•	•		•	•		86	Bergamot
•			•	•				•		•	•		90	Bergenia
	•			•			•	•					94	Bishop's Hat
•					•			•		•	•		96	Bitterroot
•				•	•		•			•			98	Bleeding Heart
•			•	•			•	•					102	Buttercup
•			•				•	•		•			104	Chrysanthemum
•			•	•			•	•		•			108	Cimicifuga
•			•	•			•	•		•			110	Clematis
•			•	•			•	•		•			116	Columbine
•				•	•		•	•		•	•		120	Coral Bells
•				•	•			•		•	•		124	Corydalis
•			•	•	•			•			•		126	Cranesbill
•			•	•				•		•			130	Crocus
•			•	•				•		•			132	Cupid's Dart
•			•	•	•	•	•	•		•			134	Daylily
•			•				•	•		•			138	Delphinium
•				•	•		•			•	•		142	Elephant Ears
•			•	•	•		•	•		•	•		146	Euphorbia
•			•					•			•	•	150	Evening Primrose
•					•	•	•	•		•	•		152	False Solomon's Seal
•			•	•				•		•	•		154	Flax
•			•	•			•	•					156	Fleece-Flower
•			•	•			•	•			•	•	158	Forget-Me-Not
•				•	•		•			•			160	Foxglove
•			•					•		•			164	Gaillardia

Height Legend: Low: < 30 cm (12") • Medium: 30–61 cm (12–24") • Tall: > 91 cm (36")

SPECIES by Common Name	White	Pink	Red	Orange	Yellow	Blue	Purple	Foliage	Spring	Summer	Fall	Low	Medium	Tall
Gentian	•					•	•			•	•	•	•	
Globe Thistle						•	•	•		•				•
Goat's Beard	•							•		•		•	•	•
Goutweed	•							•		•		•	•	
Hens and Chicks	•		•		•		•	•		•		•		
Hops								•		•				•
Hosta	•						•	•		•	•		•	•
Iris	•	•	•		•	•	•	•	•	•		•	•	•
Jacob's Ladder	•					•	•	•	•	•		•	•	
Japanese Painted Fern								•					•	
Japanese Spurge	•							•	•			•		
Joe Pye Weed	•	•					•			•	•			•
Lady's Mantle					•			•		•	•		•	
Lamb's Ears		•					•	•		•		•	•	
Lamium	•	•			•		•	•		•		•		
Liatris	•						•	•		•			•	•
Lily	•	•	•	•	•		•			•			•	•
Lily-of-the-Valley	•	•						•	•			•		
Lupine	•	•	•	•	•	•	•	•		•			•	•
Lysimachia	•				•			•	•	•		•	•	•
Mallow	•	•				•	•	•		•	•	•	•	•
Maltese Cross	•	•	•							•			•	•
Marsh Marigold	•				•			•	•	•			•	
Masterwort	•	•					•	•		•	•	•		
Meadow Rue	•	•			•	•	•		•	•			•	•
Meadowsweet	•	•						•	•	•			•	•
Monkshood	•					•	•	•		•			•	•
Mullein	•	•	•	•	•		•	•		•				•
Obedient Plant	•	•					•			•	•		•	•
Ostrich Fern								•						•
Penstemon	•	•	•		•				•	•			•	•

HARDINESS			LIGHT				SOIL CONDITIONS						Page Number	SPECIES by Common Name
Hardy	Semi-hardy	Tender	Sun	Part Shade	Light Shade	Full Shade	Moist	Well Drained	Dry	Fertile	Average	Poor		
•			•	•			•	•		•			166	Gentian
•			•				•	•			•		168	Globe Thistle
•				•	•	•	•			•			170	Goat's Beard
•			•	•	•	•		•			•	•	174	Goutweed
•			•	•				•			•	•	176	Hens and Chicks
•			•	•			•	•		•			178	Hops
•				•	•		•	•		•			180	Hosta
•			•					•		•	•		186	Iris
•			•	•			•	•		•			190	Jacob's Ladder
	•			•			•			•	•		192	Japanese Painted Fern
•					•	•		•		•			194	Japanese Spurge
•			•	•			•						196	Joe Pye Weed
•				•	•		•	•		•			198	Lady's Mantle
•			•					•			•	•	200	Lamb's Ears
•				•	•	•	•	•					202	Lamium
•			•					•		•	•		206	Liatris
•			•	•				•		•			208	Lily
•			•	•	•	•	•			•	•		214	Lily-of-the-Valley
•				•	•			•		•	•		216	Lupine
•			•	•			•	•		•			220	Lysimachia
•			•	•			•	•			•		224	Mallow
•			•	•				•			•		228	Maltese Cross
•			•	•			•			•			230	Marsh Marigold
	•		•	•			•			•			232	Masterwort
•				•	•		•	•		•			234	Meadow Rue
•				•	•		•			•			236	Meadowsweet
•				•						•			240	Monkshood
•			•					•				•	244	Mullein
•			•				•			•	•		248	Obedient Plant
•				•	•	•	•	•		•			250	Ostrich Fern
•			•					•		•	•		252	Penstemon

Height Legend: Low: < 30 cm (12") • Medium: 30–61 cm (12–24") • Tall: > 91 cm (36")

SPECIES by Common Name	COLOUR								BLOOMING			HEIGHT		
	White	Pink	Red	Orange	Yellow	Blue	Purple	Foliage	Spring	Summer	Fall	Low	Medium	Tall
Peony	•	•	•		•		•	•	•	•			•	•
Phlox	•	•	•			•	•		•	•	•	•	•	•
Pincushion Flower	•	•				•	•			•			•	
Pinks	•	•	•				•		•	•		•	•	
Poppy	•	•	•	•				•	•	•			•	•
Potentilla	•	•	•	•	•			•		•		•	•	
Prairie Mallow		•								•			•	
Prickly Pear Cactus					•			•		•		•		
Primrose	•	•	•	•	•	•	•	•	•	•		•	•	•
Purple Coneflower	•	•		•			•			•			•	•
Rudbeckia				•	•					•	•		•	•
Russian Sage						•	•	•		•	•			•
Sandwort	•				•				•	•		•		
Saxifrage	•	•	•						•	•		•	•	
Sea Holly	•					•		•		•			•	•
Sea Lavender	•					•	•			•			•	
Sedum	•	•	•		•			•		•	•	•	•	
Siberian Bugloss						•	•	•	•	•			•	
Snow-in-Summer	•							•	•	•		•		
Soapwort	•	•	•						•	•		•	•	
Solomon's Seal	•							•	•	•			•	•
Speedwell	•	•				•	•			•		•	•	
Spiderwort	•	•				•	•			•			•	
Sweet Woodruff	•							•	•	•		•		
Thrift	•	•							•	•		•	•	
Thyme	•	•					•		•	•		•	•	
Tiarella	•	•						•	•	•		•	•	
Trollius				•	•			•	•	•			•	•
Viola	•		•		•	•	•		•	•	•	•		
Windflower	•	•			•	•		•	•	•	•	•	•	

Hardy	Semi-hardy	Tender	Sun	Part Shade	Light Shade	Full Shade	Moist	Well Drained	Dry	Fertile	Average	Poor	Page Number	SPECIES by Common Name
•			•				•	•		•			256	Peony
•			•	•			•	•		•			260	Phlox
•			•				•	•		•	•		264	Pincushion Flower
•			•					•					266	Pinks
•			•					•		•	•		270	Poppy
•			•	•				•			•	•	274	Potentilla
	•		•				•	•		•	•		276	Prairie Mallow
•			•	•				•		•			278	Prickly Pear Cactus
•			•	•			•	•		•	•		280	Primrose
•			•	•	•			•		•	•		284	Purple Coneflower
•			•	•				•		•			288	Rudbeckia
	•		•					•			•	•	292	Russian Sage
•			•		•			•					294	Sandwort
•				•		•	•	•		•			296	Saxifrage
•			•					•	•		•	•	300	Sea Holly
•			•					•					302	Sea Lavender
•			•					•			•		304	Sedum
•				•	•	•	•	•		•			308	Siberian Bugloss
•			•	•				•					310	Snow-in-Summer
•			•					•			•		312	Soapwort
•				•	•	•	•	•		•			314	Solomon's Seal
•			•				•	•			•		316	Speedwell
•			•	•			•	•		•			320	Spiderwort
•				•			•			•			322	Sweet Woodruff
•			•					•			•	•	324	Thrift
•			•					•			•	•	326	Thyme
•				•	•		•			•			330	Tiarella
•				•			•			•			332	Trollius
•			•	•			•	•		•			334	Viola
•				•	•		•				•	•	336	Windflower

Glossary

Acid soil: soil with a pH lower than 7.0

Alkaline soil: soil with a pH higher than 7.0

Basal leaves: leaves that form from the crown

Basal rosette: a ring or rings of leaves growing from the crown of a plant at or near ground level; flowering stems of such plants grow separately from the crown

Crown: the part of a plant where the shoots join the roots, at or just below soil level

Cultivar: a cultivated (bred) plant variety with one or more distinct differences from the parent species, e.g., in flower colour, leaf variegation or disease resistance

Damping off: fungal disease causing seedlings to rot at soil level and topple over

Deadhead: to remove spent flowers to maintain a neat appearance and encourage a longer blooming period

Direct sow: to plant seeds straight into the garden, in the location you want the plants to grow

Disbud: to remove some flower buds to improve the size or quality of the remaining ones

Dormancy: a period of plant inactivity, usually during winter or other unfavourable climatic conditions

Double flower: a flower with an unusually large number of petals, often caused by mutation of the stamens into petals

Genus: category of biological classification between the species and family levels; the first word in a scientific name indicates the genus, e.g., *Digitalis* in *Digitalis purpurea*

Hardy: capable of surviving unfavourable conditions, such as cold weather

Humus: decomposed or decomposing organic material in the soil

Hybrid: a plant resulting from natural or human-induced crossbreeding between varieties, species or genera; the hybrid expresses features of each parent plant

Invasive: able to spread aggressively from the planting site and outcompete other plants

Knot garden: a formal design, often used for herb gardens, in which low, clipped hedges are arranged in elaborate, knot-like patterns

Marginal: plants that grow in shallow water or in consistently moist soil along the edges of ponds and rivers

Neutral soil: soil with a pH of 7.0

Node: the area on a stem from which a leaf or new shoot grows

Offset: a young plantlet that naturally sprouts around the base of the parent plant in some species

pH: a measure of acidity or alkalinity (the lower the pH, the higher the acidity); the pH of soil influences availability of nutrients for plants

Rhizome: a root-like, usually swollen stem that grows horizontally underground, and from which shoots and true roots emerge

Rootball: the root mass and surrounding soil of a container-grown plant or a plant dug out of the ground

Rosette: see Basal rosette

Self-seeding: reproducing by means of seeds without human assistance, so that new plants constantly replace those that die

Semi-hardy: a plant capable of surviving the climatic conditions of a given region if protected

Semi-double flower: a flower with petals that form two or three rings

Single flower: a flower with a single ring of typically four or five petals

Species: the original plant from which a cultivar is derived; the fundamental unit of biological classification, indicated by a two-part scientific name, e.g., *Digitalis purpurea* (*purpurea* is the specific epithet)

Sport: an atypical plant or part of a plant that arises through mutation; some sports are horticulturally desirable and propagated as new cultivars

Subshrub: a perennial plant that is somewhat shrubby, with a woody basal stem; its upper parts are herbaceous and die back each year

Subspecies (subsp.): a naturally occurring, regional form of a species, often isolated from other subspecies but still potentially interfertile with them

Taproot: a root system consisting of one main vertical root with smaller roots branching from it

Tender: incapable of surviving the climatic conditions of a given region; requiring protection from frost or cold

True: describes the passing of desirable characteristics from the parent plant to seed-grown offspring; also called breeding true to type

Tuber: a swollen part of a rhizome or root, containing food stores for the plant

Variegation: describes foliage that has more than one colour, often patched or striped or bearing differently coloured leaf margins

Variety (var.): a naturally occurring variant of a species; below the level of subspecies in biological classification; also applied to forms produced in cultivation, which are properly called cultivars

Lily

Marsh marigold

Index of Plant Names

Page numbers in **bold** indicate main flower headings.

A

Aconitum, 240–244
x *cammarum*, 242
 'Bicolor,' 242
 'Bressingham Spire,' 242
x *carmichaelii*, 243
 'Arendsii,' 243
napellus, 243
Aegopodium, 174–176
podagraria, 175
 'Variegatum,' 175
Alchemilla, 198–200
alpina, 199
mollis, 199
Alum Root. See Coral Bells
Aquilegia, 116–120
canadensis, 118
flabellata, 118
 'Cameo Mix,' 118
x *hybrida*, 118
 'Double Pleat,' 118
 'Dragonfly,' 118
 'McKana Giants,' 118
 'Ruby Port,' 118
 'Sunlight White,' 118
 'Royal Purple,' 119
viridifolia, 119
vulgaris, 119
 'Magpie,' 119
 'Nora Barlow,' 119
Anemone, 336–338
altaica, 337
blanda, 337
 'Atrocaerulea,' 337
 'Pink Star,' 337
 'White Splendor,' 337
canadensis, 337
sylvestris, 337
Arabis, 70–72
alpina subsp. *caucasica*, 71
 'Compinkie,' 71
 'Snow Cap,' 71
procurrens, 71
 'Variegata,' 71
Arenaria, 294–296
capillaris, 295
ciliata, 295
montana, 295
purpurascens, 295
Armeria, 324–326
 'Bees,' 325
maritima, 325
 'Alba,' 325
 'Dusseldorf Pride,' 325
Artemisia, 72–76

absinthium, 74
 'Lambrook Silver,' 74
lactiflora, 74
 'Guizho,' 75
ludoviciana, 75
 'Silver King,' 75
 'Silver Queen,' 75
 'Valerie Finnis,' 75
schmidtiana, 75
 'Nana,' 75
stelleriana, 75
 'Silver Brocade,' 75
vulgaris 'ORIENTAL LIMELIGHT,' 75
Aruncus, 170–174
aethusifolius, 173
dioicus, 173
 'Kneiffii,' 173
 'Zweiweltkind,' 173
 'Var. *astilbioides*,' 173
Astilbe, 76–80
x *arendsii*, 77
 'Avalanche,' 77
 'Bressingham Beauty,' 77
 'Cattleya,' 77
 'Fanal,' 78
 'Weisse Gloria,' 78
chinensis, 78
 'Pumila,' 78
 'Superba,' 78
japonica, 79
 'Deutschland,' 79
 'Peach Blossom,' 79
Astrantia, 232–234
carniolica 'Rubra,' 233
major, 233
 'Hadspen Blood,' 233
 'Lars,' 233
 'Rosea,' 233
 'Rubra,' 233
 'Sunningdale Variegated,' 233
maxima, 233
Athyrium, 192–194
nipponicum, 193
 'Pictum,' 193
 'Samurai Sword,' 193
 'Ursula's Red,' 193

B

Baptisia, 80–82
australis, 81
 'Purple Smoke,' 81
Bee Balm. See Bergamot
Bellflower, 82. See
 Campanula
Bergamot, 86. See *Monarda*
Bergenia, 90–94
cordifolia, 92

 'Bressingham Ruby,' 92
 'Bressingham White,' 93
 'Purpurea,' 93
 'Evening Glow,' 93
x *schmidtii*, 93
 'Winter Fairy Tale,' 93
Bishop's Hat, 94. See
 Epimedium
Bitteroot, 96. See *Lewisia*
Black-Eyed Susan. See
 Rudbeckia
Blanket Flower. See Gaillardia
Blazing Star. See Liatris
Bleeding Heart, 98. See
 Dicentra
Boneset. See Joe Pye Weed
Brunnera, 308–310
macrophylla, 309
 'Dawson's White,' 309
 'Hadspen Cream,' 309
Bugbane. See Cimicifuga
Buttercup, 102. See
 Ranunculus

C

Caltha, 230–232
palustris, 231
 'Alba,' 231
 'Flore Pleno,' 231
Campanula, 82–86
x 'Birch Hybrid,' 84
carpatica, 84
 'Blue Clips,' 84
 'Bressingham White,' 84
 'Jewel,' 84
 'Kent Belle,' 84
cochleariifolia, 84
 'Blue Tit,' 85
glomerata, 85
 'Acaulis,' 85
 'Superba,' 85
persicifolia, 85
poscharskyana, 85
 'Dickson's Gold,' 85
Catananche, 132–134
caerulea, 133
 'Alba,' 133
 'Bicolor,' 133
 'Blue Giant,' 133
 'Major,' 133
 'Perry's White,' 133
Cerastium, 310–312
tomentosum, 311
 'Silberteppich,' 311
 'Var. *compactae*,' 311
 'Yo Yo,' 311
Chrysanthemum, 104–108
x *morifolium* 'Morden,' 106
 'Morden Canary,' 106

'Morden Candy,' 106
'Morden Delight,' 106
'Morden Everest,' 107
'Morden Fiesta,' 107
'Morden Gaiety,' 107
'Morden Garnet,' 107
Cimicifuga, 108–110
racemosa, 109
ramosa 'Atropurpurea,' 109
'Atropurpurea,' 109
'Brunette,' 109
Cinquefoil. See Potentilla
Clematis, 110–116
heracleifolia 'Davidiana,' 113
integrifolia, 113
x *jackmanii*, 113
x 'Prairie Traveler's Joy,' 113
recta 'Purpurea,' 114
tangutica, 114
Columbine, 116. See
Aquilegia
Convallaria, 214–216
majalis, 215
'Albostriata,' 215
'Aureovariegata,' 215
'Flore Pleno,' 215
'Fortin's Giant,' 215
'Rosea,' 215
Coral Bells, 120. See
Heuchera
Corydalis, 124–126
flexuosa, 125
'Gold Panda,' 125
'Purple Leaf,' 125
lutea, 125
ochroleuca, 125
Cranesbill, 126. See
Geranium
Crocus, 130. See *Pulsatilla*
Cupid's Dart, 132. See
Catananche

D
Daylily, 134. See *Hemerocallis*
Delphinium, 138–142
x *belladonna*, 140
'Blue Bees,' 140
'Wendy,' 140
x *elatum*, 140
'Blue Dawn,' 140
'Magic Fountain Hybrids,'
    140
'Sungleam,' 140
'Turkish Delight,' 140
grandiflorum, 140
'Album,' 140
'Blue Butterfly,' 141
Dicentra, 98–102
exima, 100
'Alba,' 100
'King of Hearts,' 100
'Stuart Boothman,' 100
formosa, 100

'Adrian Bloom,' 101
'Luxuriant,' 101
'Var. *alba*,' 101
spectabilis, 101
'Alba,' 101
'Gold Heart,' 101
Dianthus, 266–270
x *allwoodii*, 268
'Beatrix,' 268
'Doris,' 268
'Laced Romeo,' 268
'Sweet Wivelsfield,' 268
deltoides, 268
'Brilliant,' 268
gratianopolitamus, 269
'Blue Hills,' 269
'Mountain Mist,' 269
'Petite,' 269
plumarius, 269
'Spring Beauty,' 269
Digitalis, 160–164
grandiflora, 162
x *mertonensis*, 162
purpurea, 163
'Alba,' 163
'Apricot Beauty,' 163
'Excelsior Hybrids,' 163
'Foxy Hybrids,' 163

E
Echinacea, 284–286
purpurea, 286
'Kim's Knee High,' 286
'Kim's Mop Head,' 286
'Magnus,' 286
'Ruby Giant,' 286
'White Lustre,' 286
'White Swan,' 286
Echinops, 168–170
ritro, 169
'Vietch's Blue,' 169
sphaerocephalus, 169
'Arctic Glow,' 169
Elephant Ears, 142. See
Ligularia
Epemidium, 94–96
grandiflorum, 95
'Lilafee,' 95
x *rubrum*, 95
x *versicolor* 'Sulphureum,' 95
x *youngianum*, 95
'Niveum,' 95
'Roseum,' 95
Eryngium, 300–302
alpinum, 301
amethystinum, 301
planum, 301
Eupatorium, 196–198
maculatum, 197
'Atropurpureum,' 197
'Bartered Bride,' 197
'Gateway,' 197
rugosum, 197

'Chocolate,' 197
Euphorbia, 146–150
dulcis, 148
griffithii, 148
'Fireglow,' 148
polychroma, 149
'Candy,' 149
'Emerald Jade,' 149
Evening Primrose, 150. See
Oenothera

F
Fall Garden Mum. See
Chrysanthemum
False Dragonhead. See
Obedient Plant
False Indigo. See Baptisia
False Solomon's Seal, 152.
See
Smilacina
Fiddlehead Fern. See Ostrich
Fern
Filipendula, 236–240
palmata 'Rubra,' 237
purpurea, 237
'Elegans,' 237
rubra, 238
'Venusta,' 238
ulmaria, 238
'Aurea,' 238
'Flore Pleno,' 238
'Variegata,' 238
vulgaris, 238
'Flore Pleno,' 238
'Rosea,' 239
Flax, 154. See *Linum*
Fleece-Flower, 156. See
Persicaria
Foam Flower. See Tiarella
Forget-Me-Not, 158. See
Myosotis
Foxglove, 160. See *Digitalis*

G
Gaillardia, 164–166
x *grandiflora*, 165
'Burgundy,' 165
'Goblin,' 165
Galium, 322–324
odoratum, 323
Gayfeather. See Liatris
Gentian, 166. See *Gentiana*
Gentiana, 166–168
acaulis, 167
clausa, 167
cruciata, 167
septemfida, 167
Geranium, 126–130
x 'Johnson's Blue,' 128
macrorrhizum, 128
'Album,' 128
'Bevan's Variety,' 128
x *oxonianum*, 128

'A.T. Johnson,' 128
'Wargrave Pink,' 128
pratense, 128
  'Mrs. Kendall Clarke,' 128
  'Plenum Violaceum,' 128
sanguineum, 129
  'Album,' 129
  'Alpenglow,' 129
  'Elsbeth,' 129
  'Shepherd's Warning,' 129
  'Var. *stratium*,' 129
Globe Flower. See Trollius
Globe Thistle, 168. See
  Echinops
Goat's Beard, 170. See
  Aruncus
Goutweed, 174. See
  Aegopodium

H
Hemerocallis, 134–138
  'Chicago Jewel,' 136
  citrina, 137
  fulva, 137
    'Kwanso,' 137
    'Kwanso Variegata,' 137
    'Luxury Lace,' 137
Hens and Chicks, 176. See
  Sempervivum
Heuchera, 120–124
  americana, 122
    'Chocolate Veil,' 122
    'Pewter Veil,' 122
    'Stormy Seas,' 122
    'Velvet Night,' 122
  x *brizioides*, 123
    'Firefly,' 123
    'June Bride,' 123
    'Raspberry Regal,' 123
  micrantha, 123
    'Bressingham Hybrids,' 123
    'Chocolate Ruffles,' 123
    'Pewter Moon,' 123
    'Var. *diversifolia* 'Palace
      Purple,' 123
  sanguinea, 123
    'Coral Cloud,' 123
    'Frosty,' 123
    'Northern Fire,' 123
    'White Cloud,' 123
Hops, 178. See *Humulus*
Hosta, 180–186
  'Blue Angel,' 181
  fortunei, 181
    'Albomarginata,' 182
    'Aureomarginata,' 182
  'Francee,' 182
  'Frances Williams,' 182
  'Gold Standard,' 182
  'Great Expectations,' 183
  'Honeybells,' 183
  plantaginea, 183
    'Aphrodite,' 183

'Royal Standard,' 184
sieboldiana, 184
  'Elegans,' 184
sieboldii, 184
  'Alba,' 185
  'Kabitan,' 185
  'Sum & Substance,' 185
Humulus, 178–180
  lupulus, 179
    'Aureus,' 179
    'Magnum,' 179
  japonicus 'Variegatus,' 179
Hybrid Garden Mum. See
  Chrysanthemum

I
Iris, 186–190
  germanica, 187
  pallida, 188
    'Aureo-variegata,' 188
    'Variegata,' 188
  pumila, 188
  setosa, 189
  sibirica, 189
    'Ruffled Velvet,' 189
    'Silver Edge,' 189

J
Jacob's Ladder, 190. See
  Polemonium
Japanese Painted Fern, 192.
  See *Athyrium*
Japanese Spurge, 194. See
  Pachysandra
Joe Pye Weed, 196. See
  Eupatorium

L
Lady's Mantle, 198. See
  Alchemilla
Lamb's Ears, 200. See *Stachys*
Lamium, 202–206
  galeobdolon, 204
    'Florentium,' 204
    'Herman's Pride,' 204
    'Silver Angel,' 204
  maculatum, 204
    'Anne Greenaway,' 204
    'Aureum,' 205
    'Beacon Silver,' 205
    'Orchid Frost,' 205
    'White Nancy,' 205
Lewisia, 96–98
  cotyledon, 97
Liatris, 206–208
  spicata, 207
    'Floristan Violet,' 207
    'Floristan White,' 207
    'Kobold,' 207
Ligularia, 142–146
  dentata, 144
    'Britt-Marie Crawford,' 144
    'Desdemona,' 144

'Othello,' 144
przewalskii, 144
stenochephala, 144
  'The Rocket,' 144
wilsoniana, 145
Lilium, 208–214
  Asiatic Hybrids, 210
  Aurelian Hybrids, 211
  Martagon Hybrids, 211
  Oriental Hybrids, 212
  cernuum, 212
  lancifolium, 212
  michiganense, 213
  regale, 213
  rubellum, 213
Lily, 208. See *Lilium*
Lily-of-the-Valley, 214. See
  Convallaria
Limonium, 302–304
  latifolium, 303
    'Blue Cloud,' 303
    'Violetta,' 303
Linum, 154–156
  perenne, 155
    'Nanum,' 155
    'Sapphire,' 155
Loosestrife. See Lysimachia
Lupin, 216. See *Lupinus*
Lupinus, 216–220
  Gallery Hybrids, 218
  Russell Hybrids, 219
Lychnis, 228–230
  chalcedonica, 229
    'Alba,' 229
    'Dusky Salmon,' 229
  coronaria, 229
    'Alba,' 229
    'Angel's Blush,' 229
    'Atrosanguinea,' 229
Lysimachia, 220–224
  ciliata, 221
    'Firecracker,' 221
  clethroides, 221
  nummularia, 222
    'Aurea,' 222
  punctata, 223
    'Alexander,' 223

M
Mallow, 224. See *Malva*
Maltese Cross, 228. See
  Lychnis
Malva, 224–228
  alcea, 226
    'Fastigiata,' 226
  moschata, 226
    'Pink Perfection,' 226
    'White Perfection,' 226
  sylvestris, 226
    'Bibor Felho,' 227
    'Braveheart,' 227
    'Mystic Mix,' 227
    'Primley Blue,' 227

'Zebrina,' 227
Marsh Marigold, 230. See
Caltha
Masterwort, 232. See
Astrantia
Matteuccia, 250–252
struthiopteris, 251
Meadow Rue, 234. See
Thalictrum
Meadowsweet, 236 See
Filipendula
Monarda, 86–90
didyma, 88
'Gardenview Scarlet,' 88
'Marshall's Delight,' 88
'Panorama,' 88
'Petite Delight,' 88
'Raspberry Wine,' 89
'Rosy Purple,' 89
'Violet Queen,' 89
Monkshood, 240. See
Aconitum
Mullein, 244. See *Verbascum*
Myosotis, 158–160
alpestris, 159
scorpioides, 159
'Spring Carpet,' 159
sylvatica, 159

O

Obedient Plant, 248. See
Physostegia
Oenothera, 150–152
fruticosa, 151
'Summer Solstice,' 151
macrocarpa, 151
speciosa, 151
'Pinkie,' 151
Opuntia, 278–280
humifusa, 279
Ostrich Fern, 250. See
Matteuccia

P

Pachysandra, 194–196
terminalis, 195
'Green Carpet,' 195
'Green Sheen,' 195
'Variegata,' 195
Paeonia, 256–260
lactiflora, 258
'Dawn Pink,' 258
'Duchesse de Nemours,' 258
'Prince of Darkness,' 258
'Sarah Bernhardt,' 259
officinalis, 259
'Alba Plena,' 259
suffruticosa, 259
'Rubra Plena,' 259
'Deep Dark Purple,' 259
'Godaishu,' 259
'High Noon,' 259
tenuifolia, 259

Papaver, 270–274
nudicale, 272
orientale, 272
'Allegro,' 272
'Brilliant,' 272
'Carneum,' 272
'Pizzicato,' 273
Pasque Flower. See Crocus
Penstemon, 252–256
barbatus, 254
'Alba,' 254
'Elfin Pink,' 254
'Hyacinth Mix,' 254
'Praecox Nanus,' 254
'Prairie Dusk,' 254
'White Bedder,' 254
digitalis, 254
'Husker Red,' 255
fruticosus 'Purple Haze,' 255
Peony, 256. See *Paeonia*
Perennial Statice. Sea Lavender
Perovskia, 292–294
atriplicifolia, 293
'Blue Spire,' 293
'Filigran,' 293
'Longin,' 293
Persicaria, 156–158
affinis 'Dimity,' 157
bistorta, 157
'Superba,' 157
microcephala 'Red Dragon,'
157
Phlox, 260–264
'Chatahoochee,' 261
maculata, 262
'Miss Lingard,' 262
'Omega,' 262
'Rosalinde,' 262
paniculata, 262
'David,' 262
'Eva Cullum,' 262
'Norah Leigh,' 262
'Starfire,' 262
'Windsor,' 262
stolonifera, 262
'Ariane,' 263
'Blue Ridge,' 263
'Sherwood Purple,' 263
subulata, 263
'Candy Stripe,' 263
'G.F. Wilson,' 263
'Rosette,' 263
Physostegia, 248–250
virginiana, 249
'Miss Manners,' 249
'Summer Snow,' 249
'Variegata,' 249
'Vivid,' 249
Pincushion Flower, 264. See
Scabiosa
Pinks, 266. See *Dianthus*
Plantain Lily. See Hosta
Polemonium, 190–192

caeruleum, 191
'Album,' 191
'Apricot Delight,' 191
'Brise d'Anjou,' 191
'Snow and Sapphires,' 191
'White Ghost,' 191
reptans, 191
Polygonatum, 314–316
commutatum, 315
falcatum 'Variegatum,' 315
multiflorum, 315
odoratum 'Variegatum,' 315
Poppy, 270. See *Papaver*
Potentilla, 274–276
nepalensis, 275
'Miss Willmott,' 275
neumanniana, 275
'Nana,' 275
tridentata, 275
Prairie Mallow, 276. See
Sidalcea
Prickly-Pear Cactus, 278. See
Opuntia
Primrose, 280. See *Primula*
Primula, 280–284
auricula, 281
denticulata, 282
florindae, 282
x *polyanthus,* 282
saxatilis, 283
vialii, 283
vulgaris, 283
Pulsatilla, 131–132
patens, 131
vulgaris, 131
'Alba,' 131
'Papageno,' 131
'Rubra,' 131
Purple Coneflower, 284. See
Echinacea

R

Ranunculus, 102–104
acris, 103
'Var. *flore-pleno*,' 103
ficaria, 103
'Albus,' 103
'Brazen Hussy,' 103
'Double Mud,' 103
repens, 103
'Buttered Popcorn,' 103
Rock Cress. See Arabis
Rockfoil. See Saxifrage
Rose Campion. See Maltese
Cross
Rudbeckia, 288–292
fulgida, 290
'Pot of Gold,' 290
Var. *sullivantii* 'Goldsturm,'
290·
hirta, 290
'Indian Summer,' 290
'Prairie Sun,' 290

'Sonora,' 291
'Toto,' 291
'Toto Gold,' 291
'Toto Rustic,' 291
laciniata, 291
'Goldquelle,' 291
Russian Sage, 292. See
Perovskia

S
Sandwort, 294. See Arenaria
Sage. See Artemisia
Saponaria, 312–314
ocymoides, 313
'Alba,' 313
'Rubra Compacta,' 313
officinalis, 313
'Rosea Plena,' 313
Saxifraga, 296–300
arendsii, 298
'Cloth of Gold,' 298
cotyledon, 298
paniculata, 298
'Foster's Red,' 299
'Minutifolia,' 299
x urbium, 299
'Aureopunctata,' 299
'Primuloides,' 299
Saxifrage, 296. See Saxifraga
Scabiosa, 264–266
caucasica, 265
'Fama,' 265
'House's Hybrids,' 265
'Miss Wilmont,' 265
columbaria, 265
'Butterfly Blue,' 265
'Pink Mist,' 265
Sea Holly, 300. See Eryngium
Sea Lavender, 302. See
Limonium
Sea Pink. See Thrift
Sedum, 304–308
acre, 306
'Aureum,' 306
'Autumn Joy,' 306
'Mohrchen,' 306
spectabile, 306
'Brilliant,' 306
'Neon,' 306
spurium, 307
'Fuldaglut,' 307
'Tricolor,' 307
telephium 'Sunset Cloud,' 307
'Vera Jameson,' 307
Sempervivum, 176–178
arachnoideum, 177
'Clairchen,' 177
'Kappa,' 177
tectorum, 177
'Atropurpureum,' 177
'Limelight,' 177
'Pacific Hawk,' 177
Siberian Bugloss, 308. See

Brunnera
Sidalcea, 276–278
malviflora, 277
'Brilliant,' 277
'Elsie Heugh,' 277
'Party Girl,' 277
Smilacina, 152–154
racemosa, 153
stellata, 153
Snow-in-Summer, 310. See
Cerastium
Soapwort, 312. See Saponaria
Solomon's Seal, 314. See
Polygonatum
Snow on the Mountain. See
Aegopodium
Speedwell, 316. See Veronica
Spiderwort, 320. See
Tradescantia
Spike Gayfeather. See Liatris
Spurge. See Euphorbia
Stachys, 200–202
byzantina, 201
'Big Ears,' 201
'Primrose Heron,' 201
'Silver Carpet,' 201
grandiflora 'Rosea,' 201
'Superba,' 201
Stonecrop. See Sedum
Sundrops. See Evening
Primrose
Sweet Woodruff, 322. See
Galium

T
Thalictrum, 234–236
aquilegifolium, 235
'Thundercloud,' 235
'White Cloud,' 235
delvayi, 235
'Album,' 235
'Hewitt's Double,' 235
Thrift, 324. See Armeria
Thyme, 326. See Thymus
Thymus, 326–330
x citriodorus, 328
'Argenteus,' 328
'Aureus,' 328
'Golden King,' 329
praecox subsp. articus, 329
'Albus,' 329
'Elfin,' 329
'Highland Cream,' 329
'Languinosis,' 329
'Minimus,' 329
'Purple Carpet,' 329
'Snowdrift,' 329
vulgaris, 329
'Silver Posie,' 329
Tiarella, 330–332
cordifolia, 331
'Dark Eyes,' 331
'Filigree Lace,' 331

'Inkblot,' 331
'Skeleton Key,' 331
wherryi, 331
'Heronswood Mist,' 331
'Oakleaf,' 331
Tradescantia, 320–332
x andersoniana, 321
'Charlotte,' 321
'Concorde Grape,' 321
'Hawaiian Punch,' 321
'Isis,' 321
'Little Doll,' 321
'Purple Dome,' 321
'Red Cloud,' 321
'Snowcap,' 321
Trinity Flower. See
Spiderwort
Trollius, 332–334
chinensis, 333
'Golden Queen,' 333
x cultorum, 333
'Cheddar,' 333
'Earliest of All,' 333
'Lemon Queen,' 333
'Orange Crest,' 333
pumilus, 333

V
Verbascum, 240–246
bombyciferum, 246
'Banana Custard,' 246
nigrum, 246
phoeniceum, 246
Veronica, 316–320
austriaca, 318
'Crater Lake Blue,' 318
'Trehane,' 318
gentianoides, 318
'Variegata,' 318
prostrata, 319
repens, 319
spicata, 319
'Blue Carpet,' 319
'Red Fox,' 319
'Subsp. incana,' 319
x 'Sunny Border Blue,' 319
whitleyi, 319
Viola, 334–336
obliqua, 335
'Royal Robe,' 335
'White Czar,' 335
sororia, 335
'Freckles,' 335
'Rubra,' 335
tricolor, 335
'Blue Elf,' 335
'Helen Mount,' 335

W
Wall Rock Cress. See Arabis
Wild Indigo. See Baptisia
Windflower, 336. See Anemone
Wormwood. See Artemisia